Improving the Department of the Army's Marketing for Recruitment, Hiring, and Retention of Civilians in Critical Occupations

BRUCE R. ORVIS, M. WADE MARKEL, JOHN ENGBERG

Prepared for the United States Army
Approved for public release; distribution unlimited

 ARROYO CENTER

For more information on this publication, visit **www.rand.org/t/RRA1337-1**.

About RAND

The RAND Corporation is a research organization that develops solutions to public policy challenges to help make communities throughout the world safer and more secure, healthier and more prosperous. RAND is nonprofit, nonpartisan, and committed to the public interest. To learn more about RAND, visit www.rand.org.

Research Integrity

Our mission to help improve policy and decisionmaking through research and analysis is enabled through our core values of quality and objectivity and our unwavering commitment to the highest level of integrity and ethical behavior. To help ensure our research and analysis are rigorous, objective, and nonpartisan, we subject our research publications to a robust and exacting quality-assurance process; avoid both the appearance and reality of financial and other conflicts of interest through staff training, project screening, and a policy of mandatory disclosure; and pursue transparency in our research engagements through our commitment to the open publication of our research findings and recommendations, disclosure of the source of funding of published research, and policies to ensure intellectual independence. For more information, visit www.rand.org/about/research-integrity.

RAND's publications do not necessarily reflect the opinions of its research clients and sponsors.

Published by the RAND Corporation, Santa Monica, Calif.
© 2022 RAND Corporation
RAND® is a registered trademark.

Library of Congress Cataloging-in-Publication Data is available for this publication.
ISBN: 978-1-9774-0971-3

About This Report

This report documents research and analysis conducted as part of two projects entitled *Improving the Army's Marketing for Recruitment, Hiring, and Retention of DA Civilians in Critical Occupations* and *DA Civilian Marketing*, both sponsored by the Assistant Secretary of the Army for Manpower and Reserve Affairs. The purpose of the first project was to identify current practices and potential changes needed to market, recruit, hire, and retain Department of the Army civilians in critical occupational specialties.[1] The purpose of the second project was to help the Army prepare for the addition of the Army Civilian brand to the Army Marketing Research Group's fiscal year 2016 contract by carrying out research to better understand the marketplace and assessing the potential employee external market's perceptions and awareness levels; identifying current and projected Department of the Army civilian shortfalls; and setting specific marketing objectives, goals, and strategies.

This research was conducted within RAND Arroyo Center's Personnel, Training, and Health Program. RAND Arroyo Center, part of the RAND Corporation, is a federally funded research and development center (FFRDC) sponsored by the United States Army.

RAND operates under a "Federal-Wide Assurance" (FWA00003425) and complies with the *Code of Federal Regulations for the Protection of Human Subjects Under United States Law* (45 CFR 46), also known as "the Common Rule," as well as with the implementation guidance set forth in DoD Instruction 3216.02. As applicable, this compliance includes reviews and approvals by RAND's Institutional Review Board (the Human Subjects Protection Committee) and by the U.S. Army. The views of sources utilized in this study are solely their own and do not represent the official policy or position of DoD or the U.S. Government.

---

[1] Key elements of the first project are summarized in this report and further detailed in M. Wade Markel, Bruce R. Orvis, Eric Apaydin, John Engberg, Anny Wong, and Philip Hall-Partyka, unpublished RAND Corporation research, 2015.

Acknowledgments

We wish to express our gratitude to the many participants in our focus groups, interviews, and surveys for their time and innumerable contributions to our project. We also are grateful to the subject-matter experts within Headquarters, Department of the Army; the Army Corps of Engineers; commands and field agencies; and the Army's Civilian Human Resources Agency for their invaluable insights during the formative stage of our work.

We want to thank the many, many individuals who helped coordinate our site visits, including Sarah Wheat, Kerry Momberger, Wendy Taylor, Sammy Bone, Sue Hickman, Sandra Foster, Blair Tuck, Shelly Heath, Carmen Finstad, Patrice Creel, Richard Price, Jo Ann Rosenfeld, Margaret Oldham, and Chris Hunt. We thank our subcontractor, Echo Cove Research, for the survey data collection efforts and other support provided to us.

We especially wish to express our thanks to our sponsor, then Deputy Assistant Secretary of the Army for Marketing and his staff, especially Jeffrey Sterling and Alicia McCleary for initiating and supporting both studies, Andrea Zucker for her assistance with the Office of Management and Budget, and John Jessup for his extensive and continuous support throughout the course of our research.

We are grateful to our past and current RAND colleagues Eric Apaydin, Anny Wong, Philip Hall-Partyka, Beth Roth, and Molly McIntosh for their contributions to this research. Finally, we thank our reviewers, Charles Goldman of RAND and Leonard Bright of Texas A&M University, for their helpful reviews of this report.

Summary

People are central to the Army's mission. Army units' operational performance depends on recruiting and training high-quality soldiers. Organizing, training, and equipping Army units depend on having high-quality soldiers and civilians to perform the functions assigned to the Secretary of the Army in Title 10, U.S. Code. This report summarizes the results of two interrelated projects that constituted a multiyear effort to assess and strengthen the Army's ability to attract high-quality applicants to its civilian workforce and retain high-quality Army civilian employees. The projects' specific objectives were to help shape the development of the Army Civilian brand and associated marketing strategy. This included enhancing Army officials' understanding of the job preferences and job search activities of individuals in the external market (job-seekers) and in the internal market (Army civilian employees), assessing potential employees' awareness of Army civilian job opportunities and their perceptions of and concerns about Army civilian jobs, comparing compensation in Army jobs with that in similar private-sector positions, identifying potential hiring needs, and recommending marketing strategies.

Research Approach

To achieve the objectives articulated above, we pursued several lines of research effort, as explained in the following sections.

Selecting Occupations for Analysis

We selected six occupations—from the 80 designated as mission-critical by the Army, U.S. Department of Defense, or federal government—for in-depth analysis, in order to produce generalizable conclusions about developing an

Army Civilian brand and marketing that brand to prospective applicants. Occupations varied along several dimensions:

- size
- demographic characteristics, including age, ethnicity, gender, proportion of veterans in the occupation, and education levels
- workforce structure, including grade, proportion of supervisors in the occupation, and salary levels
- the rate of turnover and retirements in the occupation
- geographic distribution
- input from stakeholders at Headquarters, Department of the Army, and the Army's Civilian Human Resources Agency.

Seeking to identify occupations that reflect different problem issues and hiring processes, and informed by discussions with key stakeholders, we selected the following occupations (the number in parenthesis indicates the occupation series number):

- Management Analysts (0301)
- Program Managers (0340)
- Civil Engineers (0810)
- Electronics Engineers (0855)
- Contracting Specialists (1102)
- Information Technology (IT) Managers (2210).

We do not mean to suggest these occupations are the most critical to the Army's ability to perform its statutory functions. Rather, we deemed that these occupations were sufficiently representative, along the aforementioned dimensions, of other mission-critical occupations that analysis would yield broadly applicable conclusions.

Assessing the External Market

We began by discussing the external market with various Army stakeholders. Based on those discussions, we focused on the engineering, contracting, and IT jobs for the external study. We then developed a "semistructured" questionnaire—that is, one in which most questions were open-ended. That survey provided the team with the raw material necessary to conduct a larger, more comprehensive survey of potential Army applicants, consisting of a series of mostly closed-ended questions providing comprehensive and detailed information for subsequent analysis. The survey elicited information about respondents' background and demographic characteristics; current job, including tenure, for professionals; year of school, primary area of study, and types of desired careers for students; and the importance of 16 job characteristics. For professionals, the survey then asked them to rate their current employer on the same 16 characteristics, their satisfaction with their current job, and whether they were currently looking for another job or planned to do so within the next year. Students and professionals both were asked the extent to which they would use 11 sources of information if they were to conduct a job search. They next were asked about their overall impression of the Army, awareness that civilians can work for the Army, and interest in getting more information about a civilian Army job or career. They were asked to rate Army civilian jobs on the same 16 job characteristics and, separately, on possible concerns about Army jobs. Respondents were then given additional information about Department of the Army civilian jobs. They were asked which aspects of that information were particularly attractive in terms of considering working for the Army.

Assessing the Army Civilian Brand's Image

The Army's objective is to develop an Army Civilian brand identity that attracts potential applicants to Army civilian employment and inclines those already so employed to remain with the Army. In general, brand identity is what a firm wants its customers to think and feel about the firm and its products. In this case, the product is a job with the Army. Those in the incumbent category (i.e., those already employed by the Army) will experience varying degrees of satisfaction with the product they have acquired.

To develop the Army Civilian brand identity, it is necessary to understand the brand's current image. The Army must understand what individuals currently think about the brand in order to leverage those elements that resonate with potential applicants and to cope with any issues that they have. To assess the brand image, we conducted focus groups with civilians in the selected occupations from different commands, at different installations across the Army. During the focus group sessions, we asked current employees how they came to an Army career, why they took the job in the first place, their likes and dislikes about their employment, why they have stayed, and whether they would think about leaving. The answers to these questions help explain how the Army has successfully retained at least a segment of its target demographic. In a follow-on study, we surveyed the larger population of potential employees who were not currently pursuing an Army job to understand what might appeal to them.

Comparing Army and Private Sector Compensation over Time

Pay and benefits are critical factors in prospective applicants' decisions to seek employment. Relying on data from the census and Defense Manpower Data Center, we compared pay and total compensation over the length of long careers for Army and private-sector civilians in the selected mission-critical areas. We performed a similar analysis of other occupations in the career programs from which the four mission-critical occupations were selected.

Assessing Army Hiring Needs

We used the RAND Inventory Model (RIM) to forecast future hiring needs for Army civilians in the selected mission-critical occupations. The analysis estimated the number of additional applicants the Army would need to bring on if current attrition trends persisted. We also estimated the impact on the distribution of experience within the civilian workforce if the Army were to restrict itself to hiring at entry level only.

Analyzing Marketing Approaches

We also interviewed managers, human resource officials, and others involved with recruiting and retaining Army civilians in these occupations. The focus groups, interviews, and compensation analysis enabled us to identify similarities and differences in the way that individuals in different occupations and in different commands are recruited and perceive the Army Civilian brand.

We also analyzed the inventory of workers in each occupation to determine how many additional employees might be needed, and when it would be necessary to start recruiting them. We considered alternative scenarios for the size of each occupation's workforce and the economic conditions under which recruiting would take place.

Major Findings

Findings About the External Market

Potential Applicants from Different Applicant Categories Focused on the Same Job Characteristics

As explained in Chapter Three, potential student, younger professional, and older professional applicants were generally looking for the same things from their next job: attractive salary levels, good work-life balance, generous benefits, strong job security, a generous retirement plan, and opportunities to use their talents and abilities.

Certain Affinity Groups Cluster Around Preferences for Different Combinations of Job Characteristics

Several distinct affinity groups emerged regarding preferred job characteristics. That is, there were distinct groups of potential applicants that focused on one set of job characteristics to the relative exclusion of others. Marketing should address these interests and, when possible, tailor information being provided according to a potential hire's particular focus.

Awareness of Army Civilian Opportunities Is Low in the External Market

This finding is of fundamental importance: Only about 40 percent of students and younger professionals were aware that there are civilian jobs within the Army. Only about 60 percent of older professionals were aware that civil-service jobs exist within the Army.

Potential Applicants Share Several Intuitive—but Mostly Erroneous—Concerns About Army Civilian Employment

Not surprisingly, given their limited knowledge of Army civilian jobs and confusion about serving in uniform versus as a civilian, potential applicants had a number of concerns about Army civilian employment. These concerns involve the potential for physical danger, involuntary location assignment, insecure employment, and inadequate compensation. Almost all of these fears are groundless. Appendix D provides additional detail.

Willingness to Consider Army Civilian Employment Correlates with Favorable Perceptions of the Army

Our analysis indicates that basic favorability toward the Army is strongly associated with interest in getting information about Army civilian jobs and a willingness to recommend one to a friend looking for work.

Perceived Characteristics of Army Civilian Jobs

Among the strongly preferred job characteristics, the only notable positive association was students' perception of a good retirement plan. Among lesser preferred job characteristics, there were positive associations with preference strength for exciting challenges (for professionals) and fast advancement. In contrast, persons preferring work-life balance and schedule flexibility had more concern about finding them in Army civilian jobs, and professionals, who value salary more highly, perceived Army salaries to be more problematic.

Preferred Sources of Information About Jobs

Responses to the information sources we surveyed, in preferred order, included referral, online website, potential employer, professional networking, Google, profession-specific, agency, job fair, professional organization, alumni network, and government. Preferred sources of job information were generally similar across the student and professional groups. However, students were relatively more likely to use job fairs and, compared with older professionals, to use Google. Students were relatively less likely to use an agency. Preferred information sources also generally were similar across job groups. However, younger Electronics Engineers were more likely to use

Google and older Civil Engineers were more likely to use job fairs but less likely to use an agency.

Findings About What the Army Has to Offer

The next step in assessing the Army's brand position with respect to civilian employment was to evaluate the extent to which it can meet the expectations of its potential customers in the external market.

Incumbents Identified Potential Functional, Economic, and Psychological Benefits of an Army Civilian Job

As described in Chapter Four, an employer brand consists of functional, economic, and psychological aspects. The following broad themes could be elements of an Army Civilian brand:

- career and geographic mobility
- a wide, diverse range of potential careers
- job security and stability
- good benefits
- good work-life balance
- a chance to serve soldiers and the nation.

Army Civilian Salaries Are Often Lower Than Those Available in the Private Sector

Army civilian salaries are often significantly lower than those available to members of mission-critical occupations in the private sector. Of the four occupations we analyzed, Army civilians' average salaries were lower than those available in the private sector in three occupations. Only Contracting Specialists' average salaries were higher in the Army than in the private sector. A broader examination paints a more ambiguous picture. Our analysis of the four career programs that include these four occupations indicates—to the extent comparison is both possible and valid—that relative compensation differs by occupation. Some occupations receive higher salaries in the Army, and others receive lower salaries.

Army Total Compensation Often Exceeds That Available in the Private Sector

Although private-sector *salaries* are often higher than in the Army, federal—and thus Army—*total* compensation is often higher than in the private sector. Higher total compensation is a result of a more generous benefits package, including health insurance, pension, and vacation, among other benefits.

Findings About Requirements

Hiring Needs Are Likely to Increase Significantly over the Next Decade in Certain Occupations

For the most part, the Army should be able to maintain its civilian workforce at its current size by hiring at the same levels it did between fiscal years 2015 and 2018. Additional attention may be warranted with respect to specific occupations, such as Electronics Engineers and Contracting Specialists, for which a significant increase in requirements can be anticipated.

Most Workforce Needs Can Be Met by Hiring at Entry Level

Fortunately, it appears that the Army can meet most of its needs by hiring at entry level. Our analysis of the four mission-critical occupations suggests that only one—Electronics Engineers—would need to hire or increase retention of mid-career professionals to maintain its current experience distribution.

Caveats

The foregoing findings come with important caveats. First, qualitative observations drawn from interviews and focus groups with incumbents are somewhat dated, though no comparable information of more recent vintage is available. Second, while we can estimate the costs to Army and other employers of salaries and benefits offered to incumbents and potential employees, we cannot estimate the value that employees place on available remuneration. Third, estimates of hiring requirements are highly sensitive to assumptions about the state of the economy, and the coronavirus disease

2019 (COVID-19) pandemic has rendered the world's economic future highly uncertain. Such caveats do not invalidate the foregoing findings, but they do inspire a degree of circumspection with regard to the recommendations described below.

Recommendations

Raise Awareness of Army Civilian Job Opportunities

Most prospective employees are unaware that civilian jobs with the Army even exist. The Army should therefore take steps to increase awareness. The precise method used for this purpose (e.g., mass-media advertising, targeted internet-based marketing) depends on the overall scale of the task and the potential impact on other Army recruiting priorities.

Align the Army Civilian Brand with the Army Brand

Potential applicants most likely to consider a job as an Army civilian were those with a positive view of the Army. This finding suggests that there are potential synergies to be gained by clearly aligning the Army Civilian brand with the Army brand, and few risks. Care should be taken to avoid feeding into generally held, albeit erroneous, assumptions about risks associated with Army civilian employment. This suggests caution in aligning with combat aspects of the Army brand.

Prepare Hiring Officials to Address Applicants' Concerns

We found that potential applicants have misperceptions about involuntary deployment and concerns about Army civilian employment, including, principally, the possibility of injury/death, involuntary assignment to remote and undesirable duty stations, and low pay. Recruiting and hiring officials must have the facts at hand to allay such concerns when and if potential applicants raise them.

Establish a Civilian Brand Emphasizing Career Opportunities, Benefits, and Service

The Army Civilian brand must appeal both to external audiences it is seeking to attract and to internal audiences it is seeking to retain. It must also consist of implicit promises that the Army can keep. While salary is the primary factor that applicants consider when evaluating employment opportunities, the Army cannot claim that the salaries it offers are equal to or better than those available in the private sector. However, the Army can emphasize total compensation. An Army brand including the themes articulated in Table S.1 can appeal to external audiences on the basis of benefits and work-life balance, and to internal audiences on the broad array of themes.

Conclusion: Marketing Begins with the Job Itself

Marketing involves more than simply articulating the value proposition of an existing product. It also involves decisions about the product itself. Decisions about grade structure, the location of Army civilian work centers, and the nature of the work Army civilians are doing powerfully affect the attractiveness of Army careers. When making decisions that will affect the nature of Army jobs, Army officials should consider those decisions' impact on the Army Civilian brand.

TABLE S.1
Army Civilian Brand Themes

Civilian Brand Element	Theme
Functional	• Career and geographic mobility • A wide, diverse range of potential careers
Economic	• Job security and stability • Good benefits • Good work-life balance
Psychological	• Serving soldiers and the nation

Contents

Figures and Tables

Figures

Tables

CHAPTER ONE

Introduction

People are central to the Army's mission. Army units' operational performance depends on recruiting and training high-quality soldiers. Organizing, training, and equipping those units depend on having high-quality soldiers and civilians to perform the functions assigned to the Secretary of the Army in Title 10, U.S. Code. This report summarizes the results of two interrelated projects that constituted a multiyear effort to assess and strengthen the Army's ability to attract high-quality applicants to its civilian workforce and retain high-quality Army civilian employees. The projects' specific objectives were to help shape the development of the Army Civilian brand and associated marketing strategy. This included enhancing Army officials' understanding of the job preferences and job search activities of individuals in the external market (job-seekers) and internal market (Army civilian employees), assessing potential employees' awareness of Army civilian job opportunities and their perceptions of and concerns about Army civilian jobs, comparing compensation in Army jobs with that in similar private-sector positions, identifying potential hiring needs, and recommending marketing strategies.

This work was approved under Department of Defense Instruction (DoDI) 3216.02. Approval under the DoDI means that the project was not intended to produce generalizable results, dealing instead with the improvement of internal Department of the Army (DA) civilian marketing practices. This means that the issues addressed were those raised by the sponsor. We included information and analyses that would directly address those questions plus information and analyses that would inform them more generally.

Related Literature

This project touches on three ongoing streams of research about public-sector employment and the employer brand. First, it clearly fits within the stream of government reform efforts to identify how to attract quality applicants to government service and retain them. It differs from those efforts in its topical focus, on branding and marketing, and its method, emphasizing empirical research with prospective applicants. Second, this work is related to a stream of research on public-service motivation, which investigates the degree to which generally altruistic motives among public-sector workers can compensate for perceived disadvantages in terms of salary and benefits relative to other employers. Our research diverges significantly from that research in that our focus is on how to attract enough employees to fill the ranks of the Army's mission-critical occupations from a broad spectrum of potential applicants, only some of whom might be substantially motivated by altruism. Lastly, this project makes use of the employer brand concept, but we make no claim to advance knowledge in that domain.

The project clearly fits within one stream produced by government and nonprofit organizations concerned with attracting and retaining talent to government service. Topically, this stream has been concerned with identifying and attracting the right talent and reducing structural barriers to achieving these ends, such as sclerotic hiring processes and inflexible compensation systems (see, for example, Partnership for Public Service, 2019; Partnership for Public Service and Booz Allen Hamilton, 2013; Partnership for Public Service and LinkedIn, 2017; McPhie, 2008; U.S. Merit Systems Protection Board, Office of Policy and Evaluation, 2008a, 2008b). This project adds to this vein of research in its focus on Army civilians in general and those in mission-critical occupations in particular. Methodologically, it contributes an empirical focus on incumbents and potential applicants.

Since the late 1980s, scholars have been concerned with the problem of attracting quality employees to public service and keeping them. On the one hand, some researchers have argued that those seeking employment in the public sector respond to a similar set of incentives as any other job-seeker (see, for example, Niskanen, 1971; Alfonso and Lewis, 2001; Lyons, Duxbury, and Higgins, 2016). On the other, Perry and Wise have articulated a theory of public-service motivation (PSM), which they defined in 1990 "as an individual's predisposition to respond to motives grounded primarily or uniquely in public institutions and organizations" (Perry and Wise, 1990, p. 368). At the time, they hypothesized that individuals' propensity to seek public-sector employment would increase with their level of PSM. Perry and Wise further hypothesized that recruitment strategies focused on PSM could rely on the appeal of serving the public good to motivate potential job-seekers instead of trying to compete with private-sector compensation. Over time, other scholars of public service have attempted to test these and other related hypotheses empirically. While the results of these analyses are not unambiguous, the weight of the evidence seems to suggest that public service motivation can compensate for monetary incentives—either directly or indirectly—for some potential employees (Houston, 2000; Bright, 2005, 2008, 2009; Perry, Hondeghem, and Wise, 2010; Ritz, Brewer, and Neumann, 2016; Wright, Hassan, and Christensen, 2017). As with the uniformed military, however, the resulting body of knowledge is unclear as to whether the subset of job-seekers with high PSM—and who would consider service with the Army to be a good fit to meet the objectives underlying their PSM—is large enough to meet Army requirements in critical occupations. This project, by contrast, is focused precisely on that question. Therefore, we had to consider a broader array of potential motivating factors.

Our factor analysis results show that, while some people are attracted to working for the Army in general (public service), others value the financial and security benefits offered by Army jobs, and still others are attracted by the work schedule flexibility, vacation, and work-life balance that Army jobs can offer.

This research also touches on the concept of an "employer brand." Ambler and Barrow first advanced the concept of the employer brand in 1996. The concept integrates insights about the importance of brands to marketing with human resource functions, especially recruiting and retention. It provided a useful framework for analyzing the U.S. Army's brand image in terms of its functional, economic, and psychological components. There is continuing interest in the concept of the employer brand and ample scope for further research (Backhaus, 2016). As with PSM, however, this project is concerned with addressing the practical question of establishing the Army's particular brand as a civilian employer, not with advancing knowledge with respect to that concept.

Organization of This Report

Chapter Two provides background information on the projects and selection of critical occupations for detailed analysis. Chapter Three presents our analysis of the external market. It identifies the criteria potential employees use to evaluate potential careers, analyzes the relationship between current job satisfaction, awareness of Army civilian employment and willingness to consider a job with the Army. It also identifies potential applicants' perceptions of Army jobs and their preferred sources of information. Chapter Four describes how current Army civilian employees in selected mission-critical occupations perceive the Army Civilian brand and its subbrands. Chapter Five compares Army compensation with that available in the private sector. Chapter Six presents our assessment of hiring needs. Chapter Seven explores Army online marketing to civilian job-seekers. In Chapter Eight, we discuss our overall conclusions and recommendations. Five appendixes provide additional background on methods and other analysis.

CHAPTER TWO

Background and Selection of Study Occupations

Overview

The analyses described in this report focus primarily on four occupations, chosen to represent a range of potential mission-critical occupations the Army had identified at the beginning of this effort. In conjunction with Army stakeholders, we chose occupations according to several criteria. Those criteria included factors such as the size of the Army population of that occupation, likely turnover in the field, location, salary levels and so forth. In consultation with stakeholders, we further narrowed the range of potential mission-critical occupations to four occupations (the number in parenthesis indicates the occupation series number):

- Civil Engineers (0810)
- Electronics Engineers (0855)
- Contract Specialists (1102)[1]
- Information Technology (IT) Managers (2210).

Analytic Approach

Identifying Occupations for the Project

Working with the sponsor, other Army subject-matter experts (SMEs), and the Army's civilian hiring agencies, our initial task was to identify critical

---

[1] This job series includes contract specialists, analysts, administrators, and negotiators.

occupational areas for in-depth analysis. The areas had to be of critical importance to the Army, due to their roles in supporting warfighting, existing or anticipated fill issues, or future growth needs in response to changes in the national security environment. The initial discussions revealed 80 civilian occupations identified as federal high-risk or mission-critical by the Army or the U.S. Department of Defense (DoD). See Table 2.1.

Analysis of all 80 occupations was well beyond the scope of the projects; therefore, we selected a subset of the occupations for our analysis. To the extent possible, our goal was to have them reflect different problem issues and hiring processes. The occupations selected vary in factors such as the number of vacancies, proportion of the skill filled by uniformed personnel versus civilians, the age of staff and related current requirements at entry and other levels, recent hiring patterns with respect to new Army employees versus transfers of current DoD employees, and their implications for mid- and longer-term hiring needs, issues, and approaches. Identifying the occupations for detailed study included reviewing the literature and data on near- and longer-term requirements, supply, hiring processes, and compensation for the critical DA Civilian positions in the general civilian and defense labor forces and considering how the results could affect Army hiring and shortages of both junior and more senior personnel.

More specifically, we reviewed the general employment literature, DoD, and Army documents, and extant analyses to

- identify a subset of mission-critical occupations from which study occupations would be selected
- develop a framework for narrowing the set and for future use by the Army Marketing and Research Group (AMRG).[2]

We integrated these results with detailed information on the characteristics of occupations (e.g., turnover; retirement eligibility; hiring; demographics; General Schedule [GS], education, and supervisor distribution; pay; percentage of veterans; geographic distribution) using Civilian Master

---

[2] The Army recently decided to disestablish AMRG and, in its stead, stand up the Army Enterprise Marketing Office.

TABLE 2.1
Federal High-Risk and DoD/Army Mission-Critical Civilian Occupations

Federal High-Risk	DoD/Army Mission-Critical	Army Mission-Critical
• 0110 – Economist	• 0017 – Explosive Safety Specialist	• 0028 – Environmental Protection Specialist
• 0201 – Personnel Management	• 0018 – Safety and Occupational Health Management	• 0083 – Police
• 0511 – Auditing	• 0080 – Security Administration	• 0085 – Security Guard
• 0840 – Nuclear Engineer	• 0081 – Fire Protection and Prevention	• 0101 – Social Science
• 0855 – Electronics Engineer	• 0130 – Foreign Affairs	• 0131 – International Relations
• 1102 – Contracting	• 0132 – Intelligence	• 0260 – Equal Employment Opportunity
• 2210 – Information Technology Management	• 0180 – Psychology	• 0391 – Communications Management
	• 0185 – Social Work	• 0401 – General Natural Resources Management and Biological Sciences
	• 0301 – Miscellaneous Administration and Programming	• 0505 – Financial Management
	• 0340 – Program Management	• 0601 – General Health Science
	• 0343 – Management Analysis	• 0603 – Physician Assistant
	• 0346 – Logistics Management	• 0620 – Practical Nurse
	• 0501 – Financial Administration and Programming	• 0621 – Nursing Assistant
	• 0510 – Accounting	• 0633 – Physical Therapist
	• 0560 – Budget Analysis	• 0640 – Health Aid and Technician
	• 0602 – Medical Officer	• 0642 – Nuclear Medicine Technician
	• 0610 – Nurse	• 0647 – Diagnostic Radiologic Technologist
	• 0660 – Pharmacist	• 0671 – Health Systems Specialist
	• 0801 – General Engineer	• 0681 – Dental Assistant
	• 0854 – Computer Engineer	• 0682 – Dental Hygiene
	• 1101 – General Business and Industry	• 0802 – Engineering
	• 1550 – Computer Scientist	• 0809 – Construction Control
	• 1670 – Equipment Specialist	• 0810 – Civil Engineering
	• 1811 – Criminal Investigating	• 0819 – Environmental Engineering
	• 1910 – Quality Assurance	• 0830 – Mechanical Engineering
	• 2001 – General Supply	• 0850 – Electrical Engineering
	• 2003 – Support Program Management	• 0861 – Aerospace Engineering
	• 2010 – Inventory Management	• 0893 – Chemical Engineering
	• 2101 – Transportation Specialist	• 0905 – General Attorney
	• 2130 – Traffic Management	• 0950 – Paralegal Specialist
	• 2150 – Transportation Operations	• 1035 – Public Affairs Specialist
		• 1040 – Language Specialist
		• 1173 – Housing Management
		• 1301 – General Physical Sciences
		• 1320 – Chemistry
		• 1515 – Operations Research
		• 1520 – Mathematics
		• 1701 – General Education and Training
		• 1712 – Training Instruction
		• 1740 – Education Services
		• 1801 – General Inspection, Investigation, Enforcement, and Compliance
		• 2152 – Air Traffic Control

SOURCE: Headquarters, Department of the Army, Assistant G-1 (Civilian Personnel).

7

File data.[3] We then used the results to select 15 candidate occupations for detailed study.

The next step involved discussing the framework and candidate occupations with the following key stakeholders:

- AMRG staff
- DA Civilian Conference attendees
- Deputy Assistant Secretary of the Army for Civilian Personnel and staff
- Assistant G-1 for Civilian Personnel and staff
- Commanding General, U.S. Army Corps of Engineers (USACE), and staff
- Director, Civilian Human Resources Agency, and staff.

On the basis of these analyses and discussions, we initially selected six occupations for detailed study. The framework and applicable values for the six occupations are illustrated in Table 2.2. The lower portion of Table 2.2 shows the minimum, quartile, and maximum values of each characteristic across the 80 mission-critical occupations in Table 2.1. We sought a range of values across our six study occupations for the framework variables. The variables reflect number of personnel (we set a minimum of 1,000 for consideration); total turnover rate; percentage currently retirement eligible and percentage who will become retirement eligible within five years; average age, tenure, and pay; percentages in GS levels 12–14 and 15+; percentage of veterans; percentage of the occupation's jobs considered sensitive; percentage of supervisors and of women in the occupation; percentage with bachelor's, master's, and doctoral degrees; percentage of the largest 20 sites employing DA civilians in the occupation located in urban areas and percentage of all DA civilians in the occupation located at one of the largest 20 sites (both measures of dispersion across the country, including urban versus rural areas); and percentage white (shown here for parsimony, with

---

[3]   The Civilian Master File describes the workforce as it exists at the end of each fiscal year. It is distinct from other civilian data sources, such as the Transactions File and more detailed pay records.

TABLE 2.2a

Selected Framework Characteristics of Study Occupations

Series	Occupation	Personnel	Turnover (%)	Retirement Eligible (%)	Retirement Eligible in 5 Years	Avg. Age	Avg. Tenure	Avg. Salary ($)	% GS 12–14	% GS 15
0301	Management Analyst	18,559	22.6	12.1	19.2	49.3	14.2	72,709	46.1	3.5
0340	Program Manager	2,033	22.5	20.3	25.9	51.6	19.9	109,722	48.6	17.8
0810	Civil Engineer	6,603	13.4	19.2	18.1	45.6	17.8	80,830	73.2	2.8
0855	Electronics Engineer	2,779	12.5	11.5	20.9	45.8	18.3	93,187	45.5	1.2
1102	Contract Specialist	7,329	17.1	13.2	16.6	45.1	15.5	71,374	52.7	1.8
2210	IT Manager	12,622	17.4	10.3	15.0	46.4	14.5	70,081	53.8	1.1
	Minimum	1,002	11.1	3.5	8.4	38.9	7.3	28,401	0.0	0.0
	25th percentile	1,378	15.7	8.9	13.6	44.5	11.5	58,882	22.8	0.1
	50th percentile	2,011	20.9	13.0	16.8	47.1	14.5	68,211	46.0	0.9
	75th percentile	3,543	24.2	15.9	19.1	48.7	17.3	77,696	54.1	1.8
	Maximum	18,599	38.4	29.4	25.9	52.7	19.9	109,722	89.0	41.4

TABLE 2.2b
Selected Framework Characteristics of Study Occupations

Series	Occupation	% Veterans	% Sensitive	% Supervisor	% Female	% Bachelor's Degree	% Master's Degree	% Ph.D.	% Urban in Top 20	% in Top 20	% White
0301	Management Analyst	61.6	16.2	25.7	34.9	25.1	23.0	2.2	61.6	51.4	71.6
0340	Program Manager	36.3	22.4	65.1	21.0	34.1	44.2	4.2	85.5	52.9	82.7
0810	Civil Engineer	15.0	3.3	21.8	17.4	60.7	30.2	3.6	67.9	58.4	81.8
0855	Electronics Engineer	10.5	27.4	16.3	10.7	56.0	33.8	7.9	63.9	94.6	69.3
1102	Contract Specialist	26.4	4.4	17.2	57.5	53.0	32.2	1.8	61.3	62.0	68.0
2210	IT Manager	55.3	22.4	16.4	24.1	24.6	14.1	1.1	49.5	49.4	68.1
	Minimum	7.7	0.0	0.0	2.8	2.0	0.2	0.0	21.2	38.4	46.6
	25th percentile	20.8	1.7	10.8	15.4	13.1	8.2	0.6	44.1	56.2	63.5
	50th percentile	35.6	4.4	16.8	32.5	24.9	19.6	1.5	60.5	64.2	69.6
	75th percentile	57.6	11.2	24.0	57.4	38.3	30.7	4.3	68.2	27.0	79.5
	Maximum	87.8	97.4	85.1	94.9	70.3	84.3	79.4	87.5	97.3	91.7

100 percent minus the percentage equaling the percentage of racial/ethnic minority employees).

Reducing the Number of Occupations Studied

Upon review, stakeholders agreed with the research team to reduce the original list of six occupations to four at a session hosted at RAND's Washington, D.C., office in July 2015. It was felt that results of our analysis of responses for incumbents in the management analyst and program management occupations did not indicate differences sufficient to warrant further study in this area. The four remaining occupations we studied are identified as follows:

- Civil Engineers (0810)
- Electronics Engineers (0855)
- Contracting Specialists (1102)
- IT Managers (2210).

CHAPTER THREE

External Market Project

In this chapter, we discuss the external market project, starting with the research objective, tasks, and initial steps. We then provide overviews of our qualitative data analysis, followed by our quantitative survey analysis. We next present and discuss detailed results from our quantitative analysis. We conclude with a summary of our quantitative results and their marketing implications. Supplemental data and analysis results are presented in Appendix C.

The objective of the external market project was to carry out research to better understand the external marketplace and assess potential employee perceptions and awareness levels; update current and projected DA Civilian shortfalls (see Chapter Six); and set specific marketing objectives and strategies. We first used the results of our internal analysis (see Chapter Four) to generate initial hypotheses on branding, marketing, and potential positioning platforms. Next, we reviewed the results of the analysis with SMEs from the offices, occupations, and agencies previously discussed to refine our initial hypotheses as desirable to develop concepts for testing in the external marketplace, including among students and younger and older professionals working or, for students, desiring to work in our engineering, contracting, and IT management specialties. We then carried out a limited, largely open-ended online survey of such students and professionals, and conducted follow-up sessions with a subsample of the participants based on their initial responses. We used the results to refine the questions and response alternatives for the larger survey. Through quantitative analysis of our survey of possible hires into DA Civilian occupations, together with those from the initial, internal DA Civilian project, the goal was to recommend branding and marketing objectives and strategies (including messaging) for student and professional groups to help fill DA civilian occupations.

Subject-Matter Expert Meetings

As discussed earlier, we focused the external project on occupational series 810, 855, 1120, and 2210 (Civil Engineers, Electronics Engineers, Contracting Specialists, and IT Managers, respectively) and obtained contact information for SMEs in these series. We conducted preliminary meetings and discussions with the SMEs and other series personnel. During July 2015, we held a meeting at RAND's Washington Office with the SMEs. During the meeting, we reviewed the results of the initial analysis with the SMEs and conducted additional discussions to develop materials for testing in the external marketplace, including for students and younger and older professionals.

Qualitative Analysis

We collected data for the qualitative analysis by having respondents complete a "semi structured" questionnaire. While this instrument included some closed-ended questions, the focus was on soliciting verbatim responses to open-ended questions. We recontacted selected respondents, who then answered additional questions probing some of their initial responses. The research populations consisted of professionals currently employed as Civil Engineers, Electronics Engineers, Contracting Specialists, or IT Managers, under 66 years old, and not employed by the military, and students (college juniors or seniors or graduate students) who were interested in pursuing a career in at least one of these occupations.

The questionnaire required 15–20 minutes to complete. The survey data were collected between January and February 2018. Respondents were recruited through online consumer panels:

- Professionals: The online panel included information on members' occupation, which we confirmed in the questionnaire before allowing respondents to continue.
- Students: College juniors and seniors and graduate students were screened through questions assessing their level of interest in each of the four occupations. Data collection for those who had little interest in any of the careers was terminated. Whenever possible, students

were questioned about the career for which they expressed the greatest interest.

Table 3.1 shows the composition of the samples of professionals and students. Twelve students responded to the follow-up questions, as did 16 professionals.

The survey covered the respondents' background characteristics and demographics; year of school for students and current job for professionals, including tenure and likes and dislikes; job preferences, including type of organization and the importance of various job characteristics; how they would go about looking for another job; and awareness and perceptions of working for Army as a civilian, including interest, perceived advantages and concerns, and if they were not interested, why not. The survey used in the qualitative analysis is presented in Appendix A.

Quantitative Analysis

Sample

Data for the quantitative analysis were collected by having respondents complete a 20–25- minute online survey. The survey instrument included primarily closed-ended questions, accompanied by some open-ended

TABLE 3.1
Sample Composition for Qualitative Analysis

	Professionals	Students
Total	63	60
Civil Engineers	15	16
Electronics Engineers	15	15
Contracting Specialists	15	14
IT Managers	18	
Early career (under 30)	14	
Mid-career (30–49)	37	
Late career (50–65)	12	

questions and interactive features. As with the qualitative analysis, the research populations consisted of professionals currently employed as Civil Engineers, Electronics Engineers, Contracting Specialists, or IT Managers, under 66 years old, and not employed by the military, and students (college juniors or seniors or graduate students) who were interested in pursuing a career in at least one of these occupations.

The survey data were collected during November 2018. As with the qualitative analysis, respondents were recruited through online consumer panels that included information on professionals' occupations. As before, we confirmed that professionals worked in one of the relevant occupations in the questionnaire before allowing them to continue. For students, we confirmed that they were college juniors, seniors, or graduate students interested in working in at least one of the four occupations. Again, whenever possible, students were questioned about the career for which they expressed the greatest interest.

Table 3.2 shows the composition of the samples of professionals and students.

The purpose of the survey used in the qualitative analysis was to help shape and inform the survey used for the quantitative analysis. Thus, the two surveys covered the same general areas, though the second survey did so in greater detail and with more response options. The survey covered screening and filtering questions, including respondents' background characteristics; their demographics; current job, including tenure, for professionals,

TABLE 3.2
Sample Composition for Quantitative Analysis

	Professionals	Students
Total	2,901	1,576
Civil Engineers	750	394
Electronics Engineers	750	394
Contracting Specialists	651	394
IT Managers	750	394
Early to mid-career (under 40)	1,626	
Mid- to late career (40–55)	1,275	

and year of school, primary area of study, and types of desired careers for students; and the importance of 16 job characteristics. For professionals, the survey then asked about how they would rate their current employer on the same 16 characteristics, how satisfied they were with their current job, and whether they were currently looking for another job or planned to do so within the next year. Students were asked to rate the type of employer they had chosen earlier on the same 16 characteristics. Students and professionals both were asked the extent to which they would use 11 sources of information if they were to conduct a job search. They next were asked about their overall impression of the Army, awareness that civilians can work for the Army, and interest in getting more information about a civilian Army job or career. They were asked to rate Army civilian jobs on the same 16 job characteristics and, separately, on possible concerns about Army jobs. Respondents were then given additional information about DA civilian jobs. They were asked which aspects of that information were particularly good reasons for considering working for the Army as a civilian and, now that they knew more, about their interest in getting more information about a civilian Army job or career and their willingness to consider recommending to a friend that he or she consider an Army civilian job. The survey used in the quantitative analysis is presented in Appendix B. Tables C.1–C.3 show descriptive statistics for the survey responses; more generally, Appendix C shows supplemental data and analysis results.

The members of the online consumer panels we used in the qualitative and quantitative analyses were recruited from multiple online channels, as well as by telephone. Online channels include the major social media platforms, which provide wide access to potential respondents. Based on a 2018 study conducted by the Pew Research Center (Smith and Andersen, 2018), social media are used regularly by 88 percent of 18-to-29-year-olds, 78 percent of 30-to-49-year-olds, 64 percent of 50-to-64-year-olds, and 37 percent of those who are 65 or older.

Because panel participants are recruited from multiple sources, respondent duplication is eliminated through digital fingerprinting and fraud protection services (provided by SurValidate). Checks are employed when participants are recruited to the panel and in real time during survey data collection. Online panel recruits are verified via email, and telephone recruits are verified by telephone calls placed from a centralized call center.

Business-to-business respondents are also verified against standard industry registries (e.g., MD, CPA). Panel participants are offered no more than eight surveys per month. Participation data show that fewer requests lead participants to be become less engaged, while more requests result in lower participation and lower-quality responses. Panel participants are given reward points for completing surveys, and these points can be redeemed for cash through PayPal or through more than 100 gift cards and charitable organizations.

For our survey, soft quotas were used to ensure that the samples had sufficient representation of professionals and students across the four job categories. Several procedures were used to ensure that all respondents provided "good" data. Respondents were removed from the sample if they completed the questionnaire too quickly, displayed response patterns that indicated a lack of attention, or gave "nonsense" answers to open-ended questions. These respondents were replaced so that the final sample size met our quotas.

Results of Quantitative Analysis

We next discuss in detail results from the quantitative analysis in the external market study. We begin with respondents' ratings of the importance of 16 job characteristics. The characteristics and, more generally, the quantitative survey questions were chosen based on relevant literature, our initial internal project, SME discussions, and our qualitative analysis. In Table 3.3, the ratings provided by students, younger professionals, and older professionals have each been converted to standard normal scores, with the average rating for that group set to zero and a standard deviation of 1.[1] In Table 3.3, the rows are sorted from highest to lowest rating using the values for younger professionals. The job characteristics in rows with green text in the top portion of the table were rated well above zero; that is, they all were rated as especially important relative to the other characteristics. These

---

[1] Respondents were shown 12 screens, each with a set of four job characteristics. They were asked to select the characteristic that would be the highest priority for them and the characteristic that would be the lowest priority on each screen. The results were combined mathematically and normalized using a MaxDiff analysis to obtain the ratings for each characteristic.

TABLE 3.3

Job Characteristic Preferences

Job Characteristic (z-score, 0 mid-point)	Student	Professional, Age < 40	Professional, Age 40–55
Attractive salary level	1.05	1.15	1.03
Good work-life balance	0.62	0.62	0.56
Generous benefits, insurance, etc.	0.46	0.57	0.55
Strong job security	0.58	0.55	0.61
Generous retirement pension plan	0.18	0.41	0.42
Opportunity to use your talents and abilities	0.29	0.31	0.34
Opportunity to do great things with your life	0.23	0.12	0.02
Provides many opportunities to learn and advance	0.07	0.05	−0.04
Fast career advancement	−0.08	−0.02	−0.12
Allows for flexibility in work schedule	−0.13	−0.23	−0.23
Exposure to exciting job-related challenges	−0.41	−0.26	−0.19
Generous holiday/vacation policy	−0.27	−0.32	−0.30
Colleagues you enjoy working with	−0.48	−0.57	−0.46
Opportunity to work with people like you	−0.67	−0.67	−0.58
Encourages collaboration among coworkers	−0.79	−0.83	−0.72
Opportunity to travel	−0.65	−0.85	−0.90

NOTE: The three yellow-shaded entries were notably and significantly lower statistically for the indicated group than for the other groups for that characteristic ($p < 0.0001$, $p < 0.01$, and $p < 0.0001$, respectively, by t-test). There were no notable differences in relative rankings by occupation within group.

characteristics are salary (rated well above other characteristics), work-life balance, benefits, job security, and using one's talents. While not identical, the relative and absolute ratings for the characteristics were similar across groups, with attractive salary level rated notably higher than other characteristics.

In contrast, the characteristics shown in red font in the bottom portion of the table were rated as least important. They involve the characteristics of colleagues and travel. The three yellow-shaded entries were notably and significantly lower statistically for the group shaded than the other groups for the given characteristic ($p < 0.0001$, $p < 0.01$, and $p < 0.0001$, respectively, by t-test). There were no notable differences in relative rankings by occupation within group.

Table 3.4 shows the correlation between professionals' preferred job characteristics and the characteristics of their current jobs as they perceive

TABLE 3.4

Correlation Between Preferred and Actual Job Characteristic Preferences

Job Characteristic	Professional, Age < 40	Professional, Age 40–55
Attractive salary level	−0.14	−0.15
Good work-life balance	−0.05	−0.06
Generous holiday/vacation policy	0.02	0.04
Strong job security	0.02	−0.03
Allows for flexibility in work schedule	0.03	0.07
Generous benefits, insurance, etc.	0.04	−0.09
Generous retirement pension plan	0.05	−0.08
Provides many opportunities to learn and advance	0.08	0.08
Opportunity to do great things with your life	0.13	0.20
Fast career advancement	0.16	0.24
Encourages collaboration among coworkers	0.17	0.22
Opportunity to use your talents and abilities	0.18	0.14
Colleagues you enjoy working with	0.21	0.19
Opportunity to work with people like you	0.27	0.29
Exposure to exciting job-related challenges	0.27	0.27
Opportunity to travel	0.36	0.40

them (measured on a 0 = Poor to 10 = Excellent scale). Among the strongly preferred job characteristics (green text), there is a mismatch between preferred and one's actual job characteristics for salary, and a match between preferred and perceived actual job characteristics for use of one's talents and abilities. Among lesser preferred job characteristics (black font), there is a match between preferred and perceived opportunity to do great things with one's life and fast career advancement. The relative differences between preferred and actual job characteristic are similar for the two professional groups and for the occupations within each group. Correlations near 0.09 and differences in correlations near 0.13 (both in absolute value) are statistically significant at $p < 0.001$.

Table 3.5 shows the association of (1) the difference between professionals' ratings of their preferred job characteristics and their normalized ratings of the characteristics of their current jobs as they perceive them with (2) their job satisfaction, as indicated by whether they were currently looking more information about a civilian job or career in the Army both before and after getting basic information about DA civilian jobs. The association is expressed as a correlation, with positive values meaning a positive association and negative values meaning a negative one. Job satisfaction, likeli-

TABLE 3.5

Correlation Between Difference in Preferred and Actual Job Characteristics, Satisfaction, and Looking for Job or Interest in Information About an Army Civilian Job or Career

Measure	Professional, Age < 40	Professional, Age 40–55
Overall satisfaction (0–10)	−0.43	−0.36
Currently looking (1 no/2 yes)	0.23	0.21
How likely to look in next year (0–10)	0.08	0.12
Interest in information about Army civilian jobs (0–10)	−0.11	−0.12
Interest in information about Army civilian careers (0–10)	−0.11	−0.13
Informed interest in information about Army civilian jobs (0–10)	−0.09	−0.07
Informed interest in information about Army civilian careers (0–10)	−0.10	−0.08

hood of looking for a job in the next year, and interest in getting information about Army civilian jobs or careers were measured on 0 to 10 scales, respectively: 0 = Extremely Dissatisfied to 10 = Extremely Satisfied; 0 = Extremely Unlikely to 10 = Extremely Likely; 0 = Not at All Interested to 10 = Extremely Interested. Correlations near 0.09 and differences in correlations near 0.13 (both in absolute value) are statistically significant at $p < 0.001$.

The correlations in Table 3.5 show that a mismatch between preferred and actual job characteristics is strongly associated with lower satisfaction and a greater likelihood of job search. At the same time, however, a mismatch between preferred and actual job characteristics is negatively associated with interest in getting information about civilian jobs in Army—that is, although professionals with a greater mismatch were more likely to be looking for a job, they were less likely to want information about Army civilian jobs.

There were no meaningful differences between younger and older professionals in the association of the extent of the mismatch between preferred and perceived job characteristics and job satisfaction, job search, or interest in information about Army jobs.

Among younger professionals, Civil Engineers were less satisfied overall ($p < 0.05$), and the association of the gap size with job satisfaction was smaller for them ($p < 0.01$). There were no differences across job series in looking for a job or in the association of the gap size with looking for one. Analogously, there were no differences across job types in interest in getting information about Army civilian jobs/careers or in the association of the gap size with interest in doing so. See Table C.4.

Among older professionals, IT Managers were most satisfied overall ($p < 0.05$); there were no differences in the association of the gap size with satisfaction across job types. Civil Engineers were somewhat more likely to look for work ($p < 0.05$) but were less sensitive to gap size in doing so ($p < 0.01$). Engineers, especially Electronics Engineers, were more interested in getting information about Army careers ($p < 0.01$). However, larger gaps between preferred and perceived job characteristics for Electronics Engineers had a greater association with reduced interest in getting information about Army civilian careers ($p < 0.05$). See Table C.5.

Favorability toward the Army was assessed through the question, "First, we would like your overall impression of the Army. Using the scale below, give us your overall impression of the Army." The question used a 0–10 scale: 0 = Extremely Unfavorable; 10 = Extremely Favorable. We then correlated the responses to the favorability question with the questions concerning interest in getting more information about Army civilian jobs or careers in addition to a question about the respondent's willingness to recommend to a friend looking for work that he or she consider an Army civilian job, all assessed on similar 0–10 scales. The interest-in-information questions were asked twice; the second time was after respondents were given some general information about Army civilian jobs and benefits. The recommendation question was asked once after receiving the general information about Army civilian jobs, with 0 = Extremely Unlikely and 10 = Extremely Likely. Table 3.6 shows the correlation results for the three survey groups. The results show that basic favorability toward the Army is strongly associated with interest in getting information about Army civilian jobs and willingness to recommend one to a friend looking for work. Again, correlations near 0.09 and differences in correlations near 0.13 (both in absolute value) are statistically significant at $p < 0.001$. Thus, there were no meaningful differences in correlations among students, younger professionals, and older professionals.

TABLE 3.6

Correlation Between Favorability Toward the Army and Interest in Information About an Army Civilian Job or Career

Measure (all 0–10 scale)	Student	Professional, Age < 40	Professional, Age 40–55
Interest in information about Army civilian jobs	0.56	0.53	0.54
Interest in information about Army civilian careers	0.57	0.51	0.52
Informed interest in information about Army civilian jobs	0.52	0.48	0.49
Informed interest in information about Army civilian careers	0.51	0.46	0.46
Would recommend Army job to friend	0.58	0.53	0.55

We next calculated the difference in respondents' preferred job characteristics and those they believed would be found in Army civilian jobs. We did this by calculating the difference in the rating for each of the 16 characteristics between the preferred and normalized Army ratings, and then summing the absolute values of the differences across all 16 characteristics. That absolute sum was correlated with the responses to the measures concerning interest in getting more information about Army civilian jobs or careers, as well as with willingness to recommend that a friend looking for a job consider an Army civilian job. As described above, the responses to these questions were all assessed on 0–10 scales, and the interest-in-information questions were asked twice; the second time was after respondents were given some general information about Army civilian jobs and benefits. Table 3.7 shows the correlation results for the three survey groups. The results show that the extent of the mismatch between one's preferred job characteristics and those perceived to characterize Army jobs is strongly associated with lower interest in getting information about Army civilian jobs or willingness to recommend one to a friend. Again, correlations near 0.09 and differences in correlations near 0.13 (both in absolute value) are statistically significant at $p < 0.001$.

Among students, there were no significant differences in interest or willingness to recommend consideration of a DA civilian Army job by job type. The association of the gap size with informed interest in Army civilian careers was significant ($p < 0.05$) but only slightly smaller for Electronics Engineers. See Table C.6.

Among younger professionals, Civil Engineers were somewhat less interested in information about Army civilian jobs or careers overall, though only one measure difference reached statistical significance at the $p < 0.05$ level (pre-informed career interest). There were no significant differences across job series in the association of the gap size with interest or recommendation. See Table C.7.

Among older professionals, Civil Engineers were significantly less interested in information about an Army civilian job before receiving additional information ($p < 0.05$), and IT Managers were significantly less interested on both the informed job and career information measures ($p < 0.05$). The association of the gap with the pre-informed interest measures for Civil Engineers ($p < 0.05$) and for IT Managers with both the informed job and

TABLE 3.7

Correlation Between Perceived Difference in Desired Job Characteristics Versus Those of Army Civilian Jobs and Interest in Information About an Army Civilian Job or Career

Measure (all 0–10 scale)	Student	Professional, Age < 40	Professional, Age 40–55
Interest in information about Army civilian jobs	−0.40	−0.35	−0.32
Interest in information about Army civilian careers	−0.41	−0.37	−0.35
Informed interest in information about Army civilian jobs	−0.33	−0.31	−0.23
Informed interest in information about Army civilian careers	−0.37	−0.35	−0.28
Would recommend Army job to friend	−0.39	−0.35	−0.26

informed career information interest measures was smaller ($p < 0.01$ and $p < 0.05$, respectively). See Table C.8.

We next correlated respondents' rating of their preference for each job characteristic with their rating of the extent to which they believed they would find that characteristic in an Army civilian job. Table 3.8 shows the results for the three survey groups. For strongly or moderately valued characteristics, positive correlations of 0.10 or greater are shaded green, and negative correlations of -0.10 or more are shaded red. The results indicate that among the strongly preferred job characteristics (green text), the only notable positive association between the importance of the characteristic to respondents and their perception of finding the characteristic in an Army civilian job was for students' perception that Army civilians get a good retirement plan. In contrast, respondents in the three groups who more highly valued work-life balance and schedule flexibility were less likely to believe they would get these characteristics in an Army civilian job. Professionals who valued salary more highly also were less likely to believe they would get a good salary in an Army civilian job. We note that salary and work-life balance are the most preferred job characteristics. Among the moderately preferred job characteristics (black text), there are matches with preference strength in the direction and level of the correlation for exciting

TABLE 3.8

Correlation Between Respondents' Ratings of Their Preferred Job Characteristics and the Perceived Characteristics of Army Civilian Jobs

Job Characteristic	Student	Professional, Age < 40	Professional, Age 40–55
Opportunity to work with people like you	0.07	0.19	0.24
Exposure to exciting job-related challenges	0.07	0.12	0.12
Fast career advancement	0.18	0.10	0.16
Encourages collaboration among coworkers	0.05	0.09	0.13
Opportunity to use your talents and abilities	0.09	0.08	0.04
Colleagues you enjoy working with	0.02	0.07	0.12
Opportunity to do great things with your life	0.04	0.06	0.05
Provides many opportunitioo to learn and advance	0.02	0.03	0.02
Opportunity to travel	0.03	0.03	0.10
Generous benefits, insurance, etc.	0.09	0.03	0.00
Generous retirement pension plan	0.13	0.02	0.02
Strong job security	0.09	0.02	−0.02
Generous holiday/vacation policy	−0.02	0.01	−0.01
Allows for flexibility in work schedule	−0.18	−0.09	−0.10
Attractive salary level	0.00	−0.14	−0.20
Good work-life balance	−0.17	−0.17	−0.20

challenges (professionals) and fast advancement. Again, correlations near 0.09 and differences in correlations near 0.13 (both in absolute value) are statistically significant at $p < 0.001$. The relative differences between respondents' ratings of their preferred and perceived Army job characteristics were similar across the four job series within each group.

Table 3.9 presents results concerning awareness of and misperceptions about Army civilian jobs. As can be seen in the table, only about 40 percent of the students and younger professionals knew that civilians can have jobs in the Army; for older professionals, awareness was just under 60 percent. Moreover, only 25–30 percent of the three groups knew that it is not Army practice to involuntarily deploy Army civilians. Among students and older professionals, there were no differences in awareness of the Army civilian job opportunity or of Army practice concerning involuntary deployment of Army civilians across job types. Among younger professionals, there were no differences in awareness of the Army civilian job opportunity; engineers were somewhat less informed concerning involuntary deployment ($p < 0.01$).

We next assessed respondents' concerns about Army civilian jobs using nine questions often used in relation to uniformed jobs in the Army. As described above, the responses to these questions were all assessed on 0–10 scales, in this case with 0 = Not a Concern and 10 = Major Concern. Table 3.10 shows the average rating for each concern for the three survey groups.

Involuntary transfer, undesirable location, injury/death, and low salary were the leading concerns about Army civilian jobs for all groups. In contrast, opposition from family/friends and not wanting to support the Army

TABLE 3.9
Awareness of and Misperceptions About Army Civilian Jobs (%)

Question	Student	Professional, Age < 40	Professional, Age 40–55
Must Civilians Be Uniformed?			
Civilians enlist or join the Army as officers to get a job	36.4	32.4	22.4
Not sure	23.6	23.9	18.7
Civilians have jobs in the Army	40.0	43.7	58.9
Could Army Civilians Be Involuntarily Deployed?			
Yes	46.5	48.6	50.7
Not Sure	26.3	24.8	19.6
No	27.2	26.5	29.6

TABLE 3.10

Concerns About Working in Army Civilian Jobs (%)

Concern (all 0–10 scale)	Student	Professional, Age < 40	Professional, Age 40–55
Possibility of being transferred involuntarily	7.45	7.15	7.25
Required to live in undesirable places	7.27	6.96	7.13
Possibility of injury/death	7.42	6.95	6.90
Low salary	7.16	6.86	7.04
Poor benefits packages	6.81	6.24	6.52
Too much travel	6.50	6.10	6.65
Not enough job security	6.62	6.01	6.27
Opposition by family/friends	6.20	5.77	5.84
Do not want to support the military	5.81	5.23	5.61

were at the bottom of the concerns. Still, all nine issues were rated as at least mildly concerning (above the scale midpoint of 5). There were no notable differences in relative concern rankings among the student and professional groups or by job type. Differences in within group ratings are statistically significant at $p < 0.05$ at 0.16 to 0.23 for students, 0.18 to 0.24 for younger professionals, and 0.20 to 0.27 for older professionals.

Results of Factor Analyses

Our factor analyses look for correlations among responses to the questions about job preferences, awareness of Army civilian jobs, favorability toward the Army, perceptions of Army civilian jobs, and concerns about working for the Army as a civilian. We used a principal component analysis followed by orthogonal factor rotation. The purpose of factor analysis is to reduce the number of dimensions in assessing the responses of the persons surveyed. Here, specifically, it is looking for question groupings that have similar responses and differences across the three professional and student groups. The factors and the related factor loadings are used to identify subgroups whose responses to the survey questions indicate the types of things that matter to them and the subgroups focused on those things and valuing them similarly.

The groupings and interrelationships were generally similar among younger and older professionals. See Tables C.9 and C.10, respectively. For professionals, in comparing models with three to six factors, we found the best fit for four factors:

- favorability toward the Army and perceptions of Army civilian jobs
- concerns about working in an Army civilian job
- importance of a job providing a good fit with colleagues and opportunity to collaborate versus importance of salary, benefits, and job security
- importance of a job providing the opportunity to use one's own talents, provide challenges, and offer fast advancement versus the importance of vacation, work schedule flexibility, and work-life balance.

For students, we found the best fit for five factors, similar to those we found for professionals. See Table C.11. The first three factors were the same ones we found for professionals. The fourth factor for professionals split into two factors for students, as follows:

- importance of a job providing the opportunity to use one's own talents, do great things with one's life, and to provide learning opportunities versus the importance of vacation and good benefits
- importance of a job providing challenges, fast advancement, and travel versus the importance of work schedule flexibility and work-life balance.

We next examined how the factors and awareness of Army civilian jobs were related to perceptions of Army civilian job characteristics relative to one's preferences. The results are summarized below for each of the three survey groups. See Tables C.12–C.14.

Students

- Favorability was consistently (though modestly) positively associated with perceptions of Army civilian jobs.

- Those with greater concerns about working as an Army civilian were more concerned about working with similar colleagues, working with colleagues they would enjoy working with, collaboration opportunities, and, to a lesser extent, travel and vacation policy; they were less concerned about salary, job security, fast advancement, and, to a lesser degree, retirement and other benefits.
- Those wanting to use their talents, do great things, and learn versus focusing on vacation and benefits were more concerned about achieving these goals in an Army civilian job and less concerned about retirement and other benefits, travel, and vacation policy.
- Those wanting challenges, fast advancement, and travel versus schedule flexibility and work-life balance were more concerned about achieving these goals in an Army civilian job and, to a lesser extent, about retirement and other benefits; they were less concerned about work-life balance, schedule flexibility, and, to an even lesser extent, vacation policy and enjoying working with their colleagues.
- We found limited additional effects of awareness of civilian jobs or deployment practices. Concern about job security and working with similar people (modestly lower) were found for those unaware of Army civilian jobs. Concern about travel was lower, but concern about work-life balance and, to a lesser degree, vacations and schedule flexibility were greater among those unaware of involuntary deployment policy.

Younger Professionals

- Favorability was consistently (though modestly) positively associated with perceptions of Army civilian jobs.
- Those emphasizing a good fit with colleagues and collaboration versus salary, benefits, and job security were more concerned about achieving these goals and, to a lesser degree, about travel and challenges in an Army civilian job; they were less concerned about salary and, to a lesser extent, retirement and other benefits, job security, fast advancement, and work-life balance.
- Those wanting to use their talents, those wanting to face challenges, and those with a preference for fast advancement versus vacation, work schedule flexibility, and work-life balance were more concerned about achieving these goals, doing great things, and opportunities to learn

and advance; they were less concerned about vacation policy, schedule flexibility, enjoying working with their colleagues, and, to a lesser extent, travel and work-life balance.

- There were limited additional effects of awareness of civilian jobs or deployment practices. Concern about vacation time was slightly higher and concern about using one's talents was slightly lower for those unaware of Army civilian jobs. Concern about retirement benefits, job security, and doing great things was modestly greater among those unaware of the Army civilian deployment practices.

Older Professionals

- Favorability was consistently (though modestly) positively associated with perceptions of Army civilian jobs.
- Those with higher concern levels about Army civilian jobs were modestly more concerned about frequent travel.
- Those emphasizing a good fit with colleagues and collaboration versus salary, benefits, and job security were more concerned about achieving these goals and, to a lesser degree, about travel and work schedule flexibility in an Army civilian job; they were less concerned about salary and, to a lesser extent, retirement and other benefits, job security, and fast advancement.
- Those wanting to use their talents, those wanting to face challenges, and those with a preference for fast advancement versus vacation, work schedule flexibility, and work-life balance were more concerned about achieving these goals, doing great things, and opportunities to learn and advance; they were less concerned about vacation policy, schedule flexibility, enjoying working with their colleagues, and work-life balance.
- There were limited additional effects of awareness of Army civilian jobs or deployment practices. Concern about job security was slightly higher and that about collaboration opportunities slightly lower for those unaware of Army civilian jobs. Concern about work-life balance was modestly greater among those unaware of the Army civilian deployment practices.

We next examined how the factors and awareness of Army civilian jobs were related to the gap between one's preferred job characteristics and perceptions of Army civilian job characteristics. The results are summarized below for each of the three survey groups. See Tables C.15–C.17.

Students

We found a larger gap between one's preferred job characteristics and perceptions of Army civilian job characteristics for

- those less favorable overall toward the Army and toward Army civilian job characteristics
- those focusing on salary, benefits, and job security versus those wanting to work with similar colleagues (especially larger)
- those wanting work schedule flexibility and work-life balance versus fast advancement and travel
- those wanting to use their own talents, do great things with their lives, or have the opportunity to learn new things versus those wanting vacation time and benefits
- those with concerns about working as an Army civilian (smaller effect).

No additional effect of awareness of Army civilian jobs or beliefs about Army civilian deployment practices was found on the gap between one's preferred job characteristics and perceptions of Army civilian job characteristics.

Younger Professionals

We found a larger gap between one's preferred job characteristics and perceptions of Army civilian job characteristics for

- those less favorable overall toward the Army and toward Army civilian job characteristics
- those focusing on salary, benefits, and job security versus those wanting to work with similar colleagues
- those wanting to use their own talents, do great things with their lives, learn new things, or be challenged versus those wanting work schedule flexibility, vacations, and work-life balance (smaller effect)
- those with concerns about working for Army as a civilian (smaller effect).

No additional effect of awareness of Army civilian jobs or beliefs about Army civilian deployment practices was found on the gap between one's preferred job characteristics and perceptions of Army civilian job characteristics.

Older Professionals

We found a larger gap between one's preferred job characteristics and perceptions of Army civilian job characteristics for

- those less favorable overall toward the Army and toward Army civilian job characteristics
- those focusing on salary, benefits, and job security versus those wanting to work with similar colleagues.

No additional effect of awareness of Army civilian jobs or beliefs about Army civilian deployment practices was found on the gap between one's preferred job characteristics and perceptions of Army Civilian job characteristics.

We next examined how the factors and awareness of Army civilian jobs and deployment practices were related to one's concerns about working in an Army civilian job. The results are summarized below for each of the three survey groups. See Tables C.18–C.20.

Students

- Those unaware that civilians can work for the Army were less concerned about insufficient job security, having to live in undesirable places, too much travel, poor benefits, or about supporting the military.
- Those unaware that civilians are not involuntarily deployed were less concerned about insufficient job security, low salary, family opposition, or supporting the military.
- The associations of the factors with concerns were of limited magnitudes with two exceptions:
  - Students showing greater concern levels overall showed higher, similar levels across each concern type.
  - Those wanting work schedule flexibility and work-life balance versus fast advancement and travel
    - showed greater concern levels about injury/death, living in undesirable places, and, especially, involuntary transfer

- showed lower levels of concern about supporting the military, especially, or family opposition.

Younger Professionals

- Those unaware that civilians work for the Army were relatively more concerned about injury/death and family opposition; they were less concerned about living in undesirable places, traveling too much, or low salary.
- Those unaware that civilians are not involuntarily deployed were less concerned about low salary or living in undesirable places and, to a lesser degree, about involuntary transfers, too much travel, or poor benefits.
- The associations of the factors with concerns were of limited magnitudes with one exception: Those showing greater concern overall showed higher, similar levels across each concern type.

Older Professionals

- Those unaware that civilians can work for the Army were more concerned about injury/death; they were less concerned about a low salary.
- Those unaware that civilians are not involuntarily deployed were considerably less concerned about a low salary, or, to lesser degree, about involuntary transfers, having to live in undesirable places, insufficient job security, or poor benefits.
- The associations of the factors with concerns were of limited magnitudes with one exception: those showing greater concern overall showed higher, similar levels across each concern type.

Sources of Job Information

We asked respondents to tell us how effective they thought each of 11 sources of information would be in helping them find a job, using a 0–10 scale, with 0 = Not At All Effective and 10 = Extremely Effective. We correlated the ratings across respondent groups and the job groups within them. The correlations all were very high (0.85 or above), with the exceptions of (1) students versus older professionals and (2) Civil Engineers among older professionals. We found the relative rankings more informative. They indicate the following:

- The relative rankings of preferred sources of job information were generally similar across student and professional groups. However, based on these rankings, students were generally less likely to report they would use employment agencies and more likely to report they would use job fairs. Older professionals were relatively less likely to report that they would use Google.
- Among students, the relative rankings of the preferred information sources were similar across job types, though Electronics Engineers were somewhat less likely to say they believed that Google would be helpful.
- Among younger professionals, the relative rankings of the preferred sources of information generally were similar across job types, but Civil Engineers were relatively more likely to use profession-specific sources, and Electronics Engineers were more likely to use Google but less likely to think that internet sites in general would be helpful.
- Among older professionals, the relative rankings of the preferred sources were generally similar across job types, though this was a bit less true for Civil Engineers. Civil Engineers were more likely to use job fairs and somewhat more likely to believe that professional networking would be helpful, but they were less likely to use job agencies. Electronics Engineers also were somewhat more likely to use professional networking, and, relative to Civil Engineers they were more likely to use a potential employer as an information source.

The results are shown in Table 3.11. Differences in within group ratings are statistically significant at $p < 0.05$ at 0.13 to 0.18.

Summary of Key Results

Below, we summarize key results from our quantitative survey analysis.

Awareness of Army Civilian Jobs and Concerns About Them

Only two in five students and younger professionals knew that civilians have jobs in the Army; only three in five older professionals did. Moreover, only 25–30 percent of all groups knew that Army civilians are not involuntarily deployed. There were no differences among students and older professionals in awareness across job types. There were limited differences in

TABLE 3.11

Sources of Information About Jobs (%)

Resource	Student	Professional, Age < 40	Professional, Age 40–55
Referral	7.55	7.62	7.83
Online website	7.19	7.48	7.68
Potential employer	7.20	7.39	7.69
Professional networking	7.02	7.38	7.67
Google	7.11	7.22	7.29
Profession specific	6.93	7.15	7.52
Agency	6.87	6.89	7.44
Job fair	7.08	6.85	7.10
Professional organization	6.74	6.73	7.24
Alumni network	6.91	6.71	7.11
Government	6.66	6.69	7.06

awareness of Army civilian jobs or deployment practices among job types for younger professionals: There were no differences in awareness of the Army civilian job opportunity; both groups of engineers were somewhat less informed about involuntary deployment than were Contracting Specialists and IT Managers.

For nine possible concerns about Army civilian jobs:

- All nine issues were rated as at least mildly concerning (above the scale midpoint of five); there were no notable differences in relative concern rankings among student and professional groups, or by job type.
- Involuntary transfer, undesirable location, injury/death, and low salary led the concerns about Army civilian jobs for all groups.
- Opposition to working for the Army and opposition by family or friends to doing so were ranked at the bottom of respondents' concerns.

Job Characteristic Preferences and Perceptions

Preferred job characteristics, among 16 assessed generally, were similar across student and professional groups and across occupations. Salary, especially, followed by work-life balance, benefits, job security, and using one's talents, were rated as most important. Colleague characteristics and travel were rated as least important. The relative differences between one's preferred and perceived actual job characteristics were similar across professional groups and occupations within groups. Among the most preferred job characteristics, the importance of salary was negatively associated with respondents' satisfaction with their actual salary, whereas the importance of using one's talents was positively associated with satisfaction with their actual use in one's job.

Among important but less-preferred characteristics, the importance of doing great things with one's life and fast advancement were positively associated with one's perceived actual opportunities.

The extent of a mismatch between one's preferred and actual job characteristics was strongly associated with lower job satisfaction and a greater likelihood of job search. However, it was negatively related to interest in getting information about civilian jobs in the Army. There were no meaningful differences in the effect of the size of the gap for younger versus older professionals on satisfaction, job search, or interest in Army civilian job information. There were a few differences across occupations:

- Among younger professionals, Civil Engineers were less satisfied overall, and the association between gap size and job satisfaction was smaller for them.
- Among older professionals, IT Managers were more satisfied. Civil Engineers were somewhat more likely to look for work but were less sensitive to gap size in doing so. Engineers, especially Electronics Engineers, were more interested in getting information about Army careers. However, for Electronics Engineers, larger gaps between preferred and perceived job characteristics were more likely to reduce interest in getting information about Army civilian jobs or careers.

Favorability Toward the Army and Perceptions of Army Civilian Job Characteristics

Basic favorability toward the Army was strongly positively associated with interest in getting information about Army civilian jobs and willingness to recommend that a friend looking for work consider one.

A larger overall mismatch between one's preferred job characteristics and those perceived to characterize Army civilian jobs was strongly negatively associated with interest in getting information about Army civilian jobs/careers or willingness to recommend one to a friend looking for work. The association of a perceived mismatch with interest and willingness to recommend was similar across respondent groups and job types.

With respect to the perceived match between one's specific preferred job characteristics and those believed to be found in Army civilian jobs:

- There was a negative association between the strength of one's preference for work-life balance and schedule flexibility and the extent to which they were perceived to characterize Army civilian jobs across all respondent groups; professionals more highly valuing salary also perceived salary to be more problematic.
- Among the strongly preferred job characteristics, the only notable positive association between strength of preference and perceptions of Army civilian job characteristics was students' perception of a good retirement plan.
- Among lesser preferred job characteristics, there were positive associations between preference strength and perceived Army civilian job characteristics for exciting challenges (professionals) and fast advancement.

Relationship Among Awareness of Army Civilian Job Opportunities, Deployment Practices, Job Preference Factors, Favorability Toward the Army, Perceptions of Army Civilian Job Characteristics, and Concerns About Working for the Army

Favorability toward the Army was consistently (though modestly) positively associated with perceptions of Army civilian jobs. Those wanting to use their talents, do great things, and learn versus focusing on work-life balance, vacation, or benefits were more concerned about achieving these goals in an

38

Army civilian job, doing great things, or opportunities to learn and advance; they were less concerned about retirement and other benefits, travel, work-life balance, vacation policy, schedule flexibility, or enjoying working with their colleagues. Among students, those with greater concerns about working as an Army civilian were more concerned about working with similar colleagues, working with colleagues they would enjoy working with, and collaboration opportunities, and to a lesser extent about travel and vacation policy; they were less concerned about salary, job security, fast advancement, and, to a lesser degree, about retirement and other benefits. Older professionals shared the concern about frequent travel. Students wanting challenges, fast advancement, and travel versus schedule flexibility and work-life balance were more concerned about achieving these goals in an Army civilian job and, to a lesser extent, about retirement and other benefits; they were less concerned about work-life balance, schedule flexibility, and, to a lesser extent, vacation policy and enjoying working with their colleagues. Professionals wanting a good fit with colleagues and collaboration versus salary, benefits, and job security were more concerned about achieving these goals and, to a lesser degree, about travel, work schedule flexibility, and challenges in an Army civilian job; they were less concerned about salary and, to a lesser extent, retirement and other benefits, job security, fast advancement, or work-life balance.

There were limited additional effects of awareness of civilian jobs or deployment practices. Among students, concern about job security and working with similar people was modestly lower for those unaware of Army civilian jobs. Among those unaware of involuntary deployment practices, concern about travel was lower, but concern about work-life balance and, to a lesser degree, vacations and schedule flexibility were greater. Among younger professionals, concern about vacation time was slightly higher and that about using one's talents slightly lower for those unaware of Army civilian jobs. Concern about retirement benefits, job security, and doing great things was modestly greater among those unaware of Army civilian deployment practices.

Among older professionals, concern about job security was slightly higher and that about collaboration opportunities slightly lower for those unaware of Army civilian jobs. Concern about work-life balance was modestly greater among those unaware of the Army civilian deployment practices.

A larger gap between perceived Army civilian job characteristics and one's preferred characteristics was found for persons less favorable toward the Army overall and toward Army job characteristics, and, especially, those focusing on salary, benefits, and job security versus wanting to work with similar colleagues. Also, among students, a larger gap was found for (1) those wanting work schedule flexibility and work-life balance versus fast advancement and travel and (2) to a lesser extent, for those wanting to use their own talents, do great things with their lives, or have opportunities to learn and advance versus those with concerns about working for the Army. Among younger professionals, a larger gap also was found for (1) those wanting work schedule flexibility, vacations, and work-life balance versus those wanting to use their own talents, do great things with their lives, or be challenged and (2) those with concerns about working for the Army (both smaller effects). There was no effect of awareness of Army civilian jobs or civilian deployment practices on gap size for the three respondent groups.

How are the factors related to concerns about working in an Army civilian job? We found that the associations of the factors with concerns were of limited magnitudes with one exception for all groups: Those showing greater concern overall show higher, similar levels across each type of concern. Also, for students, those wanting work schedule flexibility and work-life balance versus fast advancement and travel show greater concern about injury/death, living in undesirable places, and, especially, involuntary transfer; they show less concern about supporting the military, especially, or family opposition to doing so.

How are awareness of Army civilian jobs and deployment practices related to Army job concerns? For students, we found that persons unaware of Army civilian jobs were less concerned about insufficient job security, having to live in undesirable places, too much travel, poor benefits, or about supporting the military. Those unaware that civilians are not involuntarily deployed were less concerned about insufficient job security, low salary, family opposition, or supporting the military. Among younger professionals, those unaware of Army civilian jobs were more concerned about injury/death and family opposition; they were less concerned about living in undesirable places, too much travel, or low salary. Among older professionals, those unaware of civilian jobs also were more concerned about injury/death, and, similar to younger professionals, they were less concerned about low salary. Professionals unaware that civilians are not involuntarily deployed were less concerned about low salary, living in undesirable places, and, to lesser degree, about involuntary transfers, poor benefits, too much travel (younger), or insufficient job security (older).

Preferred Sources of Information About Jobs

The relative rankings of preferred sources of job information were generally similar across student and professional groups. However, students were generally less likely to report that they would use employment agencies and more likely to report that they would use job fairs. Older professionals were relatively less likely to report that they would use Google.

Among students, the preferred information sources were similar across job types, though Electronics Engineers were somewhat less likely to say they believed Google would be helpful. Among younger professionals, preferred sources of information generally were similar across job types, but Civil Engineers were relatively more likely to use profession-specific sources, and Electronics Engineers were more likely to use Google though less likely to use internet sites in general. Among older professionals, preferred sources were generally similar across job types, though a bit less so for Civil Engineers. Civil Engineers were more likely to use job fairs and somewhat so for professional networking; they were less likely to use job agencies. Electronics Engineers also were somewhat more likely to use professional networking, and, relative to Civil Engineers, they were more likely to use a potential employer information source.

Incumbents' Perspective on the Army Civilian Brand's Image

This chapter describes how Army civilian employees perceive the Army Civilian brand and its subbrands. We focus primarily on information obtained from persons working in the six mission-critical occupations selected for detailed analysis in the internal project. We explain our research method, describe the context in which we conducted our research, and present our findings. We begin with a discussion of selecting the data collection sites.

Identifying Sites for Data Elicitation

Most of the Army's civilians were hired by a particular organization at some Army installation. Therefore, drawing any broadly applicable conclusions beyond those from the analysis of occupation-related data discussed earlier required meeting Army civilians where they lived and worked. To collect additional information about these occupations, we identified desirable sites and agencies for interviews of hiring managers for the occupations and focus groups with incumbents in the occupations, and we developed protocols for the focus groups and interviews. As can be seen in Table 4.1, which shows the occupational series and Army commands and offices represented at each site, these sites were desirable in that they employed DA civilians in multiple occupations, typically across multiple commands. We chose the USACE sites specifically to capture the Civil Engineering occupational series, and to do so in locations in which the engineers had key, differing functions (i.e., hurricane damage–related reconstruction and prevention,

TABLE 4.1

Occupational Series and Army Commands and Offices, by Site

Site and Command	0301	0340	0810	0855	1102	2210
Aberdeen Proving Ground						
U.S. Army Test and Evaluation Command						
U.S. Army Communications and Electronics Command[a]	X	X	X	X	X	X
U.S. Army Research, Development and Engineering Command (RDECOM)[a]						
Adelphi Lab Center						
U.S. Army Research Laboratory[b]	X			X		X
Detroit Arsenal						
U.S. Army Tank and Automotive Command[a]						
U.S. Army Tank and Automotive Research, Development and Engineering Center[b]						
U.S. Army Contracting Command–Warren, MI[a]	X				X	X
U.S. Army Program Executive Office, Combat Support/Combat Service Support						
Fort Huachuca						
U.S. Army Information Systems Command[a]				X		X
U.S. Army Test and Evaluation Command						
White Sands Missile Range						
U.S. Army Test and Evaluation Command				X		X
Fort Belvoir						
U.S. Army Acquisition Support Center						
U.S. Army Program Executive Office, Enterprise Information Systems						
U.S. Army Program Executive Office, Soldier	X	X		X	X	X
Redstone Arsenal						
Headquarters, U.S. Army Materiel Command						
U.S. Army Aviation and Missile Command[a]						
U.S. Army Aviation and Missile Research, Development and Engineering Center[b]						
U.S. Army Test and Evaluation Command						

Table 4.1—continued

Site and Command	0301	0340	0810	0855	1102	2210
U.S. Army Program Executive Office, Missiles and Space						
U.S. Army Program Executive Office, Aviation	X	X		X	X	
Fort Sam Houston						
U.S. Army Installation Management Command						
U.S. Army Medical Command	X				X	X
Omaha Engineer District						
USACE				X		
Vicksburg Engineer Research and Development Center						
USACE				X		X

NOTE: Occupations are 301, Miscellaneous Administration and Program Series; 340, Program Management; 810, Civil Engineer; 855, Electronics Engineer; 1102, Contracting; 2210, IT Management.

[a] Subordinate to AMC.

[b] Subordinate to RDECOM, which in turn is subordinate to AMC.

dam building and related river flooding prevention). Again, the purpose of the site visits and detailed discussions was to identify current practices, issues, and potential improvements.

Protocol for Discussion and Analysis

The primary issues for discussion and analysis at each site are listed below. For focus group participants:

- Why did you decide to pursue your current occupation?
- Why did you decide to seek employment with the Department of the Army?
- What was your status at the time (student, intern, seeking employment, employed in other firm and/or occupation)?
  - How did you become aware of Army opportunities in your occupational series?
  - What aspects of a career as an Army civilian did you find most appealing? Least appealing?

- – To what extent were your initial impressions correct?
- – How did you compare Army opportunities with those available elsewhere? What aspects (compensation; opportunities for education, training and advancement; job security; etc.) did you find most appealing?
- – Were you hired under any special initiatives or authorities, e.g., Direct Hiring Authority or Expedited Hiring Authority?
- – To what extent do these factors differ by organization?
- Why have you stayed with the Army?
- How did you perceive the Army brand (per Wikipedia: "Brand is the personality that identifies a product, service or company [name, term, sign, symbol, or design, or combination of them] and how it relates to key constituencies: customers, staff, partners, investors etc.") when you accepted employment with the Army?
  - – In general?
  - – As it applies to individuals within your occupation?
  - – In what respects does it differ, if at all, from the overall brand of the federal civil service? From the brand of your organization? From the brand of your installation?
- How has your perception of these different brands changed over time?
- If you were trying to recruit a friend or colleague to take a position as an Army civilian within your occupational series, what aspects of your job/career field/career program would you highlight? What would you caution your friend about?

For hiring managers and HR specialists:

- Branding/marketing/recruiting methods and venues
  - – Information on and perception of Army, organizational, and activity brands, marketing, and recruiting efforts
  - – History of branding efforts, marketing strategies, hiring authorities (e.g., Direct Hiring Authority [DHA], Expedited Hiring Authority [EHA]), and other applicable human resource policies: positive and negative aspects
  - – Amenability to uniformed marketing, national civilian marketing, occupation marketing, local occupation marketing

- Recent/current difficulty in filling the occupation, including
  - Competition within DoD or from private sector
  - Turnover within the organization
  - Demographics of hires
  - Quality versus quantity issues
  - Distribution of jobs (e.g., regional, rural vs. urban, number of sites, number of agencies)
- Perceived changes in future demand, supply, or competition.

Employee Perceptions

The remainder of this chapter describes how current Army civilians in the selected mission-critical occupations perceive the functional, economic and psychological costs and benefits inherent in their jobs. An employer brand consists of these elements. It communicates to both current and potential employees how the firm can be expected to relate to them and to other stakeholders.

Our research indicated that there were common elements that incumbents from these different occupations found attractive. The occupations we studied also had unique aspects that could prove attractive to someone in that occupation but would be unavailable to Army civilians who were not members of the occupation. Professional development is an example of a functional benefit that some options can offer but others cannot or can only do so to differing degrees. Civil Engineers value opportunities for graduate education and receive them. The Army also funds graduate education for Electronics Engineers. Such opportunities are not, however, generally available to IT Managers. Contract Specialists have access to acquisition workforce training, but are somewhat divided as to its utility, especially its usefulness outside of a DoD context. This dynamic seems to suggest that it is both appropriate and necessary to develop an overall Army Civilian brand, but also to allow occupations to further elaborate upon that core brand image.

Table 4.2 depicts both elements that are common to all occupations we studied and those that are unique to the four particular occupations within the Army assessed in the external market project. Note that themes are not necessarily positive. For example, IT Managers are disappointed that they

TABLE 4.2

Elements of Brand Image According to Incumbents in Selected Mission-Critical Occupations

Brand Element	All Respondents	Civil Engineers	Electronics Engineers	Contract Specialists	IT Managers
Functional	• Army offers a wide range of career opportunities • Army offers a high degree of mobility within career fields and between locations	• Work is varied and technically challenging; offers support for skills development • Army supports professional education	• Well-resourced, technically challenging work. • Ample support for professional education	• Federal Acquisition Regulation (FAR) constitutes a unique, important domain of professional knowledge and authority • Some contracting organizations perform interesting work; others do not	• Declining opportunities to exercise and develop domain-specific skills
Economic	• Army careers offer considerable economic security and job stability • Army/Civil Service benefits are generally better than in the private sector • Incumbents perceive work-life balance to be better in the Army	• Average earnings and compensation are lower than in private sector	• Total compensation becomes better than available in the private sector at mid-career	• Army salary and total compensation are both better than in private sector	• Army salary and total compensation are both better than in private sector
Psychological	• Army offers unique opportunities to serve soldiers and the nation	• Unique opportunities to make a difference to local communities	• Often on the cutting edge of professional knowledge		

have little opportunity to develop programs as opposed to supervising contractors. This reality is hardly likely to attract a young computer scientist to the Army. On the other hand, the Army must be able to deal with this and similar issues in order to recruit effectively. The rest of the chapter will expand on Table 4.2 at greater length.

Research Context

We conducted most of our interviews and focus groups between October 2013 and March 2014. By that time, a hiring freeze had been in effect for almost nine months (Lamont, 2013), a period that also included several days of furloughs without pay and a government shutdown.[1] Nearly two years before that, Army civilian employment had reached peak levels, exceeding 294,000, obviating any immediate need to hire on a significant scale. In other words, the Army had not been hiring at scale for some time, and respondents did not believe it was likely to do so at any time in the near future. Not surprisingly, morale was lower than it might have been had our interviews preceded the 2013 government shutdown. The issue did not loom as large for later focus groups as it did for those conducted in October and November 2013.

Research Method

Focus Groups with Incumbents

As discussed earlier in Chapter Two, we initially elicited perspectives from incumbents in six occupations: Management Analysts (0301s), Program Managers (0340s), Civil Engineers (0810s), Electronics Engineers (0855s), Contract Specialists (1102s), and IT Managers (2210s). We later reduced occupations for detailed analysis in the external project to the last four on

---

[1]   The cited memo from the Office of the Assistant Secretary of the Army (Manpower and Reserve Affairs) prescribed an Army-wide hiring freeze with few exceptions. Army organizations did leverage those exceptions to fill critical vacancies, but hiring took place at a rate much lower than that needed to replace vacancies.

the list, omitting Management Analysts and Program Managers. We focus on results for these four occupations below.

To elicit the relevant information, as discussed above, we convened separate focus groups for the relevant occupations at major Army installations, such as Aberdeen Proving Ground and the New Orleans Engineer District. Volunteers were solicited from a range of commands at each location. Coordinators at each site attempted to arrange for a diverse sample of employees within the occupation, seeking employees who differed with respect to gender, ethnicity, and seniority.[2] Table 4.3 depicts the distribution of respondents within the four occupations discussed in this report by site and location. We also interviewed hiring managers and human resource officials at these sites.

It is important to note that few of the respondents were civilians who had sought a job with the Army in response to conventional marketing approaches. Many came from families in which a close relative had worked either for the Army or the federal government more generally. Others had started working for the Army indirectly, as a contractor, and then transitioned from that position into government service. Some had been advised by an acquaintance, former colleague or friend in government to consider applying. A few were veterans who were thereby aware of the existence of civil service positions with the Army. Many of those who did not fall into one of the former categories began working with the Army as a student intern, with their internship of opportunity arising from their program of civilian studies. To one degree or another, most of our respondents were already aware of the existence of civil service jobs within the Army. They were also aware of how cumbersome the application process was and that, as daunting as that process was, it need not be considered a barrier to successful application.

---

[2] Potential participants were asked to report to the focus group's location during the research team's visit. Actual participants consisted of personnel who reported and voluntarily remained after the RAND team administered the recruitment and oral consent protocols. Few if any attendees left the sessions. No records of participant identities were kept.

TABLE 4.3
Distribution of Respondents by Occupation and Location

Location	0810s	0855s	1102s	2210s	Managers/Human Resource Officials	Total
Aberdeen Proving Ground		4		2	6	12
Army Research Laboratory		4		3	4	11
Detroit Arsenal			4	5	3	12
Fort Belvoir		1		4	3	8
Fort Sam Houston			9	6	3	18
Memphis Engineer District					2	2
New Orleans Engineer District	15[a]				7	22
Omaha Engineer District	4				3	7
Redstone Arsenal		12	2	8	5	27
Engineering Research and Development Center	7			4[b]	3	14
White Sands Missile Range		6		1	1	8
Total	26	29	15	33	40	143

[a] We interviewed several 0810s who were also middle managers separately.

[b] These were actually 1550s, Computer Scientists.

Qualitative Data Analysis

We analyzed the resulting data to distill observations relating to the nature of the Army brand as experienced by respondents and group those observations into the major components of employer brands. As defined by Ambler and Barrow (1996), an employer brand consists of three aspects:

- Functional: the way that work experience with a particular firm will improve incumbents' human capital. For example, acquisition professionals have access to DoD's extensive assets for education and training.

Their education, training, and experience also enhances their attractiveness to private-sector employers. Likewise, Civil Engineers in New Orleans with whom we spoke had the opportunity to work on projects of unprecedented scale and innovation relative to many of their private-sector counterparts.

- Economic: monetary compensation to be expected with working for a particular firm, in a particular context. Obviously, this includes tangible, easily quantifiable aspects, such as pay and benefits. It can also include less-tangible aspects of compensation, such as work-life balance and job security.
- Psychological: how being associated with a particular job or firm contributes to employees' self-esteem. For example, many Army employees derive tremendous satisfaction from the idea that they are contributing to national defense and supporting soldiers. Conversely, government employees have lamented the disregard for their service indicted by repeated government shutdowns.

We identified potential elements of an Army Civilian brand based on that analysis. Almost as importantly, we identified elements that could not constitute aspects of an overall Army Civilian brand because of variation in conditions and compensation among various occupations.

General Observations

There Is No Broadly Shared Army Civilian Brand Image

Few of our respondents understood that Army civilian employment opportunities existed before a friend, family member, or professional colleague alerted them to this fact.

Incumbents agreed with human resource managers and others involved in the recruiting process that most potential applicants thought that working for the Army meant enlisting. Feedback from external audiences confirms this impression.

There were exceptions. Individuals from communities near major installations were aware that there were Army civilian jobs before they applied and were hired. For example, Aberdeen Proving Ground is known as the largest single employer in Harford County, Maryland. Yet even in communities with a large federal footprint, that large federal footprint can subsume and obscure Army opportunities. For example, respondents at Redstone Arsenal reported that neighbors were frequently surprised to learn that they worked for the Army and that such jobs existed.

If awareness of Army civilian opportunities is extremely limited, awareness of a civilian brand is even more so. Incumbents uniformly struggled to articulate an Army Civilian brand, or even to articulate potential elements of one. In part, this difficulty stemmed from a highly variable understanding of what a brand is and its significance relative to employment. Beyond such conceptual issues, incumbents had a hard time articulating potential elements of an Army Civilian brand, even when prompted with highly structured questions.

Army Employment Offers Career and Geographic Mobility

Focus group participants perceived that the Army offered a wide range of civilian careers and a high degree of mobility within them. One respondent stated, "If there's a job you're interested in, we pretty much have it." Within that universe, Army employees have the opportunity to advance according to reasonably defined career paths, changing locations and moving to their preferred locations if they so desire. Such moves are not necessarily simple or easy, but they are possible, and incumbents with whom we spoke said they felt that moving between locations was easier than it was in the private sector, especially given the range of locations available throughout the entire federal workforce. The Army's far-flung geographic dispersion makes it easier to find work where applicants want to live than it might be in the private sector. The reason that incumbents perceive that moving is comparatively simple is that civil servants retain benefits and seniority as they move from one job to the next. Incumbents recalled their own experiences to note that changing locations in the private sector often required changing firms, with the concomitant loss of seniority and benefits.

Incumbents Considered Job Security and Stability Very Important

Incumbents indicated that the security and stability associated with a "government job" were very important in their decisions to seek and accept employment with the Army. Almost every focus group emphasized this point. Several respondents claimed to have accepted considerably reduced salary in return for that security. We were, of course, unable to independently verify such claims. The 2013 government shutdown likely somewhat eroded the perception of security and stability reported by respondents. There have been shutdowns since, though we were unable to systematically assess their impact on employees' perceptions of job security.

Incumbents Valued the Army Benefit Package

Respondents perceived that the Army's benefit package was less likely to be reduced in value than that of civilian jobs. They also perceived that it was more generous than those available in the private sector. They reported valuing health insurance, retirement packages, and leave packages especially. Their perceptions are grounded in reality. The Congressional Budget Office (CBO) found that civil service benefits packages were significantly more generous than those offered in the private sector (CBO, 2017).

Incumbents Perceived That Army Careers Offered Better Work-Life Balance

Army respondents considered work-life balance very important. Work-life balance is also a significant issue for potential applicants. Incumbents felt that the Army offered better opportunities in this regard than private-sector employment. They valued the regular hours and predictable demands of their job. Those who had opportunities for flexible work schedules and telework valued them highly. Those who lacked such opportunities wanted them. Incumbents indicated that they would have been willing to trade salary to get those opportunities.

That perception is difficult to validate or invalidate, however. To begin with, the concept is difficult to operationalize. It is therefore difficult to measure, and there are no standard, generally accepted metrics for doing so (Pichler, 2008; Reiter, 2007; Guest, 2002; Kalliath and Brough, 2008). The most reliable indicator of work-life balance, however, is the number of hours worked (Tausig and Fenwick, 2001). We therefore used the Bureau of Labor Statistics' American Time Use Survey (ATUS) to compare the weekly hours worked for full-time federal, private-sector, nonprofit, and state and local government employees in categories aligned with the four occupations we studied, as indicated in Table 4.4. It was not possible to separate Army employees from federal employees in the survey data.

Figure 4.1 indicates that federal and private-sector full-time employees' average hours worked were roughly comparable on a weekly basis for our four occupational areas. Differences vary depending on the occupation. Private-sector employees in the business and financial operations category tend to work longer than their counterparts in the other sectors. They work a couple of hours more than their federal counterparts, on average. Federal employees in computer and mathematical occupations tend to work about as much as their private-sector counterparts. Both federal and private-sector employees in this category work more than their counterparts in the other two sectors. Federal employees in the architecture and engineering category tend to work more than their counterparts. Across all occupations, however, weekly hours worked seem to be roughly equal across employer types. Differences were statistically significant at the $p < 0.001$ level. This analysis is not dispositive, since it is unclear how Army civilians' work habits compare with those of the broader federal workforce of which they are a part.

TABLE 4.4

Alignment of Census Categories with Federal Occupations for Occupations Analyzed

Census Category	Federal Occupation(s)
Business and Financial Operations	Contract Specialists (1102s)
Computer and Mathematical	IT Managers (2210s)
Architecture and Engineering	Civil Engineers (0810s) Electronics Engineers (0855s)

FIGURE 4.1

Average Weekly Hours Worked for Full-Time Employees in Selected Occupational Groups: Comparison of Federal Workforce with Private-Sector, Nonprofit, and State and Local Government Workforces, 2013–2017

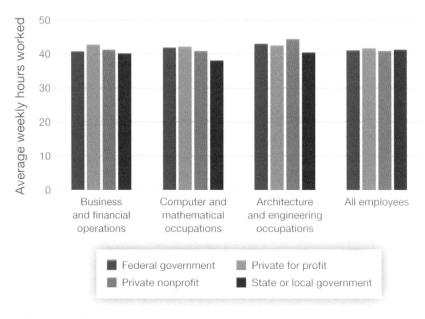

SOURCE: U.S. Bureau of Labor Statistics, 2013–2017.

We also compared Army responses to questions related to their perceived workload and work-life balance on the U.S. Office of Personnel Management's (OPM's) Federal Employee Viewpoint Survey (FEVS) to responses to those same questions in the broader federal government and the private sector. The FEVS uses three questions to assess employees' perceptions of workload and work-life balance, which are also administered to private-sector employees in another survey:

- My supervisor supports my need to balance work and other life issues.
- I have sufficient resources (for example, people, materials, budget) to get my job done.
- My workload is reasonable.

Figure 4.2 depicts the results of this comparison for the 2018 FEVS. It compares private-sector responses with those from the government as a whole, DoD generally, the Army, and the USACE. The question most directly assessing work-life balance is the question concerning supervisor support. Based on those results, it would appear that Army and USACE employees generally perceive that they receive equal or slightly greater support for work-life balance than do comparable civilian employees. While Army employees appear to believe that supervisors support work life balance at comparable rates to private-sector employees, they are less likely to believe that their workload is reasonable. They are even less likely to believe that they have sufficient resources to do their job. The accuracy and basis of their workload and resource perceptions are not addressed in the survey.

FIGURE 4.2

Private-Sector, Government-Wide, DoD, Army, and USACE Employees Responses to 2018 Work-Life Balance Questions

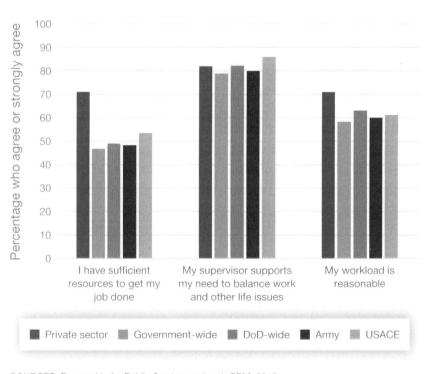

SOURCES: Partnership for Public Service, undated; OPM, 2018.

Given the foregoing results, it may behoove Army officials to move cautiously in how they include work-life balance as an element of an Army Civilian brand. On the one hand, the external market project shows it to be a highly valued job characteristic, incumbents in 2013–2014 indicated that they perceived their work-life balance to be better than what it would have been in the civilian sector, and those who most value it in the external market have concerns about finding it in an Army civilian job. On the other hand, there are indications that federal and Army work-life balance is—in general across all occupations—no better and perhaps a bit worse than in the private sector. If Army officials decide to emphasize work-life balance as an important element of the Army Civilian brand, work-life balance should receive sustained management attention to ensure that Army practice conforms to that aspiration.

Incumbents Find That Pay Banding Can Mitigate Federal Salary Disadvantages

For three of our four critical occupations, total compensation (though not salary alone) exceeds private-sector compensation for similar occupations over time (see Chapter Five). At the same time, for many occupations, average Army salary tends to be lower than that available in the private sector. Given the importance that external audiences place on salary, this no doubt puts Army marketing and recruiting efforts at a disadvantage. Recognizing the handicaps that rigid adherence to standard civil service personnel management practices imposes on managers, Congress authorized DoD to experiment with more flexible pay and promotion policies in a large-scale demonstration project with the acquisition workforce in 1999. The 2016 National Defense Authorization Act (NDAA) extended this demonstration through 2020 at least (U.S. Department of Defense, Office of the Under Secretary of Defense for Acquisition and Sustainment, 2018). Since then, the number of such demonstration practices has increased dramatically.

That flexibility translates into "broadbanding" and "pay for performance." Broadbanding reduces the number of pay grades and increases the number of steps within them, as indicated by Figure 4.3. As the figure indicates, several grades are included under each pay band. Under civil service rules, individuals need to apply for a new job to be promoted to the next

FIGURE 4.3

Acquisition Demonstration Project Pay Bands in Relation to General Schedule Pay Grades

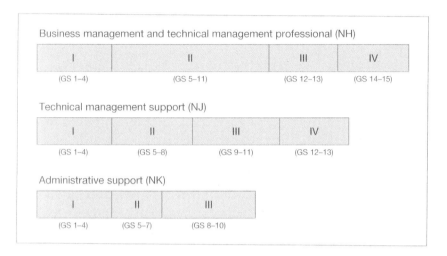

SOURCE: U.S. Department of Defense, Office of the Under Secretary of Defense for Acquisition and Sustainment, 2018.

higher grade, barring some agency reorganization. Broadbanding enables managers to promote within a larger grade without requiring incumbents to apply for positions. It also enables managers to pay for performance: promoting, awarding incentives, or increasing salary for individuals upon the attainment of certain defined criteria. Engineers and scientists particularly liked the idea of being promoted in the same position. It offered the prospect of increased compensation without having to divert their attention from research to management.

We should note, however, that a 2016 assessment of the Acquisition Demonstration Project (AcqDemo) found that broadbanding and pay for performance might not fully live up to incumbents' expectations. RAND researchers working for the Office of the Under Secretary of Defense (Acquisition, Technology and Logistics) found that pay for workers in the AcqDemo pay plan was indeed higher than for comparable employees under the GS, and that individuals whose supervisors assessed were making greater contributions to the organization received higher pay. On the other hand, it turns out that individuals under the AcqDemo pay plan were actually promoted less frequently than those under the GS. Survey respondents also questioned the criteria by which additional pay and promotions were awarded (Lewis et al., 2017).

Incumbents Value Their Service to Soldiers and the Nation

We structured focus group protocols on tangible, material benefits associated with particular occupations. Tangible benefits included compensation, developmental opportunities, and flexibility. In response to open-ended inquiries about why they chose to work for the Army, however, participants often described the psychological benefits associated with service. Those who had frequent opportunities to interact with soldiers or contribute directly to the military mission—through the development, testing, and acquisition of military technologies, for example—expressed a high degree of satisfaction. Employees at the Tank and Automotive Research, Development and Engineering Center and U.S. Army Test and Evaluation Command cited soldiers' emails and visits highlighting how a certain piece of equipment or adaptation thereof had saved their lives. On the other hand, those with less opportunity to interact with soldiers or support the military mission often expressed a degree of dissatisfaction.

The Federal Hiring System Can Deter Applicants

Our incumbents described the federal civil-service hiring process as cumbersome, slow, and difficult to navigate. According to one Civil Engineer, "The application process is a huge deterrent." Several studies over the past two decades tend to validate our respondents' perceptions. Recently, the U.S. Government Accountability Office (GAO) found that in spite of an OPM goal for time-to-hire of 80 days—established amid much fanfare in 2010—the average across the government was 106 days. Over time, Congress has increased the number of flexible hiring authorities available to agencies, but those authorities remain little used. A 2016 GAO study found that federal agencies relied on just 20 of the 105 hiring authorities available to them to make 90 percent of their appointments (GAO, 2016, 2019a, 2019b; U.S. Merit Systems Protection Board, Office of Policy and Evaluation, 2008a, 2018b, 2010; Partnership for Public Service, 2019). DoD has generally been better than the rest of the government, but the Army may lag behind. Another GAO study found that the Army used direct hire authority to staff its acquisition workforce about half as much as the Departments of the Navy and Air Force (GAO, 2019c).[3]

Worse, respondents reported that a perception exists that it is necessary to have some sort of inside connection to get an Army job. According to the respondents, it is in fact useful to know someone on the inside. That is not because an insider can influence assessment or selection decisions. Rather, the process is so cumbersome and demanding that it discourages many other applicants. Others may fail to comply fully with the arduous procedures necessary to get a government job under civil service procedures. Respondents indicated that their "insider advantage" consisted of contacts who would explain to them the importance of the procedure and coach them through the various steps. Most importantly, contacts would assure them that compliance would be rewarded. Several former contractors whose positions had been insourced said that they might well have given up had colleagues and supervisors not encouraged them to persevere.

There may be little that the Army can do about this. As indicated above, almost a decade has elapsed since OPM initiated a major effort—with White House backing—to streamline the hiring process. In the meantime, Congress has increased agencies' flexibility and authorities to expedite that process. For all that, time to hire has improved very little, if at all. Fundamental elements that make the hiring process complex—including the need for fair and open competition, competitive examination, proliferating preferences, and the need to rank and select candidates according to validated criteria—are established in the fundamental legislation governing the civil service (5 USC Part III; 5 CFR Part 332). The cumbersome nature of the hiring process is likely to remain a challenge that Army hiring managers will have to overcome.

---

[3] The Army did rely on direct or expedited hiring authorities for most of the appointments to the civilian acquisition workforce.

Direct and Expedited Hiring Authorities Can Reduce the Handicap Imposed by the Federal Hiring System

OPM allows federal agencies to bypass many of the more challenging requirements of the hiring system using direct and expedited hiring authorities (DHA/EHA). DHA enables federal managers to hire applicants much as private-sector employers do, at least when certain conditions obtain. They can fill vacant positions with the first or best-qualified candidate they can find (OPM, undated-a; McHugh, 2014). As noted, an increasing number of positions within the acquisition workforce are filled using DHA. EHA resembles normal competitive hiring processes but expedites those processes to a degree (McHugh, 2012). The Army hired many of the respondents in our focus groups using DHA or EHA. Yet while using these authorities clearly reduces the time and energy required to acquire qualified employees, there is some tension between the need to expedite hiring and the statutory requirement to draw the federal workforce "from all segments of society . . . after fair and open competition" (5 USC 2301). In 2008, the U.S. Merit System Protections Board expressed concern about the increasing use of these hiring authorities for that very reason (McPhie, 2008).

Civil Engineers (0810s): Challenging Work, Professional Development, and Service to Community

The Army Civil Engineers with whom we spoke in fiscal year (FY) 2014 said that they were attracted to the diversity, technical challenge, and scale of work available in the USACE. They reported feeling that they had greater opportunities to work on projects of national scale and importance, such as rebuilding New Orleans' levees in Hurricane Katrina's wake. They also said that their opportunities for professional education generally exceeded those of other Army civilians. In addition, respondents told us that their work provided direct benefit to the communities in which they worked and the nation as a whole, because of the USACE's focus on America's domestic infrastructure. This domestic focus contrasts with much of the rest of the Army, which is largely focused on overseas contingency operations. In some respects, the USACE's distinctive mission and organizational identity pose a challenge for Army branding efforts. The Army may need to consider presenting a significantly different brand identity to Civil Engineers it is trying to recruit or retain. In doing so, it will have to address the fact that Army Civil Engineers earn less—in general—than their private-sector counterparts.

Civil Engineers Seek Challenging Work

The engineers in our focus groups said that they appreciated the opportunity to pursue challenging, important work. Respondents seldom identified compensation as a primary issue. Most respondents expressed the belief, however, that their contemporaries earned more at private-sector architecture and engineering firms. Instead, most of our respondents spoke first about the nature of their work. Young engineers at the New Orleans district appreciated the opportunity to work on large, innovative projects that continued to address the challenges posed by Hurricane Katrina's aftermath. Those at the Omaha district cited their work on large water management projects. Engineers at the Vicksburg Engineering Research and Development Center welcomed the opportunity to pursue advanced research in Civil Engineering. According to one respondent, "what sells this place is what they do here."

That preference for challenging work can cut both ways. Some Katrina-related projects in New Orleans were nearing completion in 2014. Some of the engineers there expressed a willingness to move on to other employment to seek new challenges. Another USACE manager, from another district with Katrina-related projects, indicated that some senior engineers were beginning to seek other challenges as Katrina-related work was drying up.

Civil Engineers Value Professional Development

Like most of our respondents, Civil Engineers told us that they valued the opportunity for further professional development in their field. They cited opportunities for graduate education as a very important factor in retention. The USACE tries to provide such opportunities. Focus group participants reported that managers typically allocate a certain portion of their budget to funding subordinate engineers' further professional education and development. On the other hand, they noted that increasingly constrained budgets were reducing opportunities to attend professional conferences and further their education.

Indications are that engineers' satisfaction with professional development opportunities have not changed. Figures 4.4 and 4.5 indicate USACE employees' responses to two FEVS questions pertaining to satisfaction with developmental opportunities. Question 1 asks about employees' opportunity to improve their skills. Question 68 asks about satisfaction with training opportunities. Of course, neither question speaks directly to either Civil Engineers' responses or their opportunities for graduate education. Nonetheless, both speak broadly to the question of professional education, and Civil Engineers make up a substantial portion of USACE's workforce.

FIGURE 4.4

Responses from All Federal, DoD, Army, and USACE Employees to Federal Employee Viewpoint Survey Question 1: "I am given a real opportunity to improve my skills in my organization"

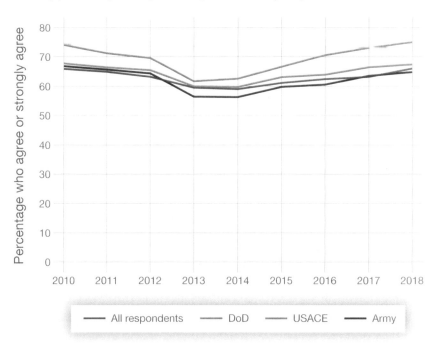

SOURCE: OPM, 2010–2018. Differences are significant to the $p < 0.001$ level.

FIGURE 4.5

Responses from All Federal, DoD, Army, and USACE Employees to Federal Employee Viewpoint Survey Question 68: "How satisfied are you with the training you receive for your present job?"

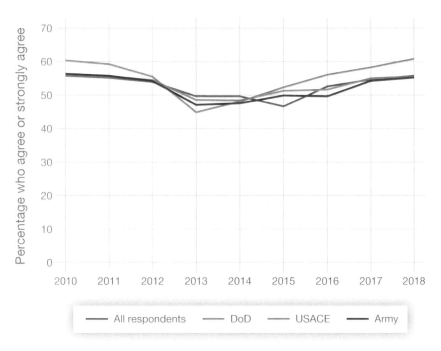

SOURCE: OPM, 2010–2018. Differences are significant to the $p < 0.001$ level.

USACE employees' responses are shown by the thick black line. In both cases, we see that employee's satisfaction achieves a nadir in the FY 2013–2014 time frame, coincident with the major government shutdowns and constraints on training budgets, and both recover from that point. These trends indicate that Civil Engineers' satisfaction with their opportunities for graduate education probably remained the same or improved since the time we conducted our focus groups. Throughout the period, USACE employees reported feeling better about their opportunities for improving their skills than the population of federal employees as a whole, as well as their counterparts in the rest of the Army and DoD. Except for FYs 2013–2014, they also reported being more satisfied with their training.

Civil Engineers Value Their Unique Opportunities to Serve Their Communities

The Army has broad responsibilities to the nation. The USACE also shares in these national responsibilities, but it also has important responsibilities of its own that affect specific local communities in the way that the rest of the Army often does not. This factor's importance became clear in focus groups at the New Orleans Engineer District. Obviously, Hurricane Katrina's impact on New Orleans clearly demonstrated how USACE activities can—for good or ill—have tremendous impacts on those communities. Young engineers cited a need to give back to the city in which many of them grew up. More-senior engineers reported feeling stung by the criticism and hostility they experienced in the wake of the disaster. All of them said that they wanted a more effective public narrative that explained their efforts and the benefits they provided to their fellow citizens.

Electronics Engineers (0855s): Cutting-Edge Work

Electronics Engineers have the opportunity to pursue cutting-edge technical work with systems related to the Army's core mission. Electronics Engineers with whom we spoke told us that these opportunities were very attractive to them. We should note, however, that similar opportunities are not generally available to the Army's civilian workforce. Further, the Army Electronics Engineers with whom we met had received relatively generous support for graduate education. Those engineers also seemed to value their membership in their broader professional community. A key signifier of this membership is the ability to attend professional and academic conferences. At the time of our meetings with them, opportunities to attend such conferences were under pressure.

Innovative Research and Development Attracts Electronics Engineers

Like Civil Engineers, Electronics Engineers reported placing a very high value on the work they do, at least as long as it is novel and exciting. This attitude was particularly prevalent in the test and evaluation community.

Engineers at the Redstone Test Center (RTC) stated that they had forgone other employment opportunities to continue the sort of hands-on work with military hardware they were doing with Army Test and Evaluation Command. Electronics Engineers with other organizations at Redstone Arsenal—such as those working in the Aviation and Missile Research, Development and Engineering Center (AMRDEC) and Program Executive Officers (PEOs)—noted that RTC's "boom video" was a powerful recruiting tool. As the name suggests, the "boom video" highlighted opportunities to blow things up as part of testing. Respondents at the Army Research Laboratory in Adelphi, Maryland, said that they valued opportunities to conduct research and development with cutting edge technologies, and that such opportunities were available virtually nowhere else. Electronics Engineers in organizations oriented on research, development, and testing—like the research, development, and engineering centers (RDECs) and test centers— usually indicated higher job satisfaction than those working in administrative and oversight organizations like PEOs. In fact, Electronics Engineers in the latter roles noted that they might advise potential applicants to seek employment elsewhere. Most respondents vastly preferred to perform technical work than to assume administrative or management roles, even within technically oriented organizations.

Electronic Engineers Value Professional Development

Respondents cited the Army's support for professional education—generous through early 2014—as an important motivation for pursuing an Army career and continuing it. They cited Army support for graduate education at the master's or doctoral level as a key reason for becoming an Army civilian in the first place or continuing as one. Although private-sector organizations also support employees' graduate education, respondents said that they generally believed Army support to be more generous. At the same time, respondents also expressed frustration with what they perceived to be increasing constraints on professional education driven by budget constraints in the 2013–2014 timeframe. Still, even this dissatisfaction highlights the potential importance of this benefit as a recruiting and marketing tool.

Contracting Specialists (1102s): A Rewarding Challenge, for Some

In general, the Army can make a better offer to individuals in this occupation than can private-sector employers. Significantly greater responsibilities related to the need for regulatory compliance inherent in government contracting are the sources of both the reward and the challenge. The Army's ability to fulfill that promise appears to vary with location and the nature of the work. In any case, Army civilians in these occupations tend to make more than their private-sector counterparts.

Army Contracting: A Potentially Rewarding Challenge, but Potential Is Indifferently Realized

Focus group participants generally agreed that Army Contract Specialists bore unique and challenging responsibilities. These responsibilities have no apparent parallel in the private sector. Several respondents observed that Contracting Specialists are the one occupation whose members are authorized to obligate money on behalf of the federal government. This occupation differs from its private-sector analog—purchasing agent—mostly because Contracting Specialists must comply with the Federal Acquisition Regulation (FAR) and its Army derivative, the Army FAR Supplement (AFARS). These regulations prescribe a complex and somewhat contingent set of rules and procedures for making government purchase decisions in a fair and cost-effective manner in various conditions. Applying these regulations and policies in a range of contexts—especially situations not clearly anticipated in the FAR or AFARS—could pose interesting and potentially enjoyable intellectual challenges for members of this occupation.

Those whose efforts directly affect the Army's combat mission find their involvement to be particularly rewarding. Respondents cited site visits by veterans as particularly moving.

Respondents differed with respect to the degree to which they had the opportunity to face and overcome interesting challenges. Respondents' perspectives varied by site and probably also by the nature of the site. Some respondents found the FAR's challenge to be unnecessarily complex and convoluted, citing examples in which other services' approach to procuring goods and services seemed to produce comparable results to those achieved by Army organizations at less cost and in less time.

Extensive Training Opportunities, but with Uncertain Utility

DoD provides civilian members in acquisition billets with extensive training under the authority of the Defense Acquisition Workforce Improvement Act (DAWIA). Training is well-resourced, extensive, and mandatory for Contracting Specialists and other members of the defense acquisition workforce. Perceptions of the utility of this training differ. Respondents who seemed to like their job said that they appreciated the opportunity to improve their knowledge and skills. Those who said that they found their current positions frustrating characterized much of the training as ill-structured and often inapplicable to their specific circumstances. In short, while Contracting Specialists have more access to professional training and education than Army employees generally, that circumstance could be either an advantage or a disadvantage depending on local circumstances.

Information Technology Managers (2210s): Declining Opportunities for Professional Practice

Declining Opportunities for Professional Practice

Perhaps the most significant issue for the IT Managers with whom we met was the outsourcing of what they perceived as their professional responsibilities. Most respondents we met said they had entered the IT field because they wanted to solve specific problems and develop applications for that purpose. At the time we conducted our interviews and focus groups, however, the Army seemed to be transferring developmental work to Computer Scientists (1550s) and problem solving to contractors. To be sure, we did not necessarily encounter a robust selection of the several subfields in this broad occupation. Those we did meet, however, reported that their role was increasingly being reduced to monitoring the compliance and performance of contractors to whom the actual work in their field was being outsourced. Incumbents felt this made their work at least a little boring and led to the atrophy of their professional skills. In short, this outsourcing is a source of professional dissatisfaction. The Army will have to cope with this dissatisfaction in order to attract and retain candidates in this field.

Caveats

We conducted most of these interviews and focus groups in late 2013 and early 2014, just after an extended government shutdown. Tensions over the resulting involuntary furloughs for some may have inflected the focus and tone of some of the observations we recorded. Of course, similar stoppages have occurred recently, so what might have been a significant but temporary irritant in FY 2014 may now be perceived as a permanent condition of employment. Also, for reasons related to preserving anonymity, we did not record demographic information about participants in these focus groups. Thus, we cannot be completely certain that they were a representative sample of Army employees within their occupation, organization or at their installation. Most importantly, several years have elapsed since we conducted this research. Certainly, there has been a steady turnover of Army employees since that time. Perceptions may well have changed, if for no other reason than the passage of time.

Conclusion

Several broad themes that could comprise elements of an Army Civilian brand emerged from the different focus groups:

- career and geographic mobility
- a wide, diverse range of potential careers
- job security and stability
- good benefits
- good work-life balance
- a chance to serve soldiers and the nation.

It is useful to consider some of these themes carefully. Recent government shutdowns may have called the perceived stability and security of federal civil-service jobs into question. Further, the evidence we reviewed with respect to Army jobs' workload and work-life balance is inconsistent. Participants in our various focus groups clearly affirmed that they considered work-life balance to be one of the chief advantages of their jobs; federal workers in the occupations we described tended to work hours comparable to those reported by their private-sector counterparts, with hours worked being one of the principal indicators of work-life balance; and Army civilians reported at least equivalent support of work-life balance from their supervisors. At the same time, there were fewer Army civilians who reported that their workload was reasonable or that they had sufficient resources to accomplish it.

Aside from these common elements, the occupations we analyzed could offer unique benefits to potential applicants. Civil Engineers had the opportunity to work on some of the country's more challenging projects. They also had the opportunity to serve their local communities and achieve lasting impact there, as opposed to the more general support provided by the Army.

Electronics Engineers could place themselves at the cutting-edge of technology. Contract Specialists could exercise substantially greater authority than their private-sector counterparts, and Electronics Engineers, Contract Specialists, and IT Managers receive greater compensation over time than their private-sector counterparts. In short, these occupations indicate that there are opportunities for hiring managers and recruiters to make targeted appeals to potential applicants.

CHAPTER FIVE

Salary and Benefit Comparison with the Private Sector, Nonprofits, and State and Local Governments

Our purpose in this chapter is fairly limited. Because potential applicants consider compensation as the most important factor in their job search, it is important for Army leaders to understand where the Army stands relative to its potential "competitors" in order to establish an Army Civilian brand and market it effectively. Depending on the occupation, compensation may or may not constitute a selling point, but it is a point that will come up. This rudimentary analysis cannot establish, however, the salary and benefit levels that would be required to compensate for some of the recent hardships of government service, such as government shutdowns, nor can it calculate the utility of the premium that some applicants might attach to the relatively high degree of job security associated with a federal job.

Compensation breaks down into two components: salary and benefits. Salary seems to be the most important factor in attracting applicants, followed by work-life balance, job security, and finally the second part of compensation, benefits. Because of the importance of compensation in attracting applicants, we assessed salary and total compensation in the four occupations we analyzed. We also analyzed salaries in other related occupations to determine the extent to which the four occupations under consideration might be representative of compensation in the larger Army. The purpose of this analysis was to inform consideration of the role that compensation might play in the Army Civilian brand.

Our analysis of compensation indicates that it is difficult to tell any consistent story with respect to Army compensation. In some occupations, including Army Civil Engineers, both salaries and total compensation lag behind those of their counterparts in the private, nonprofit, and state and local government sectors. In others, including Electronics Engineers and IT Managers, salaries are generally lower but total compensation is higher, eventually. In a few, including Army Contracting Specialists, both salaries and total compensation exceed that available in the other sectors. When one looks beyond these four occupations, one finds that relative compensation differs significantly by occupation.

Thus, the most that can probably be said about Army compensation in its civilian brand is that it does not differ egregiously from that offered in the private sector. The degree to which salaries specifically (as a component of total compensation) are competitive, however, depends on the specific job and on individual preferences that are difficult to quantify systematically. Army civilians, like other federal employees, must contend with shutdowns, furloughs without pay, negative media coverage, difficult hiring processes, poor organizational image, and politically motivated human resource management decisions. On the other hand, Army employees—like other federal employees—have extremely high levels of job security. Our analysis indicates that individuals weigh these factors differently. Detailed information in salaries and total compensation over one's career may be an area better left to targeted marketing efforts than to a broad element of the Army Civilian brand.

Research Approach

We analyzed compensation in two dimensions. First, we compared both salaries and overall compensation in each of the four occupations studied with comparable employees in the private, nonprofit, and state and local government sectors. Second, we assessed the degree to which selected occupations' compensation levels were representative of the larger career program of which they were a part, both in absolute terms and relative to private-sector analogs. The purpose of the latter analysis was solely to determine the degree to which the mission-critical occupations selected as the basis for this project could be considered to be representative of the set of career programs of which they are a part. As the subsequent analysis will show, the extent to which they were varied. Consequently, we did not extend that comparison to either the nonprofit or the state and local government sectors.

Analyzing Relative Compensation

We developed experience and compensation profiles for each of the four occupations investigated. Profiles compared salaries and total compensation, including both salary and benefits. Benefits' values were estimated as the average cost to the employer of providing them. Data on Army employees were derived from the Defense Civilian Personnel Data System (DCPDS), which is managed by the Defense Civilian Personnel Advisory Service (www.dcpas.osd.mil). Data on private-sector, nonprofit, and state and local government analogs were drawn from the U.S. Census Bureau's American Community Survey (ACS; U.S. Census Bureau, undated). For each sample, we estimated the salary to be expected at each year of experience for a typical worker with a bachelor's degree in each occupation. For each subgroup (Army, private-sector, nonprofit, and state and local government) we estimated the mean salary or compensation and a 95 percent confidence interval. In the charts that follow, a solid line represents mean salary or compensation. Dotted lines of the same color represent the confidence interval around the mean.

Analyzing the Degree to Which Selected Occupations Were Representative of Their Career Program

An issue for this project concerns the degree to which inferences drawn from the study of selected occupations can be applied to other Army occupations, especially mission-critical occupations. With respect to compensation, we compared selected occupations' compensation with that of other occupations in the career program (CP) in which the selected occupant was included. Career programs are groupings of occupations with similar skills and development patterns. For example, Civil Engineers (0810s) are part of CP 18–Engineers and Scientists (Construction). We compared Army and civilian experience and compensation profiles for all civil service occupations aligned exclusively with one CP, excluding those occupations represented in several CPs. We aligned federal occupations with private-sector counterparts using a crosswalk obtained from the U.S. Census Bureau (Census Bureau, 2013).

For example, CP 14–Contracting and Acquisition consists of 13 occupations. Only five of those occupations—Contracting (1102s), Industrial Property Management (1103), Purchasing (1105), Procurement Clerical and Technician (1106), and Grants Management (1109)—are unique to this CP. Moreover, we were only able to identify two civilian occupations that we could align with civil service occupations: purchasing agents, except wholesale, retail and farm products (aligned with 1102s and 1105s) and procurement clerks (aligned with 1106s).

Average Private-Sector Compensation Is Generally Higher Throughout Civil Engineers' Careers

Average salary and total compensation for Civil Engineers are higher for Civil Engineers in the private sector than in the DA, as indicated by Figure 5.1. Army salaries are generally lower than those available in other sectors, although they are well within the wide range of variation with respect to the nonprofit sector beginning about the 21-year mark.

Civilian private-sector salaries are about 30 percent higher at first, with the gap narrowing to about 20 percent by the mid-career point. The gap for total compensation is narrower, starting at around 17 percent higher for private-sector employees and narrowing to about 6 percent at the 30-year mark. Still, Army civilian Civil Engineers' total compensation does at least begin to fall within the 95 percent confidence interval for their counterparts in the nonprofit sector at about 11 years of service, while the average approaches parity at 26 years of service.

Civil Engineers' Relative Compensation Is Not Representative of Other Occupations in Its Career Program

Figure 5.2 depicts the ratio of CP 18 salaries relative to their private-sector counterparts over the length of their careers. The legend indicates the census category for each occupation and the OPM occupations within CP 18 that

FIGURE 5.1

Civil Engineers' Salary and Compensation Levels, by Years of Experience

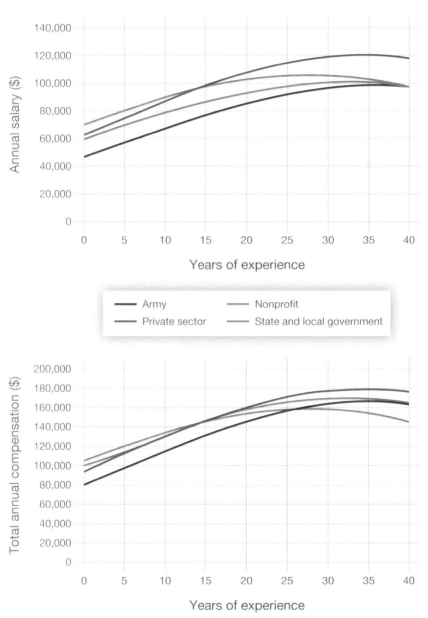

SOURCES: DCPDS; U.S. Census Bureau, undated, 2013.

FIGURE 5.2

Career Program 18 (Engineers and Scientist, Construction) Salaries as a Percentage of Private Sector Salaries

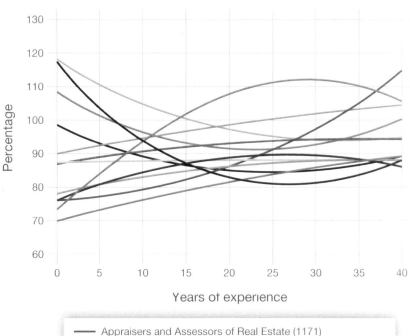

- Appraisers and Assessors of Real Estate (1171)
- Industrial Engineers, including Health and Safety (0804, 0896)
- Conservation Scientists and Foresters (0408, 0545, 0457, 0460, 0480)
- Economists (0110)
- Miscellaneous Social Scientists (0101, 0193, 0199)
- Construction and Building Inspectors (0809)
- Architects, except Naval (0807, 0808)
- Civil Engineers (0810)
- Surveying and Mapping Technicians (0817, 1361, 1371, 1374)
- Environmental Scientists and Geoscientists (0028, 1313, 1315, 1350, 1360)
- Urban and Regional Planners (0020)
- Lifeguards and other Protective Service Workers (0025)

SOURCES: DCPDS; U.S. Census Bureau, undated, 2013.

align with each category. Civil Engineers' relative salaries are indicated by the thick purple line. The specific details of each occupation depicted are less important than the chart's overall message: Each occupation's salary relative to its civilian counterpart is different. There is no standard pattern. The only similarity is that most CP 18 occupations earn less salary than their private-sector counterparts throughout most of their careers. Industrial Engineers are the only exception, reaching parity in the 15th year of a 40-year career and exceeding their private-sector counterparts thereafter.

Comparing total compensation between the Army and the private sector alters the dynamic described above somewhat. It remains true that there is no single pattern that describes the relative compensation of Army occupations in CP 18 and the civilian occupations aligned with them. Still, while salaries for most occupations are lower in the Army than in the private sector, Figure 5.3 indicates that total compensation is often higher. As noted previously, that is not true for Civil Engineers specifically, though the differences narrow over time.

Electronics Engineers' Average Compensation Is Higher in the Army Than in the Private Sector

As indicated in Figure 5.4, salaries for Electronics Engineers are generally higher in the private and nonprofit sectors. Army salaries begin to exceed those of state and local employees at about 18 years of service and fall within the confidence interval at eight years of service. The Army is more competitive with regard to total compensation. While Army compensation starts lower than its erstwhile competitors, it begins to fall within the confidence interval for the state and local government and nonprofit sectors at about 8 years of service. It starts to match its competitors at about 17 years of service, and exceeds even the private sector at about 21 years of service.

FIGURE 5.3

Career Program 18 (Engineers and Scientist, Construction) Total Compensation as a Percentage of Private-Sector Compensation

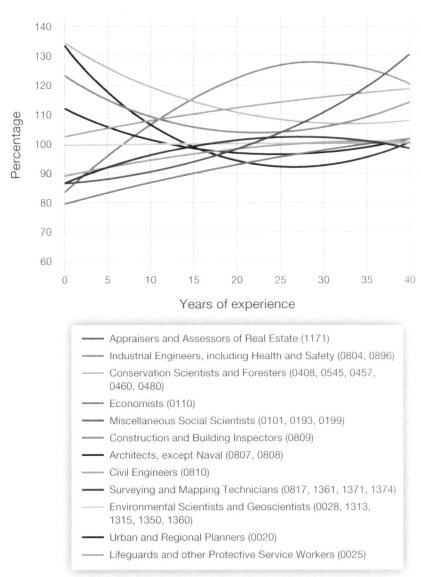

SOURCES: DCPDS; U.S. Census Bureau, undated, 2013.

FIGURE 5.4

Electronic Engineers' Salary and Compensation Levels, by Years of Experience

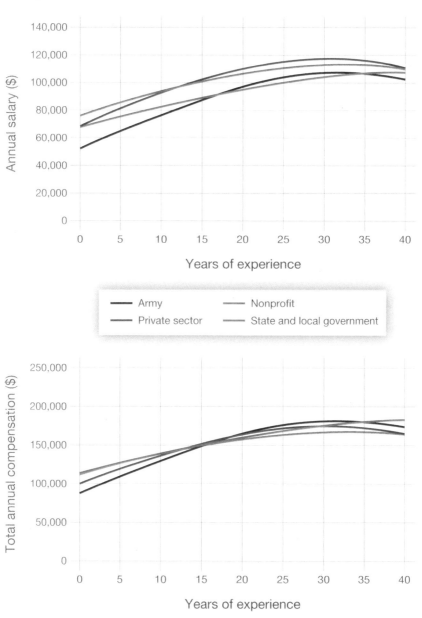

SOURCES: DCPDS; U.S. Census Bureau, undated, 2013.

Electronic Engineers' Relative Compensation Is Generally Unrepresentative of Other Occupations in its Career Program

As with Civil Engineers, we compared compensation levels for occupations in Electronics Engineers' career program—CP 16–Engineers and Scientists (Non-Construction)—with those occupations' private-sector counterparts. The legend to Figure 5.5 reflects the crosswalk for this career program. And—as with Civil Engineers—we found no particular similarities with regard to compensation amongst the different occupations. About half of the occupations generally make lower salaries than their private-sector counterparts, and half make roughly comparable or higher salaries. Electronics Engineers' relative salary is indicated by the thick purple line.

As with Civil Engineers, the pattern changes somewhat when total compensation is considered. Once again, the patterns differ across the range of occupations included in the analysis. However, most of the occupations in CP 16 have higher or comparable total compensation than their private-sector counterparts (Figure 5.6).

Army Contracting Specialists Average Compensation Is Generally Higher Than in the Private Sector

The Army tends to compensate Contracting Specialists relatively well. Average Army salaries equal or exceed those available in the state and local government and nonprofit sectors from the start of employees' careers. By the tenth year of service, they tend to exceed those available in the private sector. Army Contracting Specialists' total compensation tends to exceed that of their counterparts in the private, state and local government, and nonprofit sectors throughout their careers. Figure 5.7 depicts this dynamic.

FIGURE 5.5

Career Program 16 (Engineers and Scientist, Non-Construction) Salaries as a Percentage of Private-Sector Salaries

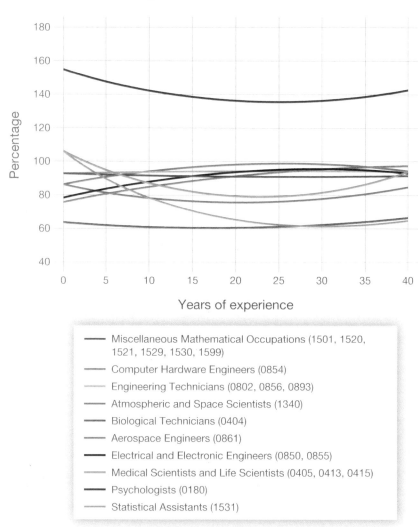

SOURCES: DCPDS; U.S. Census Bureau, undated, 2013.

FIGURE 5.6

Career Program 16 (Engineers and Scientist, Non-Construction) Total Compensation as a Percentage of Private-Sector Compensation

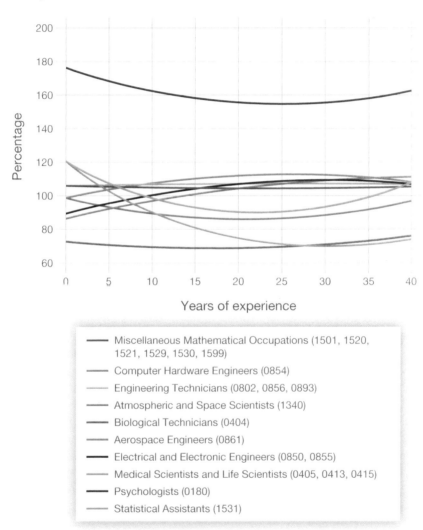

SOURCES: DCPDS; U.S. Census Bureau, undated, 2013.

FIGURE 5.7

Contracting Specialists' Salary and Compensation Levels, by Years of Experience

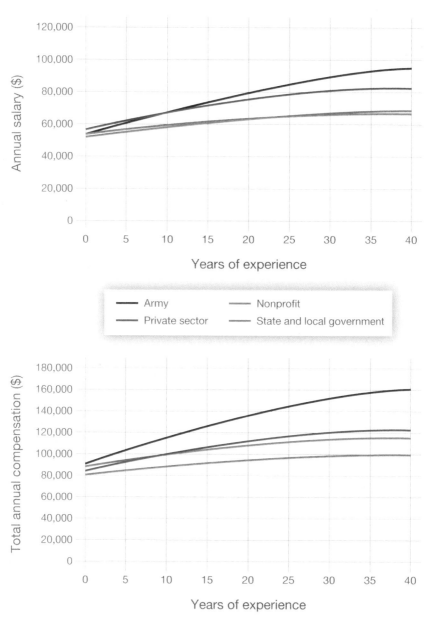

SOURCES: DCPDS; U.S. Census Bureau, undated, 2013.

Contracting Specialists' Relative Compensation Is Generally Unrepresentative of Other Occupations in Their Career Program

As noted in the introduction to this section, we were only able to align two private-sector occupations with occupations unique to CP 14–Contracting and Acquisition with civilian occupations: (1) purchasing agents, except wholesale, retail and farm products (aligned with 1102s and 1105s) and (2) procurement clerks (aligned with 1106s). We found that Army Contracting Specialists' salaries and thus compensation significantly exceeded those of private-sector counterparts, whereas procurement clerks' salaries and thus total compensation fell significantly below that of private-sector counterparts. Figure 5.8 depicts the results of this analysis.

The picture does not change markedly when total compensation is considered. Although the amounts in question differ, the facts that Contracting Specialists' compensation is higher than private-sector counterparts' and that procurement clerks' compensation is lower do not, as indicated by Figure 5.9.

Information Technology Managers' Total Compensation Exceeds Private-Sector Counterparts

IT Managers tend to earn slightly lower salaries than their private-sector counterparts, as indicated by the first of the two charts in Figure 5.10. Their salaries tend to exceed those of their counterparts in the state and local government and nonprofit sectors. As shown in the second of the two charts, however, total compensation tends to be higher throughout their careers.

Information Technology Managers' Relative Salaries Are Not Representative of Other Occupations in CP 34

As mentioned above, salaries for IT Managers tend to run slightly lower than those of their private-sector counterparts. In contrast, librarians' and library technicians' salaries tend to be higher in the Army, whereas salaries for other occupations in this CP fall further short of their private-sector counterparts. See Figure 5.11.

FIGURE 5.8

Career Program 14 (Contracting and Acquisition) Salaries as a Percentage of Private-Sector Salaries

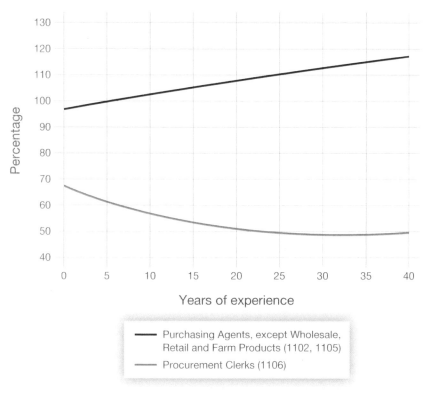

SOURCES: DCPDS; U.S. Census Bureau, undated, 2013.

FIGURE 5.9

Career Program 14 (Contracting and Acquisition) Total Compensation as a Percentage of Private-Sector Compensation

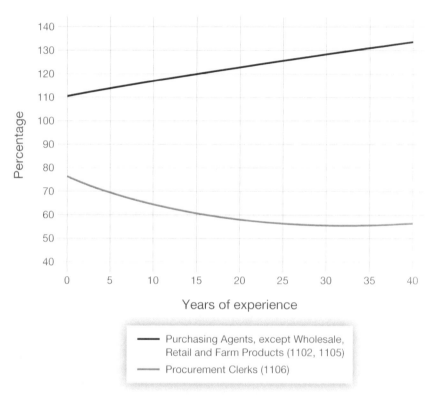

SOURCES: DCPDS; U.S. Census Bureau, undated, 2013.

FIGURE 5.10

Information Technology Managers' Salary and Compensation Levels by Years of Experience

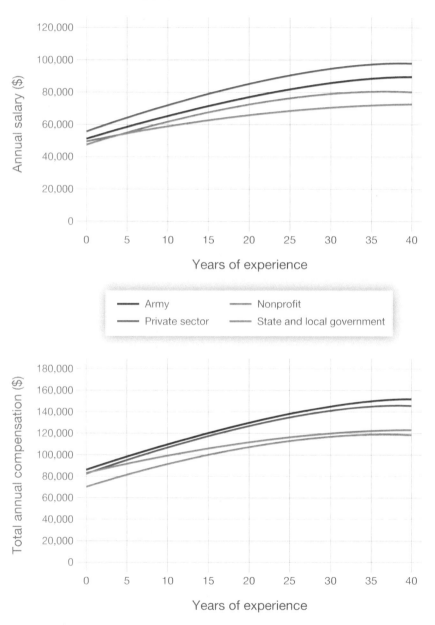

SOURCES: DCPDS; U.S. Census Bureau, undated, 2013.

FIGURE 5.11

Career Program 34 (Information Technology Management) Salaries as a Percentage of Private-Sector Salaries

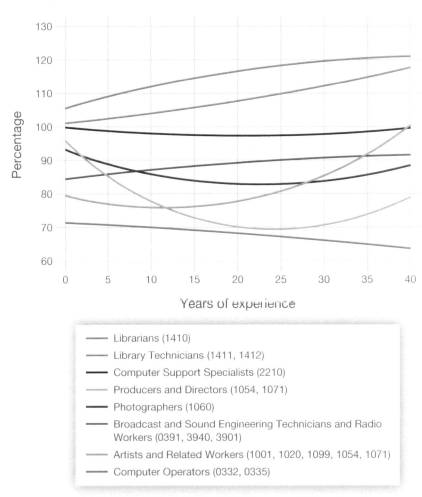

SOURCES: DCPDS; U.S. Census Bureau, undated, 2013.

Comparing total compensation yields a similar pattern, but also indicates that total compensation for many CP 34 occupations is higher in the Army than in the private sector. Figure 5.12 depicts the result of this analysis.

FIGURE 5.12

Career Program 34 (Information Technology Management) Total Compensation as a Percentage of Private-Sector Compensation

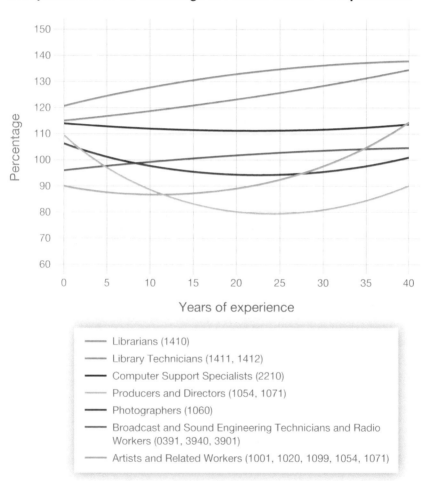

SOURCES: DCPDS; U.S. Census Bureau, undated, 2013.

Caveats

At first glance, this analysis may appear to be relatively straightforward. There are ample data available on salary. We cannot calculate the actual cost of benefits associated with each job in the samples from which we drew our estimates. Our estimates of the average cost of benefits to employers are drawn from literature that does draw on extremely large data sets. There is no reason to doubt the underlying data.

The issue, however, is that the apparent clarity and precision of the resulting estimates obscure the fact that individuals can place significantly different values on the same set of numbers. As we observed in Chapter Three, prospective applicants value benefits differently depending on their individual preferences and station in life. Younger respondents are not particularly concerned with health insurance, something which can approach primary concern for older respondents. Even salary is far from straightforward. In the interviews and focus groups described in Chapter Four, we repeatedly encountered individuals who claimed to have given up higher salaries in the private sector to obtain the stability and security offered by a government job. This is particularly true with regard to applicants with a high degree of public-sector motivation (PSM). For such individuals, the chance at public service can compensate for reduced remuneration.

In short, we can estimate with some confidence the salary and benefits that might be offered to applicants in these mission-critical occupations at different points in their careers. We cannot, however, predict what those salary and benefit levels are worth to specific applicants or incumbents. The analyses presented in this chapter do not attempt to assess what level of remuneration would be required to compensate incumbents and potential applicants for the hardships of public service. Therefore, they serve an important but limited purpose. They tell Army leaders how Army compensation levels compare with potential competitors and that it is not possible to make any overarching statement about relative levels of Army compensation that will apply to all individuals. This information can inform the development of the Army's brand position and marketing strategy.

Conclusion

There appears to be no consistent pattern across mission-critical occupations in the relationship of Army salary and compensation levels to those available in the private, nonprofit, and state and local government sectors. They are neither uniformly higher nor uniformly lower. Rather, the relationships seem to differ by occupation. For our four study occupations, we found that both salary and total Army compensation, including benefits, were lower in the Army than in the private sector for Civil Engineers. In contrast, both salary and compensation were eventually higher in the Army for Contracting Specialists. Private- and nonprofit-sector salaries for Electronics Engineers was higher throughout their careers, whereas state and local employees' salaries tended to be higher during initial stages. Army compensation eventually eclipsed that of its competitors near mid-career. For IT Managers, Army salary was lower than the private sector, but higher than that available in the state and local government and nonprofit sectors throughout careers. Army total compensation was greater throughout careers, as well. We should note that there tended to be significant variation with regard to salaries and total compensation in the nonprofit and state and local government sectors.

Our analysis of relative compensation for CP 14 (Contracting and Acquisition), 16 (Engineers and Scientists, Non-Construction), 18 (Engineers and Scientists, Construction), and 34 (IT Management) indicates that it would be difficult to make any statement about relative compensation that would be true for Army civilians across all mission-critical occupations. The CBO has found, however, that federal benefits are uniformly higher relative to salary than those available in the private sector, at least in terms of the resources invested in providing those benefits (CBO, 2017). For that reason, total compensation for Army occupations often exceeds that available in the private sector, even when private-sector salaries are higher. This rather extensive analysis of Army compensation relative to potential competitors in the private, nonprofit, and state and local government sectors is not meant to suggest that the Army should attempt to base its employer brand on salary or relative compensation. Given current levels of compensation, doing so would reflect poorly on the Army in some instances. Nor is it meant to suggest that the Army should try to increase compensation to levels approximating those of its competitors. Rather, we note that salary is the single most important consideration to a wide range of potential applicants, and that benefits are very important also. It is therefore important for Army officials to understand where the Army stands with respect to those competitors when establishing its brand position and marketing strategy.

CHAPTER SIX

Analysis of Prospective Hiring Needs

In this chapter, we assess the Army's potential future hiring needs. We also analyze the impact that hiring at the appropriate level could have on the distribution of experience within occupations. Finally, we evaluate the degree to which the occupations in question are representative of the career programs of which they are a part with respect to hiring needs. By extension, we also assess the degree to which these four occupations are representative of the Army as a whole.

This analysis can inform the Army's marketing campaign to hire future Army civilians, especially the allocation of resources. A problem that affects 50 prospective employees for a few targeted organizations annually warrants a different approach and a different level of marketing resources than one that affects thousands annually across the entire Army. This analysis can inform who gets resources, how much they get, and to what purposes those resources can be allocated. This is especially true given the Army's decentralized approach to hiring, although we do not attempt to analyze at the level of individual organizations.

Of the four occupations selected for analysis, two (Electronics Engineers and Contracting Specialists) will likely require a significant increase in hiring to maintain their current strength. Two (Civil Engineers and IT Managers) will likely be able to maintain their current strength by hiring at the same rate they have in the recent past. Overall, most of the other occupations we examined in different career programs seem to be postured to maintain their strength by hiring at or below recent historical levels.

Research Approach

We used the RAND Inventory Model (RIM) to project Army hiring needs by occupation over the next ten years. RIM estimates the number of new hires necessary to sustain a workforce of a given size based on assumptions about how likely members of that occupation will be to separate at any given stage of their career. These assumptions are based on recent historical data. They are classed as assumptions only because future performance is not guaranteed to reflect past performance. We also assumed that economic conditions—which affect recruiting and retention—would average 4.9 percent (the average national unemployment rate over 2014–2018) over the decade.[1] Finally, we assumed that the workforce would retain the same size and grade structure over that period. We compared hiring needs with average hiring over the past four years (FYs 2015–2018) to indicate how much additional effort—if any—would be required to maintain the workforce in each occupation at its current size and structure. We did not include FY 2014 in our average. Noticeably fewer employees were hired in FY 2014 than in FYs 2015–2018 for many occupations, and thus including it might have skewed the average.

We also compared the current distribution of the occupation by experience with that projected to obtain if current trends continued. In our interviews, Army leaders had expressed concern about bimodal distributions of experience, with their workforce being divided between one group of relatively newly hired employees and another group of much more experienced employees. Managers were concerned that when the latter group retired, they would be faced with an experience deficit. We used RIM to project how the continuation of current trends would affect the experience distribution of incumbents, assuming that new accessions at junior levels sufficed

---

[1] It would be unduly optimistic in a macro-economic sense to assume that the highly favorable economic conditions of 2014–2018 would continue for another decade. Good economic conditions make recruiting and retention more difficult, however. To the extent that economic conditions worsen, the Army is likely to incur fewer retirements and other voluntary losses. It will therefore need to recruit fewer new applicants. The analysis presented in this chapter therefore provides an upper bound estimate of the number of new recruits the Army will need to obtain. This rate also predates the much higher unemployment rates experienced in 2020–2021 due to the COVID-19 pandemic.

to maintain current personnel inventory levels. We made these comparisons both at the level of individual occupations and at the level of the career programs of which they are a part. The results of this analysis can project what the age distribution of the workforce could be, but not what it should be. Army officials must decide that for themselves.

Civil Engineers: Typical Hiring Needed to Maintain Fill and Current Distribution of Experience

Over the next ten years, the Army—mostly the USACE—will likely need to hire an average of 355 Civil Engineers each year in order to maintain its current strength. RIM analysis projects a requirement of 384 for FY 2019, declining to 326 in FY 2028, as indicated by Figure 6.1. These numbers approximate the Army's average hiring performance over the FY 2015–2018 time frame.

If the Army is able to hire as projected, then the future distribution of experience will resemble the current distribution thereof. Figure 6.2 compares the current distribution by experience—shown in blue—with the future distribution—shown in green. The distributions are grouped in terms of years relative to retirement eligibility (YORE). For example, "YORE –11 to –20" consists of those employees who have between 11 and 20 years until they are eligible for retirement. "YORE 0 to 4" indicates, for example, that the group includes individuals that have reached retirement eligibility (0) and have continued to work for up to four years thereafter. The distribution indicates that the future Civil Engineer workforce will be weighted slightly more toward the less experienced end of the distribution than it is today, but the differences do not appear to be hugely significant.

The Army's hiring needs for Civil Engineers'—though modest—are significantly greater than those for most of the rest of CP 18 (Engineers and Scientists—Construction). Figure 6.3 compares the likely number of new hires needed in each selected CP 18 occupation with the average hired over FYs 2015–2018. The aggregate of the different CP 18 occupations analyzed is shown as a thick black line. Civil Engineers are represented by a dashed line. Most CP 18 occupations' hiring needs are well below that average, as is

FIGURE 6.1

Civil Engineers (0810): Anticipated Hiring Needs Compared with 2015–2018 Hiring Performance

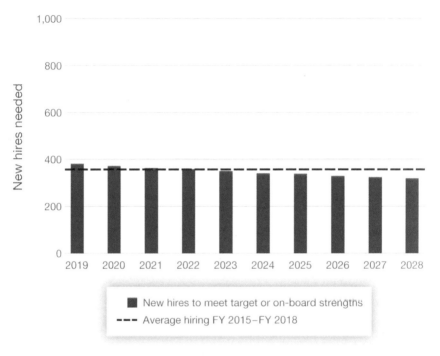

SOURCE: DCPDS.

FIGURE 6.2

Civil Engineers (0810s) Distribution of Workforce in Terms of Years Relative to Retirement Eligibility in FY 2018 Compared with FY 2028 Projection

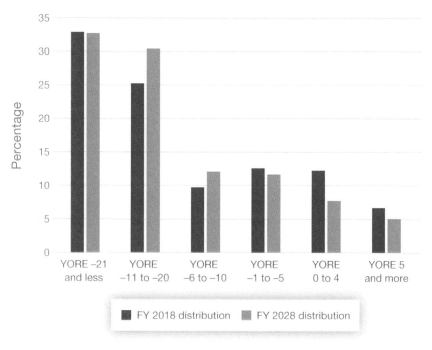

SOURCE: DCPDS.

FIGURE 6.3

Comparison of FY 2019–2028 Hiring Needs with FY 2015–2018 Average Hiring Needs for Selected Career Program 18 (Engineers and Scientists—Construction) Occupations

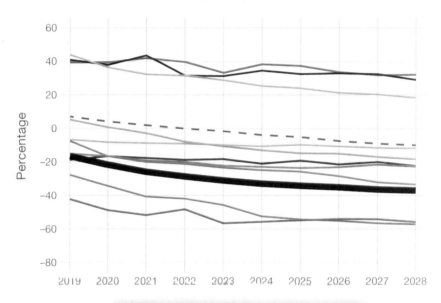

SOURCE: DCPDS.

total, which ranges from 20 percent less than its previous average to almost 40 percent less.

Electronics Engineers: Significant Increases in Hiring Needed, and Facing a Substantial Loss of Experience

As indicated by Figure 6.4, the Army will likely have to increase its hiring of Electronics Engineers by about 50 percent in order to maintain its current strength in this occupation. Over 2015–2018, the Army hired an average of

FIGURE 6.4

Electronics Engineers (0855): Anticipated Hiring Needs Compared with 2015–2018 Hiring Performance

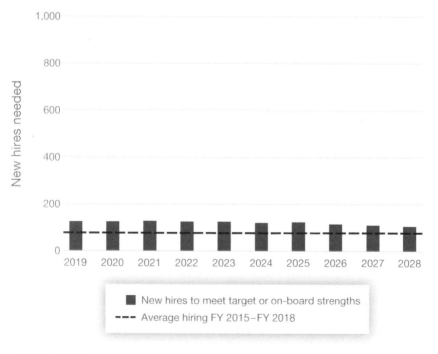

80 new Electronics Engineers each year. Going forward, it will have to hire an average of 123 new engineers every year. In absolute terms these numbers are not all that high across the entire nation. Meeting the demand may tax the organizations that employ them, however.

If the Army maintains its Electronics Engineer workforce entirely through new junior hires, Figure 6.5 indicates doing so will significantly shift the workforce's experience distribution. The current workforce has a bimodal distribution, with just under half having 11 or more years until they reach retirement, and a comparable number having five years or fewer. The projected 2028 workforce will be more weighted to the young end of that range, with more than half of the workforce having 11 or more years until retirement. To the extent that Army officials want to maintain that

FIGURE 6.5

Electronics Engineers (0855s) Distribution of Workforce in Terms of Years Relative to Retirement Eligibility in FY 2018 Compared with FY 2028 Projection

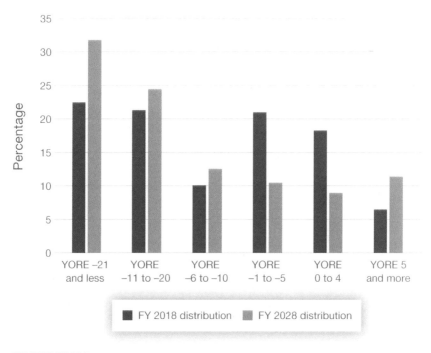

SOURCE: DCPDS.

workforce, they would need to recruit and/or retain a greater proportion of mid-career professionals.

The Army's hiring needs for Electronic Engineers are small in absolute terms but large relative to the size of the occupation and the career program of which they are a part, CP 16 (Engineers and Scientists—Non-Construction). Figure 6.6 depicts hiring needs for selected CP 16 occupations relative to their FY 2015–2018 hiring average. The aggregate of the different CP 16 occupations analyzed is shown as a thick black line. Electronics Engineers are represented by a dashed line. By 2028, hiring needs exceed the recent historical average only for Electronics Engineers.

Contracting Specialists: Significant Hiring Required to Maintain Current Workforce Size

As indicated by Figure 6.7, the Army will likely have to significantly increase hiring of Contracting Specialists to maintain the current workforce size. The Army will have to hire an average of 400 each year, compared with an average of 349 between FY 2015 and FY 2018. In relative terms, the Army would have to hire 22 percent more Contracting Specialists in FY 2019 than it did from 2015 to 2018. That percentage would decline to 9 percent by FY 2028.

As Figure 6.8 indicates, if the Army is able to maintain that pace of hiring, the future distribution of experience would closely resemble that which obtains today.

The Army will likely need to hire more Contracting Specialists relative to workforce size than it will for other occupations in its career program. Figure 6.9 compares hiring needs for FYs 2019–2028 with average hiring needs in the FY 2015–2018 time frame for three occupations in CP 14 (Contracting and Acquisition): 1102 (Contracting); 1101 (General Business Operations), and 1105 (Purchasing). The aggregate of the different CP 14 occupations analyzed is shown as a thick black line. Contracting Specialists are represented by a dashed line. It also makes the same comparison for the total of these three occupations. Of the three occupations analyzed, only 1102s have higher-than-average hiring needs. Anticipated total hiring needs for the aggregated selected occupations are slightly greater than the FY 2015–2018 average in 2019, and slightly lower in FY 2028.

FIGURE 6.6

Comparison of FY 2019–2028 Hiring Needs with FY 2015–2018 Average Hiring Needs for Selected Career Program 16 (Engineers and Scientists—Non-Construction) Occupations

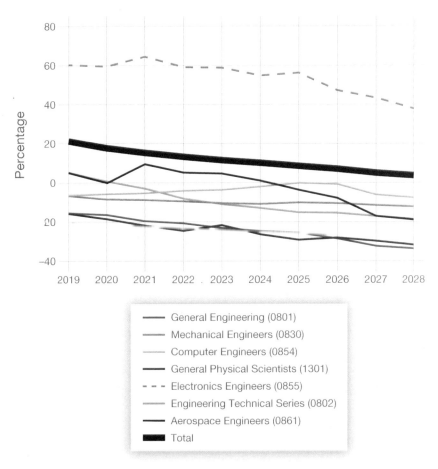

SOURCE: DCPDS.

FIGURE 6.7

Contracting Specialists (1102): Anticipated Hiring Needs Compared with 2015–2018 Hiring Performance

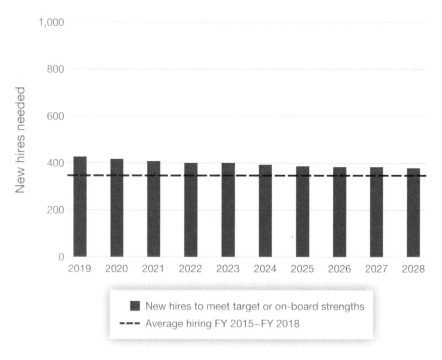

SOURCE: DCPDS.

FIGURE 6.8

Contracting Specialists (1102s) Distribution of Workforce in Terms of Years Relative to Retirement Eligibility in FY 2018 Compared with FY 2028 Projection

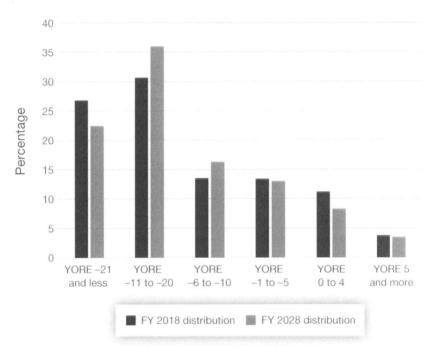

SOURCE: DCPDS.

FIGURE 6.9

Comparison of FY 2019–2028 Hiring Needs with FY 2015–2018 Average Hiring Needs for Selected Career Program 14 (Contracting and Acquisition) Occupations

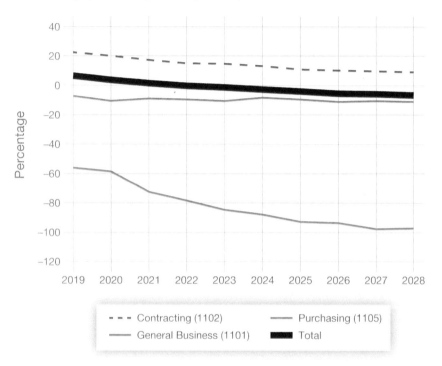

SOURCE: DCPDS.

Information Technology Managers: Continue Current Hiring Performance to Maintain Current Strength

Hiring needs for IT Managers will likely remain close to recent historical levels, as indicated by Figure 6.10.

If the Army hires at this pace, then the resulting distribution of experience will be almost identical to that which obtains today, as indicated by Figure 6.11.

For the rest of CP 34 (IT Management), Figure 6.12 indicates that hiring needs will exceed average hires in the FY 2015–2018 timeframe for the Telecommunications and Visual Information Specialists series, while it will be

FIGURE 6.10

Information Technology Managers (2210): Anticipated Hiring Needs Compared with 2014–2018 Hiring Performance

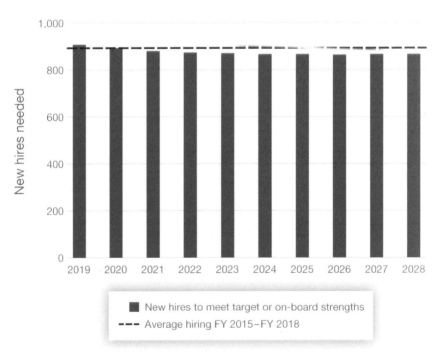

SOURCE: DCPDS.

FIGURE 6.11

Information Technology Managers (2210s) Distribution of Workforce in Terms of Years Relative to Retirement Eligibility in FY 2018 Compared with FY 2028 Projection

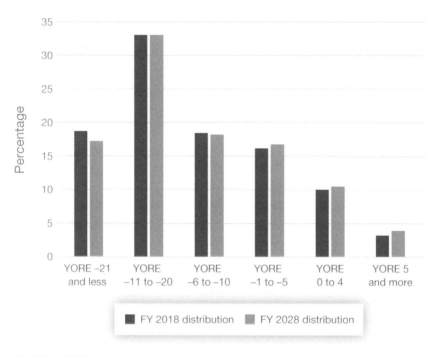

SOURCE: DCPDS.

less than that average for the Miscellaneous Administration and Program Management series. The aggregate of the different CP 34 occupations analyzed is shown as a thick black line. It reflects increased hiring needs of about 10 to 15 percent. IT Managers are represented by a dashed line.

Caveats

The analyses presented in this chapter are somewhat uncertain. They necessarily rest on assumptions about the enterprise strategy, size, and organization of the Army—which define personnel requirements—and the state of the economy. When we initiated these analyses, we assumed economic

FIGURE 6.12

Comparison of FY 2019–2028 Hiring Needs with FY 2015– 2018 Average Hiring Needs for Selected Career Program 34 (Information Technology Management) Occupations

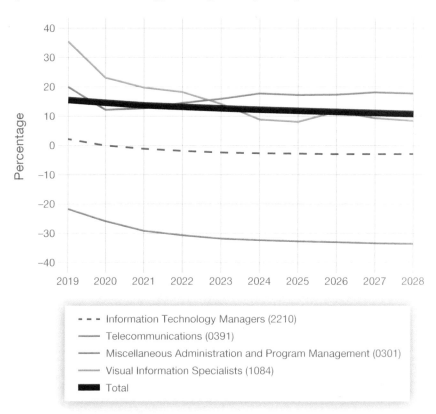

SOURCE: DCPDS.

stability and reasonable growth throughout the period. Since we performed these analyses in 2019, the COVID-19 pandemic and related, varying mitigation measures accompanying its spread have made that assumption inappropriate. The country's economic future is uncertain.

Conclusion

Our original analysis of hiring needs in these various occupations indicated that the Army would need to significantly increase hiring for some mission-critical occupations in the near term. At the same time, our projections indicate that many occupations will be able to retain their current strength by hiring at recent historical (FYs 2015–2018) levels or below. Different occupations face additional challenges. In particular, to maintain its current experience base, the Army will probably have to recruit/retain a significant number of mid-career Electronics Engineers. For the most part, however, the Army will be able to maintain its current distribution of experience by recruiting at entry level.

As noted just above, however, the analyses presented in this chapter rest on unstable assumptions about the enterprise strategy, size, and organization of the Army and the state of the economy. Since we performed these analyses in 2019, the COVID-19 pandemic and related, varying mitigation measures accompanying its spread have made our original assumptions about economic conditions inappropriate. The country's economic future is uncertain.

CHAPTER SEVEN

Exploring Army Online Marketing to Civilian Job-Seekers

In this chapter, we summarize what we learned about how the Army is currently marketing civilian employment to the general public via online platforms. We begin by describing our research approach, followed by what we found.

Research Approach

We focused on the four mission-critical occupations: Civil Engineers (0810), Electronics Engineers (0855), Contracting Specialists (1102), and IT Managers (2210). To guide our online research, we identified Army commands and locations that have high concentrations of civilian employees in each of the four mission-critical occupations.[1] In some instances, there was overlap in commands or locations across occupations. The commands and locations we included are listed in Table 7.1.

---

[1] The commands chosen include the bulk of the Army's inventory of civilians in these mission critical occupations. Where possible, we attempted to choose locations that included either significant concentrations of two or more of the occupations under consideration—such as Huntsville—or at the very least an installation with varied human resource needs. For example, even though both Fort Hamilton (Brooklyn) and Fort Shafter have lower concentrations of Civil Engineers than Portland, they both are home to other Army civilian employees. This allowed us to assess the manner in which installations might support hiring across occupational specialties.

TABLE 7.1

Job Series Studied and Their Commands and Locations

Series	Commands	Locations
Civil Engineer (0810)	• USACE • U.S. Army Materiel Command • U.S. Installation Management Command	• Fort Hamilton • Fort Shafter • Engineer Research and Development Center
Electronics Engineer (0855)	• U.S. Army Acquisition Support Center • U.S. Army Futures Command • U.S. Army Materiel Command • U.S. Army Research, Development and Engineering Command • U.S. Army Test and Evaluation Command	• Aberdeen Proving Ground • U.S. Army Research Lab • Fort Huachuca • Redstone Arsenal • White Sands Missile Range
Contracting Specialist (1102)	• USACE • U.S. Army Materiel Command • U.S. Army Medical Command	• Fort Sam Houston • Redstone Arsenal
IT Manager (2210)	• U.S. Army Cyber Command • U.S. Army Acquisition Support Center • U.S. Army Materiel Command • U.S. Army Test and Evaluation Command • U.S. Army Human Resources Command	• Fort Belvoir • Fort Bragg • Fort George G. Meade • Fort Huachuca • Fort Knox • Fort Sam Houston • Redstone Arsenal

We went to the website of each command and location and recorded the extent and the ways in which civilian employment was being marketed.[2] Next, we explored websites job-seekers might use in their employment searches—USAJOBS.gov, LinkedIn.com, Facebook.com, and Monster.com. On the USAJOBS website, we began on the "explore opportunities" tab on the homepage and then clicked on the relevant occupation and narrowed the search results to "Department of the Army." From there, we gleaned the ways in which Army civilian jobs were marketed. On the LinkedIn, we recorded marketing information from two places: job postings and organizations' LinkedIn pages. To select job postings, we began by clicking on the

---

[2] We were not able to access three websites: Fort Shafter; Research, Development, and Engineering Command; and Fort Sam Houston.

"jobs" tab and searching for the occupation of interest.[3] We narrowed the search results to Army employers by adding the search term "army" and selecting Army employers in the drop-down "company" tab. Finally, we got to the organizations' LinkedIn pages through links provided in the job postings.

We followed the same approach on Monster as we did on LinkedIn, searching for civilian marketing information among job postings (using the same occupation search terms) and organizations' Monster pages. However, we did not find any marketing specific to civilians on Monster.

On Facebook, the job search function did not produce any Army civilian job listings.

Instead, we explored the Facebook pages for each of the commands and locations listed. Facebook, like Monster, is an underutilized civilian marketing resource; compared to USAJOBS and LinkedIn, we found remarkably little civilian marketing information on Facebook. It was not uncommon for Facebook pages to have links advertising job fairs but not much else relating to civilian employment. What we did find is included in our summary below.

In the next section, we summarize our findings on what civilian marketing strategies are currently being used, overall and for each occupation of interest. Our findings are organized into two bins based on the source: findings from command/organization websites and findings from other websites job-seekers might use (i.e., USAJOBS, LinkedIn, and Facebook).

Findings from Command/Organization Websites

In this section, we discuss the variety of civilian marketing strategies we observed on the command/organization websites. We summarize the information under two headings: general civilian marketing and occupation-specific civilian marketing.

---

[3] Search terms were "civil engineer," "electronics engineer," "contract specialist," and "information technology."

General Civilian Marketing

While searching for the websites associated with commands and locations listed above, the search results pointed us first to Army-wide marketing on GoArmy.com. There, job-seekers can find information marketed specifically to civilians, from a high-level discussion about what it means to be an Army civilian and what the Army civilian mission is, to a short description of what some of the benefits of civilian service are and the special considerations given to veterans, military spouses, students and recent graduates, and disabled individuals (U.S. Army, undated). Student work programs—for students in high school, college, or graduate school—are described as an opportunity to develop specialized skills and career experience while finishing a degree. The site also links to a list of federal occupations by college major and describes internship opportunities (USAJOBS, undated-d). Lastly, the site features in-demand civilian jobs with urgent hiring needs, linking job-seekers to openings on USAJOBS, including three of the four occupations we focus on: civil engineering, contracting, and IT management (U.S. Army, undated).

Turning our attention to the command and location websites we set out to find, two among them contain—far and away—the greatest amount of general civilian marketing material, by which we mean marketing irrespective of occupation. Those two websites belong to the USACE (www.usace .army.mil) and the U.S. Army Acquisition Support Center (asc.army.mil). Both sites have a comparatively forward stance on marketing to civilians, showing a concerted effort to showcase civil service career opportunities.

The USACE website provides general information useful to job-seekers for any civilian occupation—announcing job fairs, describing special hiring initiatives, and providing information on salary ranges and benefits (e.g., leave, insurance, retirement, alternative work schedules/telework, and training/education opportunities) (USACE, undated-b). Also, the USACE website contains a robust discussion of certain elements of civilian deployments, covering topics such as accidents, casualties, danger pay, and emergencies. What is not included is information on the likelihood of civilian deployment—as discussed earlier, Army practice is not to involuntarily deploy civilians—or, moreover, on the likelihood that a deployed civilian will experience the issues that are described on the site. The level of detail provided, without shaping job-seeker's expectations of the likelihood of these events, can leave job-seekers to create their own assessment of the likelihood of being put in danger as an Army civilian, which, as discussed, may be a detractor in recruiting.[4]

Compared with the USACE website, the U.S. Army Acquisition Support Center has even more information on its website aimed at civilian employees. On the Army Acquisition Support Center website, there is a discussion of the civilian career model with a comparison to the officer and noncommissioned officer career models, including graphical representations that emphasize career development, professional/leadership development, and continuous learning. The site also contains a six-step plan for career development, as well as information on training and education requirements and opportunities. Moreover, the website highlighted a fall 2019 initiative being spearheaded by the Civilian Human Resources Agency and the Army Director, Acquisition Career Management to create the Army Acquisition Workforce Recruitment and Sustainment Center of Excellence. This initiative was described as "a revolutionary change regarding the recruitment, hiring and sustainment of civilian Army Acquisition Workforce professionals." The goals for this initiative include supporting Army civilian hiring reform, reducing time-to-hire, and leveraging direct and expedited hiring authorities more fully, all in an effort to better hire and retain qualified Army Acquisition Workforce professionals.

The Army Acquisition Support Center site also highlighted AcqDemo, "a Congressionally-mandated project designed to show that the DoD Acquisition, Technology, and Logistics (AT&L) workforce can be improved by providing employees with a flexible, responsive personnel system that rewards employee contribution and provides line managers with greater authority over personnel actions." The site discussed how AcqDemo operates, with particular attention paid to the resources available for personal professional development, selection boards, onboarding, leadership development, and mentoring. At a higher level, the site also discusses the AcqDemo human capital strategic plan and talent management framework.

---

[4] Similarly, the Fort Bragg website, in the "For Civilians" tab, refers to civilians serving in all theaters and being deployed worldwide to support missions (U.S. Army Fort Bragg, undated).

While the Army Acquisition Support Center site is rich in content aimed at civilian job- seekers, there might be so much information available that it will overwhelm and therefore turn off candidates who are unfamiliar with DoD civil service. Instead, the Army Acquisition Support Center website might be more useful as a resource for current acquisition workforce members who can make better use of the breadth of information on the site.

Finally, the majority of the websites we accessed contained minimal references to civilian jobs in general—most often, sites contained links to USAJOBS and offered a few basics about how to find civilian employment opportunities. Other sites mentioned civilians in their command histories or missions, included information for onboarding civilians in their "newcomers" section, and highlighted the role the Civilian Personnel Advisory Center can play in helping civilian employees. Still other sites featured recent news articles about career opportunities and training programs for civilian employees or testimonies from current employees on their experiences as civil servants.

Occupation-Specific Civilian Marketing

Among the websites we reviewed, there were a handful of instances where the occupations of interest in our project were specifically called out. For example, the USACE website gave a brief description of the kind of work that Civil Engineers and Contracting Specialists—two of the occupations of interest in this project—do for the organization (USACE, undated-b). Moreover, as described briefly in the previous section, the U.S. Army Acquisition Support Center website includes a comparison of the civilian, officer, and noncommissioned officer career models, with graphical representation for engineering, contracting, and IT. Figure 7.1 shows an example—the civilian contracting career model.

Also, the U.S. Army Research Laboratory website provides information on internships, apprenticeships, and fellowship programs, as well as the use of DHA, for science, technology, engineering, and mathematics (STEM) candidates, with an explicit mention of Electronics Engineers (U.S. Army Research Laboratory, undated). Finally, for the IT Management occupation series, the U.S. Army Cyber Command website features a video about Army Cyber Teams and to the role civilians play. In addition, the site connects

FIGURE 7.1

Civilian Contracting Career Model, U.S. Army Acquisition Support Center

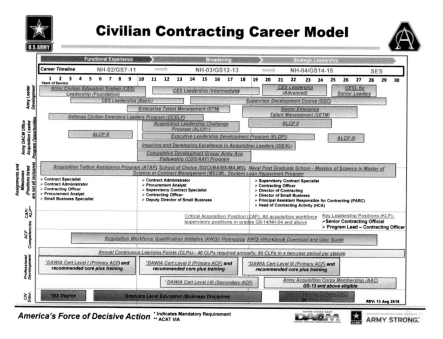

SOURCE: U.S. Army Acquisition Support Command, undated-b.

job-seekers to a LinkedIn page that shows current civilian openings at Army Cyber Command.

Findings from Other Websites Job-Seekers Might Use

In this section, we summarize the civilian marketing strategies we observed on other websites job-seekers might use—USAJOBS, LinkedIn, and Facebook. Across the three sites, we culled information from relevant job postings and organizational pages, as described above. The overwhelming majority of the civilian marketing strategies we observed are not specific to an occupation of interest. Instead, where we observed variation, it was in the strategies used by different organizations, particularly in the information made available on their organizational LinkedIn pages. In synthesizing our findings, some key civilian marketing themes emerged—compensation and benefits, career and geographic mobility, wide range of potential careers, work-life balance, and service to soldiers and the nation. In this section, we summarize our findings for each theme and provide examples from different organizations of the kinds of civilian marketing strategies that fall under each theme.

Compensation and Benefits

In all cases, organizations mentioned compensation—either salary ranges or pay bands—and nearly all discussed some aspect of benefits. As a baseline, there is benefits stock language included in LinkedIn job postings from the USACE, U.S. Army Network Enterprise Technology Command, and U.S. Army Contracting Command:

> A career with the U.S. Government provides employees with a comprehensive benefits package. As a federal employee, you and your family will have access to a range of benefits that are designed to make your federal career very rewarding. Learn more about federal benefits. (LinkedIn, undated-b)

Also, on their Facebook pages, the Engineer Research and Development Center and Fort Belvoir included information about leadership training and an internship program, respectively (U.S. Army Engineer Research and Development Center, undated; Fort Belvoir, undated).

Career and Geographic Mobility

We noticed one ubiquitous feature on LinkedIn that relates to career and geographic mobility—that is, on all organization pages, LinkedIn displays data on LinkedIn members who are associated with the organization on the website, providing information such as where the members live (i.e., metropolitan area) and what they do (i.e., occupations). Although this is not a marketing strategy employed by the organizations, it serves to provide some information to job-seekers about the kinds of occupations they might have and where they might live if they worked at a particular organization.

Some organizations provided additional details on their LinkedIn pages about locations worldwide. One USACE post described the Pacific Ocean Division doing work in Hawaii, Alaska, Korea, and Japan, while another depicted civilians working in a variety of locations to include Texas, Florida, and Puerto Rico (USACE, undated-c). The Engineer Research and Development Center's Facebook page boasts seven labs across four states (U.S. Army Engineer Research and Development Center, undated). And, relating to career mobility, a post on the Army Contracting Command LinkedIn page highlights its talent management framework (U.S. Army Contracting Command, undated-a).

Wide Range of Potential Careers

In terms of the range of potential careers, this was mentioned explicitly in USACE's USAJOBS postings, which describes its work environment as "challenging and rewarding careers across a variety of disciplines" (USA-JOBS, undated-b). Moreover, the Engineer Research and Development Center's Facebook page describes a variety of mission areas "including Soldier support, military installations, environmental research, water resources and information technology" (U.S. Army Engineer Research and Development Center, undated).

Work-Life Balance

The only organization that we observed appealing to work-life balance in an overt way is the USACE, highlighting work-life balance in its USAJOBS job postings: "As rated by their employees, USACE supervisors strongly support employee development and opportunities to demonstrate leadership skills, while also maintaining an optimal work/life balance" (USAJOBS, undated-b). Moreover, a USACE LinkedIn post that says "The Corps is its people. Corps personnel not only serve the community; they and their families are a part of that community" (USACE, undated-c).

More indirectly, several organizations made references in their USA-JOBS postings to attractive features of the local area—e.g., opportunities for recreation and sightseeing and proximity to an international airport (USA-JOBS, undated-c).

Service to Soldiers and the Nation

A connection to service—to soldiers or the nation—was a common thread across the organizations. Nearly all USAJOBS postings we reviewed contained language tying the job to service: "Civilian employees serve a vital role in supporting the Army mission. They provide the skills that are not readily available in the military, but crucial to support military operations. The Army integrates the talents and skills of its military and civilian members to form a Total Army" (USAJOBS, undated-b).

The USACE's LinkedIn page includes its mission, "to provide vital public engineering services in peace and war to strengthen our Nation's security, energize the economy, and reduce risks from disasters," as well as posts that link civilians to supporting uniformed service members, the National Governors Association, and the Federal Emergency Management Agency (USACE, undated-c). The Engineer Research and Development Center's Facebook page describes the USACE as playing "a crucial role for the Nation and Warfighter with its Civil Works and Military Missions, as well as R&D, in support of other federal agencies, and international stakeholders. The innovative work and research performed today continues to propel the Corps towards the realm of the possible" (U.S. Army Engineer Research and Development Center, undated).

The Army Contracting Command LinkedIn page included posts showing civilian employees executing billion-dollar contracts that support soldiers and their families, donating excess computers to schools and educational nonprofits through a Defense Logistics Agency program, and volunteering at a Food Bank (U.S. Army Contracting Command, undated-a). Moreover, the Army Contracting Command "about" page on LinkedIn describes the command as a "combat multiplier, the Army Contracting Command is doing its part in to keep the Army strong" (U.S. Army Contracting Command, undated-b).

Caveats

The analysis presented in this chapter represents conditions at a particular point in time. In the months since we began writing this report, changes to Army civilian employers' web presence could have occurred.

Conclusion

Stepping back from the details of actual site content, it appears that the Army and its major civilian employers provide a wealth of information about Army civilian career opportunities. For the most part, however, potential employees have to "pull" information from civilian websites. The degree to which Army organizations are able to "push" information to job-seekers in different occupations is unclear. Thus, the information is useful primarily to those who are already interested in and aware of Army civilian career opportunities. The actual content of marketing materials mirrors the larger dynamic, in that websites like GoArmy.com or the Acquisition Support Center's website provide ample information from which potential applicants can draw their own conclusions without necessarily articulating a compelling case.

CHAPTER EIGHT

Conclusions

In this chapter, we review our major findings on refining the Army Civilian brand and marketing for Army civilian careers. We summarize major conclusions about the civilian environment, focusing on the perspectives of potential employees. We also review estimates of compensation relative to the private sector and of hiring requirements over the next decade. Last, we synthesize recommendations on the Army Civilian brand from both internal and external perspectives and make recommendations on marketing.

Major Findings

This project's purpose was to help the Army improve its ability to market civilian job opportunities to potential applicants. Our findings therefore fall into one of three major categories:

1. *Findings about the external market.* These rest on our project to better understand this market and describe the results of surveys that asked about

    – for professionals, respondents' current job, the importance of 16 job characteristics, satisfaction with their current job, and whether they were currently looking for another job or planned to within the next year

    – for students, year of school, primary area of study, types of desired careers, and the importance of 16 job characteristics

    – for professionals and students, the extent to which they would use 11 sources of information if they were to conduct a job search, their overall impression of the Army, awareness that civilians can work for the Army, and interest in getting more information about a civilian Army job or career.

Professionals and students were also asked to rate Army civilian jobs on the same 16 job characteristics, and separately, about possible concerns about Army jobs.

2. *Findings about what the Army has to offer.* These rest on our prior project to identify what current Army civilian employees value about their jobs, checks of additional data on working conditions, and compensation comparisons with the private sector. These findings describe how and to what degree the Army is able to fulfill the hopes and expectations of both their internal and external "customers."

3. *Findings about requirements.* These rest on inventory modeling of how the Army's workforce size and composition are likely to vary over the next decade, in response to changes in the external environment and aging of the current workforce. This category includes conclusions about the number and type—by occupation, career program, and in some cases career stage—of employees the Army will need to recruit in order to maintain its current civilian workforce.

Findings About the External Market

It is necessary to understand potential customers' overall perceptions of the Army, awareness of Army civilian jobs, their preferred job characteristics and perceptions of those characteristics in Army jobs, possible concerns about working for the Army, motivation to seek employment, and the sources of information they use in doing so in order to market effectively. We fielded a detailed quantitative survey to gather data on these issues.

Potential Applicants from Different Applicant Categories Focus Mostly on the Same Job Characteristics

As explained in Chapter Three, potential applicants—whether students, younger professionals, or older professionals—are generally looking for the same things from their jobs: attractive salary levels, good work-life balance, generous benefits, strong job security, a generous retirement plan, and opportunities to use their talents and abilities. Colleague characteristics and travel were rated as least important. In addition, job characteristic preferences generally were similar across our study occupations: Actual and intended career field did not seem to significantly affect either which characteristics were important or their relative importance. Most of these characteristics affect the economic dimension of the employer brand. With the exception of the opportunity to use one's talents and abilities, they all involve money that the firm must pay directly to the individual or for the provision of benefits. Strong job security mitigates employees' risks with respect to compensation. Enabling work-life balance often requires firms to reduce their access to employees—to enable employees to fill nonwork requirements or pursue leisure activities—when retaining access might bring more immediate value to the firm. The commonality of interests suggests that a segmented approach to branding may not be necessary to attract external audiences. The extent of a mismatch between one's preferred and actual job characteristics was strongly associated with lower job satisfaction and a greater likelihood of job search. However, it was negatively related to interest in getting information about civilian jobs in the Army. This, together with low awareness rates of potential Army jobs, suggests that information on Army civilian jobs likely needs to be pushed to potential applicants, even those dissatisfied with their current opportunities.

Certain Affinity Groups Cluster Around Preferences for Different Combinations of Job Characteristics

Several distinct affinity groups emerged regarding preferred job characteristics. Marketing should address these interests and, when possible, tailor information being provided according to a potential hire's particular focus. The affinity groups distinguished persons focusing on fit with colleagues and desire to collaborate versus those focusing more on salary, benefits, and job security. They also distinguished persons focusing on using one's own talents, being challenged on the job, and fast advancement versus persons focusing more on vacation, work schedule flexibility, and work-life balance. Student groups further distinguished persons focusing on using their own talents, doing great things with their lives, and learning opportunities versus others focusing more on vacation and benefits, and persons focusing on being challenged, fast advancement, and travel versus those focusing more on work schedule flexibility and work-life balance. Overall, the groupings of job characteristics and the interrelationships among them were generally similar among younger and older professionals and for students, as well as across job types.

Awareness of Army Civilian Opportunities Is Low in the External Market

Only about 40 percent of students and younger professionals are aware that there are civilian jobs with the Army, and under 60 percent of older professionals are aware that civil service jobs exist within the Army. Increasing this awareness will be critical to expanding the pool of qualified applicants. As we will discuss in the next paragraph, even among those aware of Army civilian jobs, this awareness is troubled by misperceptions.

Potential Applicants Share Several Intuitive—but Mostly Erroneous—Concerns About Army Civilian Employment

Not surprisingly, potential applicants have a number of concerns about Army civilian employment. Key among these concerns are

- possibility of being transferred involuntarily
- being required to live in undesirable places
- possibility of injury/death
- low salary.

As we describe in Chapter Five and Appendix D, almost all of these concerns are erroneous. Although DoD can require civilians to transfer and to deploy, it almost never does. Low salary—or at least, lower than may be available in the private sector—is a reality for many occupations. Salaries are not entirely out of the range of acceptability, however, and total compensation is often better for Army occupations. Yet, while these particular concerns may be ill-founded, their existence is a reality with which Army marketing and branding efforts must contend. Opposition to working for the Army and opposition by family or friends to doing so were ranked at the bottom of respondents' concerns.

Willingness to Consider Army Civilian Employment Correlates with Favorable Perceptions of the Army

Our analysis indicates that basic favorability toward the Army is strongly associated with interest in getting information about Army civilian jobs and willingness to recommend one to a friend looking for work. Our analysis also showed that a mismatch between one's preferred job characteristics and those perceived to characterize Army civilian jobs was negatively associated with favorability. These findings imply that a strong association between the Army Civilian brand and noncombat aspects of the Army brand and the many missions it carries out likely would not hurt recruiting and could probably help. They also underscore the importance of marketing the positive aspects of Army civilian jobs, including tailoring messages to the most salient interests of the distinct affinity groups, as discussed above.

Preferred Sources of Information About Jobs

The relative rankings of sources of job information were generally similar across student and professional groups. In order of preference, those sources were

- referral
- online website
- potential employer
- professional networking
- Google
- profession specific
- agency
- job fair
- professional organization
- alumni network
- government.

Students were generally less likely to report they would use employment agencies and more likely to report they would use job fairs. Older professionals were relatively less likely to report that they would use Google.

Among students, the preferred information sources were similar across job types, though Electronics Engineers were somewhat less likely to say they believed Google would be helpful. Among younger professionals, preferred sources of information generally were similar across job types, but Civil Engineers were relatively more likely to use profession-specific sources, and Electronics Engineers were more likely to use Google but less likely to use Internet sites in general. Among older professionals, preferred job information sources were generally similar across job types, though a bit less so for Civil Engineers. Civil Engineers were more likely to use job fairs and somewhat more likely to use professional networking; they were less likely to use job agencies. Electronics Engineers also were somewhat more likely to use professional networking, and, relative to Civil Engineers, they were more likely to use a potential employer information source.

Findings About What the Army Has to Offer

The next step in assessing the Army's brand position with respect to civilian employment is to evaluate the extent to which it can meet the expectations of its potential customers in the external market. Here, our analysis largely recapitulates the research done in 2013–2014 to capture incumbents' perceptions of different potential aspects of an Army Civilian brand. That analysis rested on an extensive series of focus groups and interviews with incumbent employees from different mission-critical occupations and their managers at various sites around the Army. We also refreshed our analysis of how well Army civilians' compensation compares with that available in the private sector. Analysis of the internal market, however, is important not merely because of its implications for reaching the external market. Retaining current employees is also an important goal for Army marketing and branding efforts.

Incumbents Identified Potential Functional, Economic, and Psychological Aspects of an Army Civilian Brand

As described in Chapter Four, an employer brand consists of functional, economic, and psychological aspects. Several broad themes that could constitute elements of an Army Civilian brand emerged from focus groups consisting of different occupations, employed by different organizations, at different installations:

- **Career and geographic mobility:** Army employees have the ability to rise rapidly to positions of significant responsibility. Given the Army's worldwide dispersion and that of the federal government of which it is a part, it is easier in the Army than in the private sector to find employment in other places if the employee wants to move. Obviously, not all do.

- **A wide, diverse range of potential careers:** The Army offers positions in just about every career field imaginable. It also offers the opportunity to transition to another occupation if the applicant is otherwise qualified.

- **Job security and stability:** Occasional government shutdowns notwithstanding, otherwise qualified Army civilians face almost no chance of involuntary unemployment.

- **Good benefits:** Federal—and therefore Army—benefits with respect to health insurance and retirement are significantly better than those offered in the private sector.

- **Good work-life balance:** Incumbents reported that their work-life balance was generally better than that which they might have been able to achieve in the private sector. Indeed, many had transitioned from private-sector jobs to Army employment precisely for this reason, even accepting reduced salaries in consequence. However, the data on hours worked—one of the principal indicators of work-life balance— are somewhat more ambiguous: Federal workers in the occupations we described tended to work hours comparable to those reported by their private-sector counterparts. Army civilians also reported at least equivalent support of work-life balance from their supervisors. At the same time, there were fewer Army civilians who felt their workload was reasonable or that they had sufficient resources to accomplish it.

- **A chance to serve soldiers and the nation:** Incumbents derived considerable satisfaction and a sense of purpose from supporting soldiers and—through them—national defense.

Army Civilian Salaries Are Often Lower Than Those Available in the Private Sector, but Army Total Compensation Often Exceeds That Available in the Private Sector

Salary and benefits are very important to potential job applicants. Our survey indicated that salary is the single most important factor in potential applicants' assessment of job opportunities. It is thus critical for Army leaders to understand the relationship of Army civilian salaries and compensation to that in the private sector.

There does not appear to be a consistent pattern in the relationship of Army occupations' salary and compensation to that available in the private, nonprofit, and state and local government sectors that applies across all mission-critical occupations. Army salaries and total compensation are neither uniformly higher nor uniformly lower. Rather, the relationships seem to differ by occupation. For our four study occupations, we found that both salary and total Army compensation—including benefits—were lower in the Army than in the private sector for Civil Engineers. In contrast, both salary and compensation were higher in the Army for Contracting Specialists after a few years. Private-sector salary for Electronics Engineers was higher throughout their careers, but Army compensation eclipsed private-sector compensation near mid-career. For IT Managers, Army salary was lower, but Army compensation was greater, throughout their careers.

Our analysis of relative compensation for CPs 14 (Contracting and Acquisition), 16 (Engineers and Scientists, Non-Construction), 18 (Engineers and Scientists, Construction), and 34 (IT Management) indicates that it would be difficult to make any statement about relative compensation that would be true for Army civilians in mission-critical occupations. The CBO has found, however, that federal benefits, including health insurance, pension and vacation among other benefits, are uniformly higher relative to salary than those available in the private sector, at least in terms of the resources invested in providing those benefits (CBO, 2017). For that reason, total compensation for Army occupations often exceeds that available in the private sector, even though Army salaries are lower at least as often as not.

Because we did not undertake a systematic—and difficult to summarize—analysis of Army salaries and compensation across all Army mission-critical occupations, we urge caution in generalizing from these results. Nonetheless, the evidence seems sufficient to also urge caution in including salary as a key element of an Army Civilian brand, though it may be reasonable to consider addressing total compensation in some form. Again, this type of information should be considered in discussions with potential applicants. As discussed earlier, the weight given to specific features of Army civilian jobs varies across individuals and career stage, among other factors.

Findings About Requirements

Our original analysis of hiring needs in these various occupations indicated that the Army would need to significantly increase hiring for some mission-critical occupations in the near term. At the same time, our projections indicated that many occupations would be able to retain their current strength by hiring at recent historical (FYs 2015–2018) levels or below. Different occupations face additional challenges. In particular, to maintain its current experience base, the Army will probably have to recruit/retain a significant number of mid-career Electronics Engineers. For the most part, however, the Army will be able to maintain its current distribution of experience by recruiting at entry level.

As noted earlier, however, the analyses presented in Chapter Six, on hiring needs, rest on unstable assumptions about the enterprise strategy, size, and organization of the Army, and the state of the economy. Since we performed these analyses, the COVID-19 pandemic and related, varying mitigation measures accompanying its spread have made our original assumptions about economic conditions inappropriate. The country's economic future is uncertain.

Caveats

These findings come with important caveats:

- We conducted our focus groups and interviews several years ago, mostly in late 2013 and early 2014.
- Salary and compensation analyses yield relatively precise and accurate estimates of what it costs employers—the Army among them—to remunerate employees. These estimates cannot, however, tell

us how incumbents and prospective employees actually value that compensation.

- Estimates of hiring needs are sensitive to assumptions about the projected state of the economy, as well as the Army's enterprise strategy, size, and organization.

Such caveats by no means invalidate the foregoing findings, but they should inspire caution in identifying the appropriate policy responses to them.

Recommendations

Raise Awareness of Army Civilian Job Opportunities

Branding and marketing are often used to differentiate one product from another, similar product. In the case of Army civilian employment, most prospective employees are unaware that the product—civilian jobs with the Army—even exists. The Army should therefore take steps to increase awareness. The precise method used for this purpose—mass-media advertising, targeted internet-based marketing, etc.—depends on the overall scale of the task and the potential impact on other Army recruiting priorities. We note that awareness is low in spite of the fact that sites such as GoArmy. com, the USACE website, and U.S. Army Acquisition Support Center website highlight opportunities for civilian service. Raising awareness could involve more emphasis on "pushing" information to potential applicants rather than relying on them to "pull" it.

Align the Army Civilian Brand with the Army Brand

Potential applicants most likely to consider a job as an Army civilian were those with a positive view of the Army. This finding suggests that there are potential synergies to be gained by clearly aligning the Army Civilian brand with noncombat aspects of the Army brand, including the many careers and missions in the Army, and the low risk associated with Army civilian jobs. Care should be taken to avoid feeding into generally held— albeit erroneous—assumptions about risks associated with Army civilian employment.

Prepare Hiring Officials to Address Applicants' Concerns

We found that potential applicants have possible concerns about Army civilian employment, including the possibility of injury/death, involuntary assignment/reassignment to remote and undesirable duty stations, low pay, and, to a lesser extent, inadequate benefits and poor job security. As demonstrated in Appendix D, these concerns are largely unfounded. In general, highlighting these concerns—even to refute them—as part of a general marketing campaign seems unlikely to increase interest in Army careers. Recruiting and hiring officials must have the facts at hand to do so when and if potential applicants raise them, however, and marketing the variety of possible job assignment locations available to choose from and benefits provided to Army civilian employees may be effective in assisting recruiting efforts.

Our analysis suggests that it is difficult to fully generalize about Army salaries and compensation. Army civilian salaries are often lower, whereas total compensation often is greater, than that of comparable private-sector positions. From a global perspective, a lot depends on the occupation in question. Our analysis omitted many potentially relevant factors, however. Our analyses of compensation over the length of entire careers necessarily included historical patterns of grade structure and compensation that may no longer apply over the next decade in either the private or public sector. A global analysis also omits the influence of location on salaries. In many cases, Army compensation relative to the local cost of living might be as good or better than that offered by private-sector employers. Given the paramount importance of salary and compensation to potential applicants, recruiting and hiring officials should have those facts available to them as they try to attract applicants to Army careers.

Establish a Civilian Brand Emphasizing Career Opportunities, Benefits and Service

To be sure, the external market is interested in salary, benefits, and the opportunity to apply their talents. The most promising branding approach would be one that highlights these characteristics as applicable, and then tailors messages to applicants' job area and interests.

Assuming that current conditions persist, the Army is unlikely to be able to make good on promising a competitive salary in many occupations. However, as discussed, total compensation including benefits often exceeds that of comparable jobs in the private sector. And, as noted, members of the external market are interested in benefits, even though they do not prioritize benefits as highly as salary.

That is not to say that the external audience's perspective is the only one that matters. The Army needs to retain civilian employees as well as attract them. Thus, the internal audience's perspective also matters. For that reason, it remains important to continue to emphasize aspects such as career and geographic mobility and service to soldiers and the nation, even if such themes may have less attraction to external audiences. Other potential elements of a civilian brand that may have salience to both internal and external audiences include the Army's strong—though imperfectly realized—commitment to developing employees' human capital. The Army's existing infrastructure of career programs also provides the potential for some degree of segmentation, as career program officials communicate unique aspects of their occupation to incumbents.

We therefore recommend that the Army Civilian brand emphasize the themes represented in Table 8.1.

TABLE 8.1
Army Civilian Brand Themes

Civilian Brand Element	Theme
Functional	• Career and geographic mobility • A wide, diverse range of potential careers
Economic	• Job security and stability • Good benefits • Good work-life balance
Psychological	• Serving soldiers and the nation

Conclusion: Marketing Begins with the Job Itself

Marketing includes decisions about the product and thus the product's value proposition beyond the manner in which it is to be articulated (branding) and conveyed to prospective customers. In the case of Army civilian employment, these "product" decisions involve grade structure, working conditions, and developmental opportunities. For example, the issue of work-life balance hangs in a delicate balance. On the one hand, incumbents reported—as late as 2014—that the Army offers good work-life balance; it was one of the reasons that many chose an Army career over other potential opportunities. On the other hand, a smaller proportion of Army than private-sector respondents to the 2018 Federal Employment Viewpoint Survey reported that their workload was reasonable and that they had the resources they needed to do their job, even though they also reported that their supervisors fully supported their efforts to balance competing responsibilities. To the extent that Army officials want to make work-life balance an important element of their marketing efforts, then, they may have to provide additional resources. Similar considerations apply to other occupation characteristics. Civil and Electronics Engineers were both attracted to interesting, cutting-edge work, implying high levels of investment in research and development. Conversely, IT Managers were discouraged by the lack of opportunities to exercise skills obtained during their education. In the final analysis, marketing Army civilian employment depends on the nature of the jobs on offer. There are some common themes that marketing can draw on (as listed in Table 8.1), but there are other aspects that depend on the nature of specific jobs.

Survey Questionnaire for Qualitative Analysis

Programing Notes
Programing instructions are in upper/lower case light blue font.

Introduction
Thank you for taking the time to participate in our study. The following questions focus on your job and career. They cover several topics, including what you value in employment and what you think it would be like to work for different types of organizations.

Most of these questions are open-ended, meaning we will ask you a question, and look for you to write a thoughtful answer in your own words. Please take your time to provide detailed answers.

Screening and Background

1. Do you currently work for any branch of the Armed Forces?

Yes	1 TERMINATE
No	2

2. Which of the following best describes your profession/job?

Randomize	
Electrical/Electronic Engineer	1
Civil Engineer	2
Contracting/Procurement Specialist	3
Information Technology Manager	4
Other (Specify)	5 TERMINATE

3. What is your gender?

Male	1
Female	2

4. Which of the following categories includes your age?

(Change for student version)

Under 25	1
25-29	2
30-39	3
40-49	4
50-64	5
65-70	6
Over 70	7

First, we are going to ask you a few questions about your current job.

5. How long have you held your current position?

Less than a year	1
1-3 years	2
4-5 years	3
6-10 years	4
11-15 years	5
16-20 years	6
Over 20 years	7

6. How long have you been at your current company/organization?

Less than a year	1
1-3 years	2
4-5 years	3
6-10 years	4
11-15 years	5
16-20 years	6
Over 20 years	7

7. Which of the of the following best describes the type of company/ organization you work for?

Randomize	
Non-profit organization	1
Start-up company	2
Government	3
Small company (under 100 employees)	4
Mid-size company (100 to 1,000 employees)	5
Large company (over 1,000 employees)	6
Other (please specify) (Anchor)	8

8. What do you like about your current job? Please list the things that come first to mind, and tell us why?

What you like: Why you like it:
(Insert text boxes for each)

9. What do you **not** like about your current job? Please list the things that come first to mind, and tell us why?

What do you not like: Why you do not like it:
(Insert text boxes for each)

10. Next, imagine that for some reason you chose to, or had to, look for another job in another company/organization. Please describe how you would go about a job search, give as much detail as possible about where you would look, the people you would talk to, and the process you would use. (Insert large text box)

11. Again, imagine you were looking for a job at another organization. If you were offered a job you wanted at each of the following types of organizations, at which one would you prefer to work? If we have not listed your preference, please add it next to "other."

Randomize	
Non-profit organization	1
Start-up company	2
Government	3
Small company (under 100 employees)	4
Mid-size company (100 to 1,000 employees)	5
Large company (over 1,000 employees)	6
Other (please specify) (Anchor)	8

a. Please explain why you would prefer to work in a (Insert selection from above). Give us as much detail as possible. (Insert large text box)

12. Here is a list of things that people might think are important when considering a job. Please look at this list and add any additional items that are not on the list, but are important to you. Add one item per text box. Use as many boxes as you need. (Insert 5 text boxes below the last item)

Randomize	
Strong retirement/pension plan	1
Very good benefits (insurance, etc.)	2
High salary	3
Opportunity to "own" part of the company	4
Opportunity to travel	5
Job security	6
Fast career advancement	7
Exposure to exciting job-related challenges	8
Flexibility to change jobs and/or careers	9
Generous holiday/vacation policy	10
Being "family friendly" (e.g., work schedule flexibility, ability to work from home in emergencies)	11

(Insert five text boxes below the list)

13. Here is the list you just saw, along with your additions. Please look this over and select the four that are most important to you. (Insert above list, including items added by the respondent)

14. Here are the four job characteristics you selected as most important. Please explain why each one is important to you, providing as much detail as possible.

Most important: (Insert selected items,) **Why it is important:** (Insert large text boxes including "others")
(Insert large text box)

On a different topic….

We are asking different people about what they think it would be like to work for different types of organizations. We are going to ask you about the <u>U.S. Army</u>. The Army employs many civilians in many types of occupations/professions, including (Insert job from Q2).

15. First, did you know that the Army hired civilians as (Insert job from Q2)s?

Yes	1
No	2

16. Imagine again that you were looking for another job. Would you be interested in working for the Army as a civilian (Insert job from Q2) if there was an opening that matched the type of work you were looking for?

Yes	1
No	2
Maybe	3

(If yes or maybe)
17. What do you think you would like about working for the Army? Please be as specific as possible. If you aren't sure, just give us your first thoughts based upon your impressions. (Insert large text box)

(If yes or maybe)

18. What concerns might you have, if any, about working as a civilian for the Army? Please list your concerns, even if you are not sure they are accurate. Enter each concern in a separate text box. If you wouldn't have any concerns, check the box below. (Insert check box labeled "I would not have any concerns") (Insert five text boxes)

(If no)

19. Why wouldn't you be interested in working as a civilian in the Army? Please give us your issues or concerns, even if you are not sure they are accurate. Enter each issue/concern in a separate text box. (Insert five text boxes)

Here are a few final background questions.

(All Respondents)

20. What is your marital status?

Never Married	1
Married	2
Separated	3
Divorced	4
Widowed	5

(If Q20 ≠ 2)

21. Do you live with a spouse/partner? (If Q20=2 auto-code as Yes)

Yes	1
No	2

22. Has your spouse/partner ever served in the U.S. military?

Yes, currently serving	1
Yes, but not currently	2
No	3

23. Are you the parent of any children ages 18 or younger that live with you in your household?

Yes	1
No	2

(If Q23 = 1)

a. Please indicate how many children you have in each of the age ranges shown below. (Insert text box next to each age category)

0-2 years old	1
3-5 years old	2
6-10 years old	3
11-15 years old	4
16-17 years old	5
18 years old	6

24. Would it be alright if we re-contacted you if we have a couple of follow-up questions?

Yes	1
No	2

That Completes Our Questionnaire. Thank You for Your Time.

Survey Used in Quantitative Analysis

Introduction
Thank you very much for taking our survey. The following questions focus on your job and career. They cover several topics, including what you value in employment and what you think it would be like to work for different types of organizations.

As always, your responses are completely confidential. It will take about 20 minutes to complete the questionnaire.

(Student Sample)
Thank you very much for taking our survey. The following questions focus on your thoughts about jobs and careers. They cover several topics, including what you value in employment and what you think it would be like to work for different types of organizations. We know that your views may change in the future, but we are interested in how you are thinking right now.

As always, your responses are completely confidential. It will take about 20 minutes to complete the questionnaire.

Screening and Filtering Questions

(Professional Sample)
1. Which of the following best describes your occupation?

Randomize	
Civil Engineer	1
Electronics Engineer	2
Information Technology Manager	3
Contracting/Procurement Specialist	4
Other	5 TERMINATE

(If Professional Sample and Q1_2=Yes)
a. Does the following description describe the type of work that you do?

Managing, supervising, leading, and/or performing professional engineering and scientific work involving electronic circuits, circuit elements, equipment, systems, and associated phenomena concerned with electromagnetic or acoustical wave energy or electrical information for purposes such as communication, computation, sensing, control, measurement, and navigation.

Yes, completely	1
Yes, partially	2
No	3 TERMINATE

(If Professional Sample and Q1_4=Yes)
a. Does the following description describe the type of work that you do?

Manage, supervise, perform, or develop policies/procedures for professional work involving the procurement of supplies, services, construction, or research and development using advertising or negotiation procedures; the evaluation of contract price proposals; and the administration/termination/close out of contracts. Requires knowledge of the legislation, regulations, and methods used in contracting; and knowledge of business and industry practices, sources of supply, and cost factors.

Yes, completely	1
Yes, partially	2
No	3 TERMINATE

(Create variable: Career; Compute ProCar=Q1)

(All)
2. Do you currently work for any branch of the Armed Forces either on active duty or in the drilling reserve?

Yes, on active duty	1 TERMINATE
Yes, in drilling reserve	2
No	3

(If Q2=3)
a. Have you ever served in the military? If yes, which branch?

Randomize	
No, never served in the military (anchor)	1
Yes, Army	2
Yes, Navy	3
Yes, Air Force	4
Yes, Marines	5

(Professional)
3. To begin, we'd like to ask you a few questions so that we can present the appropriate questions to you later in the survey. First, which of the following categories includes your current age?

Under 22	1
22-29	2
30-39	3
40-49	4
50-55	5
Over 55	6 TERMINATE

(Professional)
a. What was the last level of education that you completed?

Less than high school	1 TERMINATE
High school graduate or equivalency	2 TERMINATE
Some college	3 TERMINATE
Two-year college graduate	4
Four-year college graduate	5
Masters or other post-graduate degree	6

(Student Sample)
4. Are you currently a student?

Yes	1
No	2 TERMINATE

(Student Sample)
5. What year are you in?

Undergrad: Freshman	1 TERMINATE
Undergrad: Sophomore	2 TERMINATE
Undergrad: Junior	3
Undergrad: Senior	4
Grad school: 1st year	5
Grad school: 2nd year	6
Grad school: 3rd year or higher	7

(Student Sample)

a. Which of the following areas of study is your primary focus?

Randomize	
Science	1
Technology	2
Engineering	3
Math	4
Liberal Arts	5
Computer Science	6
Music	7
Religion/Philosophy	8
Law/Pre-Law	9
Medical School/Pre-Med	10
Linguistics	11
Foreign Languages	12
Law Enforcement	13
Other	14

(Student Sample)

6. We would like to know the types of careers you might be interested in pursuing. On each of the 4 following screens you'll see a type of career. We will ask you how interested you might be in learning more about this career.

(Show one description per screen. Above each description on each screen include this question: **As you think about your future, how interested might you be in learning more about this career?** (Insert 0–10 scale, labels—0: "Not at all Interested"; 10: "Very Interested")

(For the Information Technology Screen: show the non-highlighted text. If respondent hovers over the job title, include the highlighted text—per respondent instructions)

(Randomize Jobs)

Civil Engineer Managing, supervising, leading and/or performing professional engineering and scientific work involving: • Construction, renovation, inspection, decommissioning, and/or demolition of structures, infrastructures, and their environmental systems above or under the earth's surface; • Investigation and evaluation of the earth's physical, natural, and man-made features; • Transportation, utilities, building and construction industries.	1
Electronics Engineer Managing, supervising, leading and/or performing professional engineering and scientific work involving electronic circuits, circuit elements, equipment, systems, and associated phenomena concerned with electromagnetic or acoustical wave energy or electrical information for purposes such as communication, computation, sensing, control, measurement and navigation.	2

Information Technology Manager (For more detail–hold mouse over job title) Administrative positions that manage, supervise, lead, administer, develop, deliver, and support information technology (IT) systems and services. Includes the automated acquisition, storage, manipulation, management, movement, control, display, switching, interchange, transmission, assurance, or reception of information. Covers computers, network components, peripheral equipment, software, firmware, services, and related resources. IT Manager specialties include: **Policy and Planning**–Strategic planning, capital planning and investment control, workforce planning, policy and standards development, resource management, knowledge management, architecture and infrastructure planning and management, auditing, and information security management. Can apply to an entire organization. **Enterprise IT Architecture**–Analysis, planning, design, implementation, documentation, assessment, and management of the enterprise structural framework to align IT strategy, plans, and systems with the mission, goals, structure, and processes of the organization. **Security**–Ensuring the confidentiality, integrity, and availability of systems, networks, and data through the planning, analysis, development, implementation, maintenance, and enhancement of information systems security programs, policies, procedures, and tools. **Systems Analysis**–Applying analytical processes to the planning, design, and implementation of new and improved information systems to meet the business requirements of customer organizations. **Applications Software**–Design, documentation, development, modification, testing, installation, implementation, and support of new or existing applications software. **Operating Systems**–Planning, installation, configuration, testing, implementation, and management of the systems environment in support of the organization's IT architecture and business needs. **Network Services**–Planning, analysis, design, development, testing, QA (quality assurance), configuration, installation, implementation, integration, maintenance, and/or management of networked systems used for the transmission of information in voice, data, and/or video formats. **Data Management**–Planning, development, implementation, and administration of systems for the acquisition, storage, and retrieval of data. **Internet**–Technical planning, design, development, testing, implementation, and management of Internet, intranet, and extranet activities, including systems/applications development and site mgt. technical management of Web sites. **Systems Administration**–Planning/coordinating the installation, testing, operation, troubleshooting and maintenance of hardware and software. **Customer Support**–Planning and delivery of customer support services: installation, configuration, troubleshooting, customer assistance and training.	3

Contracting Specialist Manage, supervise, perform or develop policies/procedures for professional work involving: • Procurement of supplies, services, construction or research and development using advertising or negotiation procedures • Evaluation of contract price proposals • Administration/termination/close out of contracts • Requires knowledge of the legislation, regulations, and methods used in contracting; and knowledge of business and industry practices, sources of supply, and cost factors. Note: Highlighted portions visible when cursor held over text. (IF Q6_1 & Q6_2 & Q6_3 & Q6_4 = 0-4: TERMINATE) (IF Q6_1 & Q6_2 & Q6_3 & Q6_4 = 0-4: TERMINATE) (Create new variables: If Q6_1 = 8-10, then CivEng=3 If Q6_1 = 6-7, then CivEng=2 If Q6_1 = 5, then CivEng=1 If Q6_1 = 0-4, then CivEng=0) If Q6_2 = 8-10, then ElecEng=3 If Q6_2 = 6-7, then ElecEng=2 If Q6_2 = 5, then ElecEng =1 If Q6_2 = 0-4, then ElecEng=0 If Q6_3 = 8-10, then ITM =3 If Q6_3 = 6-7, then ITM=2 If Q6_3 = 5, then ITM=1 If Q6_3 = 0-4, then ITM=0 If Q6_4 = 8-10, then ConSpec=3 If Q6_4 = 6-7, then ConSpec=2 If Q6_4 = 5, then ConSpec=1 If Q6_4 = 0-4, then ConSpec=0	4

(Students)

(Assign respondents to value in StdntCar using least-fill technique. Respondents can be assigned to any value for which they are scored GE "1" in variables CivEng thru ConSpec; default to highest value)
(If CivEng and Conspec and ElecEng and ITM = 0-4: TERMINATE)

(Professionals and Students)
(Create new variable: Career; Career = ProCar OR StdntCar)

(Student)
You said you might be interested in learning more about a career as a (Career). In many of the following questions, we are going to ask your thoughts about a career as a (Career).

(If Professional)

7. Next, we have a couple of questions about your current job. How long have you worked at the organization where you are now employed?

Less than a year	1
1-3 years	2
4-5 years	3
6-10 years	4
11-15 years	5
16-20 years	6
Over 20 years	7

Job Characteristic Preferences

8.

(Student)

Different people look for different things in their jobs and careers, and we would like to know what you think you will look for. While your priorities might change, answer this question based on how you feel now.

(Professionals)

Different people look for different things in their jobs and careers, and we want to know what you personally value in a job and career. Please answer this question based on your current priorities.

(Add extra space before the paragraph)

On the following 12 screens you will see sets of four job characteristics. (If professional: Assuming you were looking for another job,) (If student: Think about when you start looking for a job and) select the characteristic that would be the highest priority for you, and the characteristic that would be the lowest priority for you.

(Advance to next screen)

(Place the text below at the top of the first screen respondent sees with Max Diff choice. On subsequent screens just show the Max Diff choice.)

(If student: Think about when you start looking for a job and) select the characteristic that would be the <u>highest</u> priority for you, and the characteristic that would be the <u>lowest</u> priority for you.)

(If professional: Assuming you were looking for another job, select the characteristic that would be the <u>highest</u> priority for you, and the characteristic that would be the <u>lowest</u> priority for you.)

Randomize	
Generous retirement/pension plan	1
Generous benefits (insurance, etc.)	2
Attractive salary level	3
Opportunity to travel	4
Strong job security	5
Fast career advancement	6
Exposure to exciting job-related challenges	7
Good work-life balance	8
Opportunity to do great things with your life	9
Opportunity to use your talents and abilities	10
Opportunity to work with people like you	11
Generous holiday/vacation policy	12
Collaboration among co-workers	13
Flexible work schedule	14
Many opportunities to learn and advance	15
Colleagues you enjoy working with	16

Types of Organizations: Evaluations and Preferences

(Professionals)
9. Now we want to know how you feel about the organization where you currently work.

Think about the organization where you work, and rate it on each of the following characteristics. (Insert 0–10 scale: 0=Very Poor; 10=Excellent)

Randomize	
Generous retirement/pension plan	1
Generous benefits (insurance, etc.)	2
Attractive salary level	3
Opportunity to travel	4
Strong job security	5
Fast career advancement	6
Exposure to exciting job-related challenges	7
Good work-life balance	8
Opportunity to do great things with your life	9
Opportunity to use your talents and abilities	10
Opportunity to work with people like you	11
Generous holiday/vacation policy	12
Encourages collaboration among co-workers	13
Allows for flexibility in work schedule	14
Provides many opportunities to learn and advance	15
Colleagues you enjoy working with	16

(Professionals)
10. Overall, how satisfied are you with your current job? (Insert 0–10 scale: 0=Extremely Dissatisfied; 10=Extremely Satisfied)

11. Are you looking for another job currently?

Yes	1
No	2

(If Q11=2)
12. How likely are you to look for another job within the next 12 months? (Insert 0–10 scale: 0=Extremely Unlikely; 10=Extremely Likely)

(If Q 11=1 or Q12=5-10)
a. Why are you (If Q11=1: looking for another job) (If Q12=5-10: likely to look for another job)? Please be as specific as possible. (Insert text box)

(Professionals and Students)
(Professionals)

13. Now we want to know how you might go about conducting a job search, assuming you were looking for another job.

(Students)
14. Now we want to know how you might go about conducting a job search when the time comes.

(Add space above this paragraph)

Here is a list of activities that people often use when conducting a job search. For each of the following tell us how effective you think it would be in helping you find a job (Professionals: at a different organization). Base your answers on either your experiences or general impressions. (Insert 0–10 scale: 0=Not At All Effective; 10=Extremely Effective)

Randomize	
Online employment/career website that serves multiple industries (e.g., Indeed, Glassdoor, Monster.com, Careerbuilder.com)	1
Google	2
Employment agency/headhunter	3
Job/Career fairs	4
Government websites (e.g., USAJOBS.com, usace.army.mil/careers)	5
Profession-specific online employment/career website (e.g., EngineeringDaily.net, Engineer.net)	6
Websites of potential employers	7
Referral by an employee of the company/organization	8
Professional organization/Professional journals	9
Professional Networking (e.g., LinkedIn)	10
Alumni networks or collegiate academic departments	11

14.

(Student) Which of following types of organizations would you prefer to work in? Even if you aren't sure, base your opinion on your thoughts and impressions. (Select one)

(Professionals) Regardless of where you are working now, which of the following types of organizations would you prefer to work in. (Select one)

Randomize	
Non-profit	1
Start-up company	2
State or local government	3
Federal government	4
Small company (under 100 employees)	5
Medium company (100 to 1,000 employees)	6
Large company (over 1,000 employees)	7
Other (please specify) (Anchor)	8

We are asking different people to give us their impressions of what they think it would be like to work as a (Insert variable: Career) in different types of organizations. Base your answers either on your experiences or your general impressions.

15.
(Students)
Think about working as a (Insert variable: Career) at a (Insert type of organization selected in Q14). Rate this type of organization (as an employer) on the following characteristics. If you don't have any experiences, just give us your impression. (Insert 0–10 scale: 0=Very Poor; 10=Excellent)

Randomize	
Generous retirement/pension plan	1
Generous benefits (insurance, etc.)	2
Attractive salary level	3
Opportunity to travel	4
Strong job security	5
Fast career advancement	6
Exposure to exciting job-related challenges	7
Good work-life balance	8
Opportunity to do great things with your life	9
Opportunity to use your talents and abilities	10
Opportunity to work with people like you	11
Generous holiday/vacation policy	12
Encourages collaboration among co-workers	13
Allows for flexibility in work schedule	14
Provides many opportunities to learn and advance	15
Colleagues you enjoy working with	16

(Professionals and Students)
a. Now we want you to think about what it might be like to work as a (Insert variable: Career) in the <u>Federal Government</u>. Rate the Federal Government (as an employer) on the following characteristics. If you don't have any experiences, just give us your impressions. (Insert 0–10 scale: 0=Poor; 10=Excellent)

Randomize	
Generous retirement/pension plan	1
Generous benefits (insurance, etc.)	2
Attractive salary level	3
Opportunity to travel	4
Strong job security	5
Fast career advancement	6
Exposure to exciting job-related challenges	7
Good work-life balance	8
Opportunity to do great things with your life	9
Opportunity to use your talents and abilities	10
Opportunity to work with people like you	11
Generous holiday/vacation policy	12
Encourages collaboration among co-workers	13
Allows for flexibility in work schedule	14
Provides many opportunities to learn and advance	15
Colleagues you enjoy working with	16

Knowledge of Civilian Employment in the Army
Moving on to another topic, we are interested in people's thoughts about different branches of the armed forces, and we are going to ask you about <u>the Army</u>.

16. First, we would like your overall impression of the Army. Using the scale below, give us your **overall impression of the Army.** (Insert 0–10 scale: 0=Extremely Unfavorable; 10=Extremely Favorable)

17. As far as you know, can civilians work for the Army as civilians or do they have to join the Army as enlisted service members or officers in order to get an Army job?

Randomize	
Civilians have jobs in the Army	1
Civilians enlist or join the Army as officers to get a job	2
Not sure (Anchor)	3

Army as Employer: Attitudes and Perceptions
(If Q17=1: As you know) (If Q17=2, 3: Actually), many civilians have professional careers in the Army, including (Insert variable: Career). These civilian professionals are not in uniform, and live in their own housing, just as they would if they were employed by any other organization. (Display text on same screen as Q18)

18. (If professional: Assuming you were looking for another job, given) (If student: Given) this information, how interested would you be in learning more about...

(Show a & b on same screen)
a. ...civilian <u>jobs</u> in the Army?
b. ...civilian <u>careers</u> in the Army?

(Insert 0–10 scale: 0=Not at All Interested; 10=Extremely Interested)

19. Now we want your impression of what it would be like working as a civilian in the Army. Here are the same job characteristics you saw earlier. Please rate civilian employment in the Army on each one. It's likely you won't know for sure, so answer based on your impressions. (Insert 0–10 scale: 0=Poor; 10=Excellent)

Randomize	
Generous retirement/pension plan	1
Generous benefits (insurance, etc.)	2
Attractive salary level	3
Opportunity to travel	4
Strong job security	5
Fast career advancement	6
Exposure to exciting job-related challenges	7
Good work-life balance	8
Opportunity to do great things with your life	9
Opportunity to use your talents and abilities	10
Opportunity to work with people like you	11
Generous holiday/vacation policy	12
Encourages collaboration among co-workers	13
Allows for flexibility in work schedule	14
Provides many opportunities to learn and advance	15
Colleagues you enjoy working with	16

20. Now here are some reasons people have given for <u>not</u> wanting to work for the Army. These reasons are based on their perceptions and may not reflect the reality of working for the Army as a civilian.

Look at each reason in the list below and tell us how much it would concern you personally if you were considering working for the Army as a civilian. (Insert 0–10 scale: 0=Not a Concern; 10=Major Concern)

Randomize	
Possibility of injury or death	1
Possibility of being transferred involuntarily	2
Required to live in undesirable places	3
Opposition by family/friends	4
Not enough job security	5
Too much travel required	6
Low salary	7
Poor benefits package	8
Do not want to be part of or support the military	9

21. If the Army were mobilized in the case of a war, do you think that Army civilian employees could be involuntarily deployed?

Randomize	
Could <u>not</u> be involuntarily deployed	1
Could be involuntarily deployed	2
Not Sure (Anchor at bottom)	3

(If Not Sure)
a. You said you are not sure if Army civilian employees could be involuntarily deployed in the case of war. To what extent do you believe that would be a possibility? (Insert 0–10 scale: 0=Not At All Possible; 10= Very Possible)

22. Do you think that being a civilian employee of the Army is basically the <u>same</u> as or <u>different</u> than being a federal government employee? If you aren't sure, give your best guess.

Randomize	
The same	1
Different	2
Not Sure (Anchor at bottom)	3

Next, please read the paragraph below carefully. It gives some facts about civilian employment in the Army.

Civilian Careers in The Army
More than 330,000 men and women work in a wide variety of careers through Army Civilian Service.

What Is an Army Civilian?
An Army civilian is an employee of the United States Army who fills critical Department of Defense roles in more than 500 careers, including cyber security, engineering, medicine and administration. Army Civilian Service is one of the largest, busiest and most successful element within the Department of Defense. Army civilians are an integral part of the Army team. They provide mission-essential support to Soldiers by providing a workforce of talented, qualified civilians to fill critical non-combat roles.

Benefits of Civilian Service
Army Civilian Service employees receive a benefits package designed to provide a comfortable and secure work-life balance. These benefits include:
- Competitive salaries
- Paid holidays, sick leave, and vacation time
- A flexible work environment
- Comprehensive health and life insurance options with a substantial employer contribution to premiums
- A three-tiered retirement program with matching employer contribution
- Bonuses, awards and other incentives for job performance
- Challenging, stable job opportunities that may transfer from installation to installation.

Military Veterans and Military Spouses in Civilian Service
Veterans may be eligible for preference in hiring over non-veteran applicants.

Military spouses may be eligible for noncompetitive appointment or preference when seeking federal employment through Army Civilian Service.

Students and Recent Graduates
Army Civilian Service will fill more than 100,000 jobs in the next three to five years, providing many opportunities that can align with college majors. Army Civilian Service has an established culture of growing leaders. The Career Intern Program prepares entry-level employees for advancement in professional, administrative and technological career fields.

Employment for Disabled Individuals
Disabled individuals may qualify for Army Civilian Service competitive positions based on a special appointing authority. Applicants must be able to perform the essential duties of the job with reasonable accommodation. Noncompetitive employment is also available for individuals with severe physical, psychiatric or intellectual disabilities. Candidates must provide documentation of their disability and proof of job readiness.

23. Now that you have learned more about civilian employment in the Army, how interested would you be in learning more about...

(Show a & b on same screen)
a. ... civilian jobs in the Army?
b. ...civilian careers in the Army?

(Insert 0–10 scale: 0=Not at All Interested; 10=Extremely Interested)

24. Below is the paragraph you just read. Please read it again and click on any words or phrases that you think are especially good reasons for a civilian to consider working for the Army. (All to advance even if nothing highlighted.)

25. Suppose a friend or colleague was looking for a job. How likely would you be to recommend they consider a civilian position in the Army? (Insert 0–10 scale: 0=Extremely Unlikely; 10=Extremely Likely)

Demographics:
We have a few final questions, so we can learn a bit more about you.

26. Have you ever held a job with federal, state or local government?

Yes	1
No	2

(If Yes)
a. Why did you leave that position? (If you have had more than one job, think about the most recent.) (Insert text box)

27. What is your gender?

Male	1
Female	2

(If Student)
28. Do you currently have a part-time or full-time job?

Yes	1
No	2

(If Q28=1)
Is this job in a field related to your studies or career interests?

Yes	1
No	2

(Professionals or Q28a=1)
29. Which of the following best describes the organization where you work?

Randomize	
Non-profit	1
State or local government	2
Federal government	3
Small company (under 100 employees)	4
Medium company (under 100 to 1,000 employees)	5
Large company (over 1,000 employees)	6
Other (please specify) (Anchor)	7

(Professionals or Q28a=1)
30. Which of the following describes your position?

Executive	1
Senior manager	2
Mid-level manager	3
Engineer	4
Assistant	5
Intern	6
Other (Please specify) (Insert text box)	8

(All Respondents)
31. What is your marital status?

Never Married	1
Married	2
Separated	3
Divorced	4
Widowed	5

(If Q31 ≠ 2)
a. Do you live with a spouse/partner? (If Q31=2 auto-code as Yes, "1")

Yes	1
No	2

(If Q31a=1)
32. Is your spouse/partner employed?

Yes	1
No	2

33. What state do you live in? (Add drop-down box) (create variable coding states into census regions)

34. About how many people live in your city, town or village? If you don't know for sure, use your best guess.

Under 1,000	1
1,000 to 4,999	2
5,000 to 9,999	3
10,000 to 99,999	4
100,000 to 499,999	5
500,000 to 1,000,000	6
Over 1,000,000	7

35. Are you the parent of any children ages 18 or younger that live with you in your household?

Yes	1
No	2

(If Q35=1)
a. Please indicate how many children you have in each of the age ranges shown below. (Insert text box next to each age category)

0-2 years old	1
3-5 years old	2
6-10 years old	3
11-15 years old	4
16-17 years old	5
18 years old	6

36. Are you Spanish/Hispanic/Latino?

Yes	1
No	2

37. What is your race? (Mark one or more races to indicate what you consider yourself to be.)

Randomize	
White	1
Black or African American	2
American Indian or Alaska Native	3
Asian	4
Native Hawaiian or Other Pacific Islander	5

(Professionals)
38. Please provide your best estimate of your household's total 2017 income before taxes.

Less than $25,000	1
$25,000 - $49,999	2
$50,000 - $74,999	3
$75,000 - $99,999	4
$100,000 - $199,999	5
$200,000 or more	6
Prefer not to answer	7

(Students) (If Q5=3,4)
39. Do you intend to get a graduate degree?

Yes	1
No	2

(If Q39=1)
a. Will you most likely pursue the degree directly after college or after working for a while?

Randomize	
Directly or very soon after finishing undergraduate	1
After working for a while	2

(Professionals and Students) (If Q31a=1)
40. Has your spouse/partner ever served in the U.S. military?

Yes, currently serving	1
Yes, but not currently	2
No	3

(If Q40=1,2)
a. Which service?

Randomize	
Army	1
Air Force	2
Navy	3
Marines	4

41. Have your parents ever served in the U.S. military?

Yes, currently serving	1
Yes, but not currently	2
No	3

(If Q41=1,2)
a. Which service?

Randomize	
Army	1
Air Force	2
Navy	0
Marines	4

That completes our questionnaire. Thank you very much for your time.

APPENDIX C

Supplemental Data and Analysis Results

This appendix presents descriptive statistics for the three respondent groups and additional tabular results from our analyses for tables not shown in the main text in Chapter Three. We begin with descriptive statistics for the student, younger professional, and older professional groups, in Tables C.1–C.3.

In these tables, the names of the preferred job characteristic variables follow certain conventions. For example, "advancement" refers to the normalized rating for the group for fast career advancement. "Advancement_ArmyMinusPref" refers to difference in the within-group normalized rating for the extent to which the respondent perceived Army civilian jobs to offer fast career advancement relative to his or her rated preference for fast advancement. "ArmyAdvancement" is the unnormalized (raw) rating of the extent to which respondents perceived Army civilian jobs to offer fast career advancement. "CareerInterestChange" refers to the change in interest level of receiving more information about Army civilian careers after being given basic information about them. "JobInterestChange" is the analogous measure for receiving more information about Army civilian jobs. "Factor1_students" is the within group normalized rating of the factor score for factor 1 (see discussion in Chapter Three); "Factor1_students_raw" is the score on factor 1 before being normalized. Factor scores are the sum of products of the factor loadings for each of the variables included in the factor analyses times the respondents' ratings of those variables.

Variables beginning with "Q" refer to the question number in the questionnaire (see Appendix B). When appropriate, the name also indicates the response alternative being tabulated, e.g., Q13r1. Q17 and Q21 were recoded, with the correct answer being assigned a value of 3, unsure a value of 2, and the wrong answer assigned a value of 1. "SAD_ArmyMinusPref" is the summed absolute differences between a respondent's normalized ratings of perceived Army civilian job characteristics minus the normalized preferences of that respondent for the same characteristics. Professionals also have "SAD_ActualMinusPref" for their current jobs versus preferences. They also have variables representing the difference in the within group normalized ratings for their actual jobs versus preferences separately for each of the job characteristics, e.g., advancement_ActuMinusPref.

TABLE C.1

Descriptive Statistics for Students

Variable	Mean	SD
advancement	−0.079727	0.872554
advancement_ArmyMinusPref	0.0078295	1.192137
ArmyAdvancement	7.0501269	2.13051
ArmyBalance	6.7810914	2.393838
ArmyChallenges	7.3204315	2.019772
ArmyCollaboration	7.231599	2.101921
ArmyColleagues	7.0076142	2.149331
ArmyFlexibility	6.5583756	2.561823
ArmyGreatthings	7.4048223	2.04485
ArmyInsurance	7.5482234	2.018381
ArmyLearnandadvance	7.3464467	1.982918
ArmyPension	7.5019036	2.095497
ArmyPeople	7.0069797	2.197968
ArmySalary	7.3020305	2.153216
ArmySecurity	7.5609137	2.041187
ArmyTalents	7.3267766	1.987694
ArmyTravel	7.4428934	2.074005
ArmyVacation	6.9060914	2.361073
balance	0.6180699	0.827026

Table C.1—continued

Variable	Mean	SD
balance_ArmyMinusPref	−0.814047	1.486801
CareerInterestChange	0.2062183	1.69068
challenges	−0.405278	0.832415
challenges_ArmyMinusPref	0.4580445	1.20702
collaboration	−0.792424	0.832476
collaboration_ArmyMinusPref	0.8042213	1.24381
colleagues	−0.481685	0.718973
colleagues_ArmyMinusPref	0.3901804	1.213501
factor1_students (favorability)	$-1.52\text{E}{-16}$	9.791483
factor1_students_raw	98.022215	20.91653
factor2_students (colleagues)	$-4.63\text{E}{-17}$	4.554247
factor2_students_raw	−4.224321	4.420867
factor3_students (concerns)	$2.738\text{E}{-16}$	4.783109
factor3_students_raw	50.633029	12.12811
factor4_students (use own talents)	$-4.69\text{E}{-18}$	3.129468
factor4_students_raw	0.7500783	2.591759
factor5_students (challenges)	$2.121\text{E}{-16}$	3.152767
factor5_students_raw	7.2573143	4.455998
FamilyOpposition	6.1979695	2.98528
flexibility	−0.126152	0.868604
flexibility_ArmyMinusPref	−0.172541	1.585481
greatthings	0.2349	0.810439
greatthings_ArmyMinusPref	−0.143213	1.221486
InfoInterestCareers	6.8090102	2.587824
InfoInterestJobs	6.6173858	2.560789
InformedInfoInterestCareers	7.0152284	2.555745

Table C.1—continued

Variable	Mean	SD
InformedInfoInterestJobs	6.784264	2.516567
insurance	0.4615335	0.80433
insurance_ArmyMinusPref	−0.30371	1.173512
JobInterestChange	0.1668782	1.784076
learnandadvance	0.0663662	0.739596
learnandadvance_ArmyMinusPref	−0.001602	1.161988
LowSalary	7.1567259	2.454964
MuchTravel	6.4974619	2.76233
NoJobSecurity	6.6211929	2.679831
pension	0.1846756	0.63827
pension_ArmyMinusPref	−0.048214	1.088526
people	−0.668924	0.772029
people_ArmyMinusPref	0.5771266	1.229624
PoorBenefits	6.8140863	2.621344
PossibleDeath	7.4238579	2.494039
PossibleTransfer	7.4467005	2.23671
Q13r1	7.1852792	2.064653
Q13r10	7.0203046	2.239239
Q13r11	6.9073604	2.22175
Q13r2	7.1046954	2.258771
Q13r3	6.8661168	2.211765
Q13r4	7.0831218	2.131266
Q13r5	6.6548223	2.388095
Q13r6	6.9270305	2.153861
Q13r7	7.2043147	2.052673
Q13r8	7.553934	1.964998

Table C.1—continued

Variable	Mean	SD
Q13r9	6.7366751	2.222214
Q14	5.0177665	1.867262
Q15ar1	7.3032995	1.96558
Q15ar10	7.6427665	1.789188
Q15ar11	7.2658629	1.939007
Q15ar12	7.2258883	1.891935
Q15ar13	7.2963198	1.942118
Q15ar14	7.2290609	2.030608
Q15ar15	7.5126904	1.811734
Q15ar16	7.2430203	1.918651
Q15ar2	7.5406091	1.884507
Q15ar3	7.6979695	1.79598
Q15ar4	6.8045685	2.307724
Q15ar5	7.5196701	1.903946
Q15ar6	7.1294416	1.977588
Q15ar7	7.4549492	1.822749
Q15ar8	7.3870558	1.962489
Q15ar9	7.4238579	1.930024
Q15br1	7.6072335	1.964426
Q15br10	7.3134518	2.001135
Q15br11	7.0469543	2.087989
Q15br12	7.2899746	2.027506
Q15br13	7.1085025	2.01399
Q15br14	6.7709391	2.387043
Q15br15	7.2772843	1.953723
Q15br16	6.8997462	2.092793

Table C.1—continued

Variable	Mean	SD
Q15br2	7.6681472	1.914596
Q15br3	7.569797	1.982835
Q15br4	6.9841371	2.213466
Q15br5	7.6230964	1.927268
Q15br6	7.0317259	2.128628
Q15br7	7.2284264	1.989459
Q15br8	7.0545685	2.169238
Q15br9	7.2493655	2.026021
Q16	7.1332487	2.165827
q17.recode	2.036802	0.87355
Q18ra	6.6173858	2.560789
Q18rb	6.8090102	2.587824
Q19r1	7.5019036	2.095497
Q19r1.norm	0.1364612	0.966441
Q19r10	7.3267766	1.987694
Q19r10.norm	0.0556929	0.916722
Q19r11	7.0069797	2.197968
Q19r11.norm	−0.091797	1.013701
Q19r12	6.9060914	2.361073
Q19r12.norm	−0.138327	1.088925
Q19r13	7.231599	2.101921
Q19r13.norm	0.011797	0.969404
Q19r14	6.5583756	2.561823
Q19r14.norm	−0.298693	1.18151
Q19r15	7.3464467	1.982918
Q19r15.norm	0.0647647	0.91452

Table C.1—continued

Variable	Mean	SD
Q19r16	7.0076142	2.149331
Q19r16.norm	−0.091505	0.991269
Q19r2	7.5482234	2.018381
Q19r2.norm	0.1578239	0.930876
Q19r3	7.3020305	2.153216
Q19r3.norm	0.0442799	0.993061
Q19r4	7.4428934	2.074005
Q19r4.norm	0.1092458	0.956529
Q19r5	7.5609137	2.041187
Q19r5.norm	0.1636766	0.941394
Q19r6	7.0501269	2.13051
Q19r6.norm	−0.071898	0.982589
Q19r7	7.3204315	2.019772
Q19r7.norm	0.0527665	0.931517
Q19r8	6.7810914	2.393838
Q19r8.norm	−0.195977	1.104036
Q19r9	7.4048223	2.04485
Q19r9.norm	0.0916874	0.943083
Q2	2.8832487	0.321226
Q20r1	7.4238579	2.494039
Q20r2	7.4467005	2.23671
Q20r3	7.267132	2.288763
Q20r4	6.1979695	2.98528
Q20r5	6.6211929	2.679831
Q20r6	6.4974619	2.76233
Q20r7	7.1567259	2.454964

Table C.1—continued

Variable	Mean	SD
Q20r8	6.8140863	2.621344
Q20r9	5.8109137	3.210464
Q21	1.9917513	0.731553
q21.recode	1.8064721	0.83646
Q22	1.7557107	0.691421
Q23ra	6.784264	2.516567
Q23rb	7.0152284	2.555745
Q25	6.8483503	2.324303
Q26	1.927665	0.259124
Q27	1.4714467	0.499342
Q28	1.553934	0.49724
Q31	1.2861675	0.625358
Q31a	1.7233503	0.447484
Q34	4.6338832	1.599951
Q35	1.8362944	0.370126
Q36	1.7785533	0.415352
Q37r1	0.715736	0.451206
Q37r2	0.1630711	0.369548
Q37r3	0.0279188	0.164792
Q37r4	0.0850254	0.279008
Q37r5	0.0260152	0.159231
Q41	2.5488579	0.72866
Q5	4.9282995	1.404505
Q6_1	5.7652284	2.796725
Q6_2	5.7956853	2.85081
Q6_3	6.7195431	2.358913

Table C.1—continued

Variable	Mean	SD
Q6_4	5.946066	2.594061
RecommendArmyFriend	6.8483503	2.324303
SAD_ArmyMinusPref	17.219575	6.860374
salary	1.0483501	1.105279
salary_ArmyMinusPref	-1.00407	1.486975
security	0.5772082	0.980519
security_ArmyMinusPref	−0.413532	1.294633
SupportMilitary	5.8109137	3.210464
talents	0.2854774	0.684489
talents_ArmyMinusPref	−0.229785	1.091956
travel	−0.652043	1.215015
travel_ArmyMinusPref	0.7612887	1.520679
UndesiredLiving	7.267132	2.288763
vacation	−0.270348	0.852988
vacation_ArmyMinusPref	0.1320208	1.395174

NOTE: N = 1,576.

TABLE C.2
Descriptive Statistics for Younger Professionals

Variable	Mean	SD
ActualAdvancement	6.800738	2.570536
ActualBalance	7.5227552	2.108395
ActualChallenges	7.2189422	2.227942
ActualCollaboration	7.2115621	2.196392
ActualColleagues	7.4323493	2.09836
ActualFlexibility	7.4397294	2.266084
ActualGreatthings	7.2939729	2.27704
ActualInsurance	7.2515375	2.40309
ActualLearnandadvance	7.3646986	2.213905
ActualPension	7.0645756	2.547303
ActualPeople	7.2367774	2.157754
ActualSalary	7.399139	2.293262
ActualSecurity	7.6082411	2.16936
ActualTalents	7.5658057	2.065014
ActualTravel	6.301968	2.918243
ActualVacation	7.0707257	2.365244
advancement	−0.023869	0.855801
advancement_ActuMinusPref	−0.234664	1.320306
advancement_ArmyMinusPref	−0.122198	1.29003
Allowsforflexibilityinworkschedule	−0.313158	1.202087
ArmyAdvancement	7.1635916	2.180823
ArmyBalance	6.7736777	2.475071
ArmyChallenges	7.4440344	2.080149
ArmyCollaboration	7.4483395	2.067203
ArmyColleagues	7.095326	2.18586
ArmyFlexibility	6.6180812	2.619669

Table C.2—continued

Variable	Mean	SD
ArmyGreatthings	7.4384994	2.17685
ArmyInsurance	7.6931119	1.99844
ArmyLearnandadvance	7.4827798	2.029629
ArmyPension	7.7312423	2.029559
ArmyPeople	7.1223862	2.22277
ArmySalary	7.2773678	2.236468
ArmySecurity	7.7361624	2.048912
ArmyTalents	7.4729397	2.075396
ArmyTravel	7.5910209	2.154784
ArmyVacation	7.0934809	2.342358
Attractivesalarylevel	1.5868326	1.728726
balance	0.6159264	0.810906
balance_ActuMinusPref	−0.550319	1.274056
balance_ArmyMinusPref	−0.950312	1.555227
CareerInterestChange	0.1543665	1.971217
challenges	−0.264268	0.748728
challenges_ActuMinusPref	0.1934825	1.076077
challenges_ArmyMinusPref	0.2536472	1.181127
collaboration	−0.829901	0.722573
collaboration_ActuMinusPref	0.7558023	1.116305
collaboration_ArmyMinusPref	0.8213594	1.179904
colleagues	−0.571556	0.741272
colleagues_ActuMinusPref	0.5965772	1.06894
colleagues_ArmyMinusPref	0.3925185	1.2462
Colleaguesyouenjoyworkingwith	−0.79113	1.026046
Encouragescollaborationamongcoworkers	-1.148723	1.000162

Table C.2—continued

Variable	Mean	SD
Exposuretoexcitingjobrelatedchallenges	−0.365791	1.036366
factor1_young (favorability)	-1.03E-15	9.786183
factor1_young_raw	96.574463	21.33384
factor2_young (colleagues)	-7.13E-18	5.150494
factor2_young_raw	1.9452134	5.195846
factor3_young (concerns)	-6.01E-17	5.041742
factor3_young_raw	48.969789	13.92194
factor4_young (challenges)	-2.84E-17	3.257074
factor4_young_raw	4.6925462	2.81249
FamilyOpposition	5.7662977	3.181987
Fastcareeradvancement	−0.033039	1.184573
flexibility	−0.226242	0.868454
flexibility_ActuMinusPref	0.2545764	1.315558
flexibility_ArmyMinusPref	−0.183292	1.594688
Generousbenefitsinsuranceetc	0.7855631	0.957102
Generousholidayvacationpolicy	−0.440507	1.010772
Generousretirementpensionplan	0.5665615	0.86102
Goodworklifebalance	0.852546	1.12243
greatthings	0.1150646	0.723902
greatthings_ActuMinusPref	−0.152166	1.174888
greatthings_ArmyMinusPref	−0.128359	1.241654
InfoInterestCareers	6.8905289	2.693869
InfoInterestJobs	6.7127921	2.665203
InformedInfoInterestCareers	7.0448954	2.607648
InformedInfoInterestJobs	6.8573186	2.644576
insurance	0.5675343	0.691464

Table C.2—continued

Variable	Mean	SD
insurance_ActuMinusPref	−0.623686	1.255236
insurance_ArmyMinusPref	−0.457857	1.172912
JobInterestChange	0.1445264	1.959126
learnandadvance	0.0532156	0.688892
learnandadvance_ActuMinusPref	−0.058566	1.162615
learnandadvance_ArmyMinusPref	−0.045123	1.17845
LowSalary	6.8616236	2.696763
MuchTravel	6.095326	3.044918
NoJobSecurity	6.0116851	3.035663
Opportunitytodogreatthingswithyourlife	0.1592689	1.002002
Opportunitytotravel	-1.182261	1.679871
Opportunitytouseyourtalentsandabilities	0.424008	0.876719
Opportunitytoworkwithpeoplelikeyou	−0.934221	1.11377
pension	0.4093154	0.622048
pension_ActuMinusPref	−0.549402	1.271556
pension_ArmyMinusPref	−0.281222	1.149405
people	−0.674933	0.804649
people_ActuMinusPref	0.6121544	1.082202
people_ArmyMinusPref	0.5089644	1.209695
PoorBenefits	6.2429274	2.950363
PossibleDeath	6.9501845	2.897741
PossibleTransfer	7.1549815	2.54739
Providesmanyopportunitiestolearnandadvance	0.0736594	0.953543
Q10a	7.4889299	2.052886
Q11	1.6740467	0.468874
Q13r1	7.4772448	2.09228

Table C.2—continued

Variable	Mean	SD
Q13r10	7.3776138	2.1954
Q13r11	6.7121771	2.386281
Q13r2	7.2195572	2.288784
Q13r3	6.8936039	2.391343
Q13r4	6.8542435	2.464075
Q13r5	6.6894219	2.553328
Q13r6	7.1543665	2.256785
Q13r7	7.3936039	2.051655
Q13r8	7.6236162	2.045581
Q13r9	6.7281673	2.438644
Q14	5.3468635	1.688763
Q15br1	7.795203	1.942687
Q15br10	7.4286593	2.00188
Q15br11	7.1260763	2.155088
Q15br12	7.4544895	2.037062
Q15br13	7.1777368	2.113056
Q15br14	6.799508	2.515018
Q15br15	7.3751538	2.058103
Q15br16	7.0547355	2.181055
Q15br2	7.8234932	1.911317
Q15br3	7.5344403	2.129149
Q15br4	7.1316113	2.36511
Q15br5	7.8523985	1.965953
Q15br6	7.0725707	2.304969
Q15br7	7.2712177	2.095768
Q15br8	7.1857319	2.160614

Table C.2—continued

Variable	Mean	SD
Q15br9	7.3056581	2.134708
Q16	7.295203	2.291429
q17.recode	2.1125461	0.865192
Q18ra	6.7127921	2.665203
Q18rb	6.8905289	2.693869
Q19r1	7.7312423	2.029559
Q19r1.norm	0.1280933	0.980225
Q19r10	7.4729397	2.075396
Q19r10.norm	0.0033398	1.002363
Q19r11	7.1223862	2.22277
Q19r11.norm	−0.165969	1.073541
Q19r12	7.0934809	2.342358
Q19r12.norm	−0.179929	1.131299
Q19r13	7.4483395	2.067203
Q19r13.norm	−0.008541	0.998406
Q19r14	6.6180812	2.619669
Q19r14.norm	−0.409535	1.265233
Q19r15	7.4827798	2.029629
Q19r15.norm	0.0080923	0.980259
Q19r16	7.095326	2.18586
Q19r16.norm	−0.179038	1.055714
Q19r2	7.6931119	1.99844
Q19r2.norm	0.1096773	0.965195
Q19r3	7.2773678	2.236468
Q19r3.norm	−0.091116	1.080157
Q19r4	7.5910209	2.154784

Table C.2—continued

Variable	Mean	SD
Q19r4.norm	0.06037	1.040705
Q19r5	7.7361624	2.048912
Q19r5.norm	0.1304696	0.989572
Q19r6	7.1635916	2.180823
Q19r6.norm	−0.146067	1.053282
Q19r7	7.4440344	2.080149
Q19r7.norm	−0.010621	1.004658
Q19r8	6.7736777	2.475071
Q19r8.norm	−0.334386	1.195396
Q19r9	7.4384994	2.17685
Q19r9.norm	−0.013294	1.051363
Q2	2.8560886	0.351108
Q20r1	6.9501845	2.897741
Q20r2	7.1549815	2.54739
Q20r3	6.9594096	2.519746
Q20r4	5.7662977	3.181987
Q20r5	6.0116851	3.035663
Q20r6	6.095326	3.044918
Q20r7	6.8616236	2.696763
Q20r8	6.2429274	2.950363
Q20r9	5.2300123	3.434842
Q21	1.9833948	0.716638
q21.recode	1.7785978	0.838422
Q22	1.7380074	0.660252
Q23ra	6.8573186	2.644576
Q23rb	7.0448954	2.607648

Table C.2—continued

Variable	Mean	SD
Q25	7.0590406	2.350559
Q26	1.7792128	0.414905
Q27	1.4206642	0.493818
Q3	2.5239852	0.537553
Q31	1.7324723	0.668696
Q31a	1.295818	0.45655
Q34	4.7466175	1.435293
Q35	1.4852399	0.499936
Q36	1.7699877	0.42097
Q37r1	0.7619926	0.425995
Q37r2	0.1476015	0.354814
Q37r3	0.0313653	0.174357
Q37r4	0.0799508	0.2713
Q37r5	0.0159902	0.125476
Q38	3.9114391	1.180156
Q3a	5.0854859	0.642647
Q41	2.7257073	0.504543
Q7	3.204182	1.072226
Q9r1	7.0645756	2.547303
Q9r1.norm	−0.140086	1.143576
Q9r10	7.5658057	2.065014
Q9r10.norm	0.0849342	0.92706
Q9r11	7.2367774	2.157754
Q9r11.norm	−0.062779	0.968694
Q9r12	7.0707257	2.365244
Q9r12.norm	−0.137325	1.061844

Table C.2—continued

Variable	Mean	SD
Q9r13	7.2115621	2.196392
Q9r13.norm	−0.074099	0.98604
Q9r14	7.4397294	2.266084
Q9r14.norm	0.028334	1.017327
Q9r15	7.3646986	2.213905
Q9r15.norm	−0.00535	0.993902
Q9r16	7.4323493	2.09836
Q9r16.norm	0.0250208	0.94203
Q9r2	7.2515375	2.40309
Q9r2.norm	−0.056152	1.078834
Q9r3	7.399139	2.293262
Q9r3.norm	0.0101115	1.029529
Q9r4	6.301068	2.918243
Q9r4.norm	−0.482448	1.310105
Q9r5	7.6082411	2.16936
Q9r5.norm	0.103985	0.973904
Q9r6	6.800738	2.570536
Q9r6.norm	−0.258532	1.154007
Q9r7	7.2189422	2.227942
Q9r7.norm	−0.070785	1.000204
Q9r8	7.5227552	2.108395
Q9r8.norm	0.0656073	0.946535
Q9r9	7.2939729	2.27704
Q9r9.norm	−0.037101	1.022246
RecommendArmyFriend	7.0590406	2.350559
SAD_ActuMinusPref	16.798219	6.120074

Table C.2—continued

Variable	Mean	SD
SAD_ArmyMinusPref	18.012776	6.695427
salary	1.1464158	1.248927
salary_ActuMinusPref	-1.136304	1.727129
salary_ArmyMinusPref	-1.237532	1.762968
security	0.5493476	0.963971
security_ActuMinusPref	−0.445363	1.353392
security_ArmyMinusPref	−0.418878	1.370709
Strongjobsecurity	0.7603896	1.334299
SupportMilitary	5.2300123	3.434842
talents	0.3063268	0.63339
talents_ActuMinusPref	−0.221393	1.026874
talents_ArmyMinusPref	−0.302987	1.139511
travel	−0.854131	1.213632
travel_ActuMinusPref	0.3716822	1.432244
travel_ArmyMinusPref	0.9145005	1.576439
UndesiredLiving	6.9594096	2.519746
vacation	−0.318247	0.730237
vacation_ActuMinusPref	0.1809215	1.275065
vacation_ArmyMinusPref	0.1383176	1.340651

NOTE: N = 1,626.

TABLE C.3

Descriptive Statistics for Older Professionals

Variable	Mean	SD
ActualAdvancement	7.1145098	2.413216
ActualBalance	7.6933333	1.907001
ActualChallenges	7.5796078	1.958893
ActualCollaboration	7.6658824	1.870968
ActualColleagues	7.7984314	1.724602
ActualFlexibility	7.7341176	1.966131
ActualGreatthings	7.4407843	2.119706
ActualInsurance	7.5945098	2.022899
ActualLearnandadvance	7.48	2.003968
ActualPension	7.4407843	2.218496
ActualPeople	7.6172549	1.875903
ActualSalary	7.7129412	1.923362
ActualSecurity	7.8862745	1.871145
ActualTalents	7.8776471	1.820197
ActualTravel	6.667451	2.821063
ActualVacation	7.5819608	1.991384
advancement	−0.11895	0.883406
advancement_ActuMinusPref	0.0012809	1.219956
advancement_ArmyMinusPref	0.0946377	1.180124
Allowsforflexibilityinworkschedule	−0.31193	1.214774
ArmyAdvancement	7.4156863	1.93815
ArmyBalance	7.4478431	2.024435
ArmyChallenges	7.7294118	1.718321
ArmyCollaboration	7.707451	1.754536
ArmyColleagues	7.5443137	1.835514
ArmyFlexibility	7.1921569	2.250052

Table C.3—continued

Variable	Mean	SD
ArmyGreatthings	7.6454902	1.822535
ArmyInsurance	7.8760784	1.679225
ArmyLearnandadvance	7.6580392	1.780962
ArmyPension	7.9466667	1.650929
ArmyPeople	7.4972549	1.947252
ArmySalary	7.5623529	1.983011
ArmySecurity	8.0031373	1.627855
ArmyTalents	7.7882353	1.780503
ArmyTravel	7.7207843	1.802797
ArmyVacation	7.6219608	1.897653
Attractivesalarylevel	1.4283762	1.744331
balance	0.5589737	0.857646
balance_ActuMinusPref	−0.416788	1.24807
balance_ArmyMinusPref	−0.567755	1.421201
CareerInterestChange	0.1129412	1.622965
challenges	−0.192242	0.748616
challenges_ActuMinusPref	0.2833722	0.986041
challenges_ArmyMinusPref	0.3194509	1.049233
collaboration	−0.716873	0.686897
collaboration_ActuMinusPref	0.846735	0.958647
collaboration_ArmyMinusPref	0.8334755	1.01637
colleagues	−0.459584	0.723787
colleagues_ActuMinusPref	0.6489525	0.955659
colleagues_ArmyMinusPref	0.4973958	1.07578
Colleaguesyouenjoyworkingwith	−0.636142	1.001843
Encouragescollaborationamongcoworkers	−0.992273	0.950781

Table C.3—continued

Variable	Mean	SD
Exposuretoexcitingjobrelatedchallenges	−0.266095	1.036211
factor1_old (favorability)	-4.26E-16	10.27758
factor1_old_raw	104.33091	19.34067
factor2_old (concerns)	-3.74E-18	6.595892
factor2_old_raw	58.05914	16.49071
factor3_old (colleagues)	1.105E-16	5.442033
factor3_old_raw	7.5529146	5.993039
factor4_old (challenges)	-8.24E-18	3.612819
factor4_old_raw	3.551765	3.161584
FamilyOpposition	5.8407843	3.257244
Fastcareeradvancement	−0.164647	1.222782
flexibility	−0.225356	0.87762
flexibility_ActuMinusPref	0.3858513	1.198139
flexibility_ArmyMinusPref	0.0930846	1.462776
Generousbenefitsinsuranceetc	0.763475	1.006182
Generousholidayvacationpolicy	−0.412241	0.989206
Generousretirementpensionplan	0.5812774	0.905566
Goodworklifebalance	0.7737138	1.187126
greatthings	0.021714	0.718602
greatthings_ActuMinusPref	0.0070936	1.072456
greatthings_ArmyMinusPref	0.0649633	1.107415
0InfoInterestCareers	7.4729412	2.325515
InfoInterestJobs	7.2596078	2.260345
InformedInfoInterestCareers	7.5858824	2.265249
InformedInfoInterestJobs	7.3764706	2.181932
insurance	0.5515766	0.726922

Table C.3—continued

Variable	Mean	SD
insurance_ActuMinusPref	−0.453756	1.215776
insurance_ArmyMinusPref	−0.353531	1.089769
JobInterestChange	0.1168627	1.601017
learnandadvance	−0.035052	0.645125
learnandadvance_ActuMinusPref	0.0814645	1.064164
learnandadvance_ArmyMinusPref	0.1277897	1.063675
LowSalary	7.0407843	2.507427
MuchTravel	6.6486275	2.799779
NoJobSecurity	6.2705882	2.892046
Opportunitytodogreatthingswithyourlife	0.0300558	0.994666
Opportunitytotravel	-1.252137	1.70839
Opportunitytouseyourtalentsandabilities	0.4661745	0.900052
Opportunitytoworkwithpeoplelikeyou	−0.797275	1.115578
pension	0.419947	0.654231
pension_ActuMinusPref	−0.391139	1.2349
pension_ArmyMinusPref	−0.187809	1.018916
people	−0.575995	0.805956
people_ActuMinusPref	0.684027	0.985197
people_ArmyMinusPref	0.5910788	1.080418
PoorBenefits	6.5223529	2.836203
PossibleDeath	6.9043137	2.846178
PossibleTransfer	7.2509804	2.46732
Providesmanyopportunitiestolearnandadvance	−0.048517	0.892962
Q10a	7.6509804	1.99483
Q11	1.7788235	0.415202
Q13r1	7.6792157	1.794331

Table C.3—continued

Variable	Mean	SD
Q13r10	7.6658824	1.896801
Q13r11	7.1137255	2.304611
Q13r2	7.2878431	2.316984
Q13r3	7.4407843	2.035069
Q13r4	7.0964706	2.343556
Q13r5	7.0596078	2.345956
Q13r6	7.5176471	1.896943
Q13r7	7.6933333	1.781885
Q13r8	7.8258824	1.67523
Q13r9	7.2352941	2.159534
Q14	5.3905882	1.653569
Q15br1	8.0266667	1.540427
Q15br10	7.6713725	1.825879
Q15br11	7.4305882	1.904841
Q15br12	7.7607843	1.674923
Q15br13	7.4329412	1.923787
Q15br14	7.2768627	2.179047
Q15br15	7.5113725	1.857689
Q15br16	7.4039216	1.980077
Q15br2	7.9811765	1.540543
Q15br3	7.654902	1.945521
Q15br4	7.2290196	2.147089
Q15br5	8.0572549	1.678383
Q15br6	7.307451	2.087843
Q15br7	7.465098	1.913596
Q15br8	7.5686275	1.886652

Table C.3—continued

Variable	Mean	SD
Q15br9	7.4556863	1.985474
Q16	7.7356863	1.855013
q17.recode	2.3654902	0.824317
Q18ra	7.2596078	2.260345
Q18rb	7.4729412	2.325515
Q19r1	7.9466667	1.650929
Q19r1.norm	0.2321377	0.797356
Q19r10	7.7882353	1.780503
Q19r10.norm	0.1556195	0.859937
Q19r11	7.4972549	1.947252
Q19r11.norm	0.0150834	0.940473
Q19r12	7.6219608	1.897653
Q19r12.norm	0.0753131	0.916518
Q19r13	7.707451	1.754536
Q19r13.norm	0.1166027	0.847396
Q19r14	7.1921569	2.250052
Q19r14.norm	−0.132271	1.086717
Q19r15	7.6580392	1.780962
Q19r15.norm	0.0927381	0.860159
Q19r16	7.5443137	1.835514
Q19r16.norm	0.0378116	0.886506
Q19r2	7.8760784	1.679225
Q19r2.norm	0.1980454	0.811022
Q19r3	7.5623529	1.983011
Q19r3.norm	0.0465241	0.957743
Q19r4	7.7207843	1.802797

Table C.3—continued

Variable	Mean	SD
Q19r4.norm	0.1230424	0.870705
Q19r5	8.0031373	1.627855
Q19r5.norm	0.2594116	0.786212
Q19r6	7.4156863	1.93815
Q19r6.norm	−0.024312	0.936077
Q19r7	7.7294118	1.718321
Q19r7.norm	0.1272092	0.829905
Q19r8	7.4478431	2.024435
Q19r8.norm	−0.008781	0.97775
Q19r9	7.6454902	1.822535
Q19r9.norm	0.0866772	0.880238
Q2	2.9341176	0.248174
Q20r1	6.9043137	2.846178
Q20r2	7.2509804	2.46732
Q20r3	7.1341176	2.480705
Q20r4	5.8407843	3.257244
Q20r5	6.2705882	2.892046
Q20r6	6.6486275	2.799779
Q20r7	7.0407843	2.507427
Q20r8	6.5223529	2.836203
Q20r9	5.6054902	3.383467
Q21	1.8996078	0.694873
q21.recode	1.7890196	0.871783
Q22	1.6831373	0.633935
Q23ra	7.3764706	2.181932
Q23rb	7.5858824	2.265249

Table C.3—continued

Variable	Mean	SD
Q25	7.6133333	1.945968
Q26	1.8345098	0.371768
Q27	1.2737255	0.446045
Q3	4.5717647	0.495017
Q31	2.1145098	0.752433
Q31a	1.1686275	0.374569
Q34	5.0023529	1.439789
Q35	1.3560784	0.479027
Q36	1.8666667	0.340068
Q37r1	0.8298039	0.375952
Q37r2	0.0988235	0.298542
Q37r3	0.0188235	0.135955
Q37r4	0.052549	0.223219
Q37r5	0.0062745	0.078994
Q38	4.3333333	1.051027
Q3a	5.2454902	0.675985
Q41	2.6776471	0.51699
Q7	4.7568627	1.387494
Q9r1	7.4407843	2.218496
Q9r1.norm	0.0288076	0.995963
Q9r10	7.8776471	1.820197
Q9r10.norm	0.2249311	0.817153
Q9r11	7.6172549	1.875903
Q9r11.norm	0.1080316	0.842161
Q9r12	7.5819608	1.991384
Q9r12.norm	0.0921868	0.894004

Table C.3—continued

Variable	Mean	SD
Q9r13	7.6658824	1.870968
Q9r13.norm	0.1298622	0.839946
Q9r14	7.7341176	1.966131
Q9r14.norm	0.1604955	0.882668
Q9r15	7.48	2.003968
Q9r15.norm	0.0464129	0.899654
Q9r16	7.7984314	1.724602
Q9r16.norm	0.1893683	0.774236
Q9r2	7.5945098	2.022899
Q9r2.norm	0.0978205	0.908153
Q9r3	7.7129412	1.923362
Q9r3.norm	0.1509886	0.863467
Q9r4	6.667451	2.821063
Q9r4.norm	−0.31837	1.266478
Q9r5	7.8862745	1.871145
Q9r5.norm	0.2288043	0.840025
Q9r6	7.1145098	2.413216
Q9r6.norm	−0.117669	1.08338
Q9r7	7.5796078	1.958893
Q9r7.norm	0.0911305	0.879418
Q9r8	7.6933333	1.907001
Q9r8.norm	0.142186	0.856122
Q9r9	7.4407843	2.119706
Q9r9.norm	0.0288076	0.951613
RecommendArmyFriend	7.6133333	1.945968
SAD_ActuMinusPref	15.690125	5.634673

Table C.3—continued

Variable	Mean	SD
SAD_ArmyMinusPref	16.426385	5.728533
salary	1.0319381	1.260201
salary_ActuMinusPref	−0.880949	1.631872
salary_ArmyMinusPref	−0.985414	1.729515
security	0.6055501	0.963106
security_ActuMinusPref	−0.376746	1.294025
security_ArmyMinusPref	−0.346139	1.255734
Strongjobsecurity	0.8381834	1.333102
SupportMilitary	5.6054902	3.383467
talents	0.3367902	0.650247
talents_ActuMinusPref	−0.111859	0.970717
talents_ArmyMinusPref	−0.181171	1.05745
travel	−0.904613	1.234235
travel_ActuMinusPref	0.5862431	1.372386
travel_ArmyMinusPref	1.0276553	1.436496
UndesiredLiving	7.1341176	2.480705
vacation	−0.297826	0.714657
vacation_ActuMinusPref	0.3900124	1.120967
vacation_ArmyMinusPref	0.3731387	1.165798

NOTE: N = 1,275.

Tables C.4 and C.5 show the relationship between satisfaction with one's current job and interest in getting information about an Army civilian job by the standardized difference between one's actual and preferred job characteristics by respondent group and job type.

Tables C.6–C.8 show the relationship between the perceived difference in Army civilian job characteristics and one's preferences and interest in getting information about an Army civilian job or recommending a friend consider one by respondent group and job type.

TABLE C.4

Satisfaction and Army Job Information by Standardized Difference Between One's Actual and Preferred Job Characteristics and Job Type for Younger Professionals

Item	Dependent Variable						
	Overall Satisfaction	Currently Looking for Job	Likely to Look in Next Year	Info Interest Army Jobs	Info Interest Army Careers	Informed Info Interest Army Jobs	Informed Info Interest Army Careers
SAD_ActuMinusPref	-0.169***	-0.022***	0.048	-0.048**	-0.054***	-0.039*	-0.051**
	(0.014)	(0.004)	(0.034)	(0.021)	(0.021)	(0.021)	(0.020)
Civil Engineer	-0.778**	-0.057	0.539	0.579	0.302	-0.070	-0.264
	(0.386)	(0.095)	(0.776)	(0.554)	(0.560)	(0.551)	(0.542)
Electronics Engineer	-0.078	-0.154	-0.031	-0.514	-0.187	0.162	0.115
	(0.398)	(0.098)	(0.828)	(0.572)	(0.578)	(0.569)	(0.560)
Information Technology Manager	-0.041	-0.111	0.838	0.115	-0.412	0.289	0.055
	(0.383)	(0.094)	(0.793)	(0.550)	(0.556)	(0.547)	(0.538)
SAD_ActuMinusPref: Civil Engineer	0.057***	0.008	-0.046	-0.034	-0.021	0.011	0.023
	(0.022)	(0.005)	(0.047)	(0.031)	(0.032)	(0.031)	(0.031)
SAD_ActuMinusPref: Electronics Engineer	0.024	0.008	-0.017	0.036	0.015	-0.011	-0.001
	(0.022)	(0.005)	(0.050)	(0.032)	(0.032)	(0.032)	(0.031)
SAD_ActuMinusPref: Information Technology Manager	0.027	0.005	0.0004	0.001	0.022	-0.001	0.009
	(0.020)	(0.005)	(0.046)	(0.029)	(0.029)	(0.029)	(0.028)
Constant	10.106***	2.035***	3.205***	7.446***	7.801***	7.422***	7.793***
	(0.278)	(0.068)	(0.589)	(0.399)	(0.403)	(0.397)	(0.391)

Table C.4—continued

Item	Dependent Variable						
	Overall Satisfaction	Currently Looking for Job	Likely to Look in Next Year	Info Interest Army Jobs	Info Interest Army Careers	Informed Info Interest Army Jobs	Informed Info Interest Army Careers
R^2	0.193	0.063	0.036	0.015	0.014	0.010	0.012
Adjusted R^2	0.190	0.058	0.030	0.010	0.010	0.006	0.007
Residual Std. Error	1.848	0.455	2.646	2.651	2.680	2.637	2.598
	(df = 1,618)	(df = 1,618)	(df = 1,088)	(df = 1,618)	(df = 1,618)	(df = 1,618)	(df = 1,618)
F Statistic	55.423***	15.412***	5.868***	3.428***	3.332***	2.340**	2.722***
	(df = 7; 1,618)	(df = 7; 1,618)	(df = 7; 1,088)	(df = 7; 1,618)	(df = 7; 1,618)	(df = 7; 1,618)	(df = 7; 1,618)

NOTE: N = 1,626. SAD is the sum of the absolute values of the differences in perceptions of one's actual job characteristics minus one's ratings of the corresponding preferred job characteristics across the 16 job characteristics. $^*p < 0.10$; $^{**}p < 0.05$; $^{***}p < 0.01$.

TABLE C.5

Satisfaction and Army Job Interest by Standardized Difference Between One's Actual and Preferred Job Characteristics and Job Type for Older Professionals

Item	Dependent Variable						
	Overall Satisfaction	Currently Looking for Job	Like y to Look in Next Year	Info Interest Army Jobs	Info Interest Army Careers	Informed Info Interest Army Jobs	Informed Info Interest Army Careers
SAD_ActuMinusPref	-0.125***	-0.016***	0.089***	-0.046**	-0.020	-0.016	-0.006
	(0.016)	(0.004)	(0.033)	(0.020)	(0.020)	(0.019)	(0.020)
Civil Engineer	-0.684	-0.163	-.908**	-0.112	0.449	0.835	1.254**
	(0.478)	(0.105)	(0.841)	(0.576)	(0.586)	(0.559)	(0.576)
Electronics Engineer	0.241	0.059	0.765	0.371	1.438***	0.756	1.367***
	(0.431)	(0.094)	(0.808)	(0.520)	(0.529)	(0.505)	(0.520)
Information Technology Manager	0.927**	-0.005	0.753	-0.959*	-0.336	-0.785	-0.828
	(0.444)	(0.097)	(0.803)	(0.536)	(0.545)	(0.520)	(0.536)
SAD_ActuMinusPref: Civil Engineer	0.050	0.014**	-0.151***	0.025	0.007	-0.040	-0.055
	(0.031)	(0.007)	(0.055)	(0.037)	(0.038)	(0.036)	(0.037)
SAD_ActuMinusPref: Electronics Engineer	-0.001	-0.001	-0.059	-0.013	-0.065**	-0.035	-0.066**
	(0.026)	(0.006)	(0.053)	(0.032)	(0.033)	(0.031)	(0.032)
SAD_ActuMinusPref: Information Technology Manager	-0.039	0.001	-0.013	0.036	-0.007	0.036	0.032
	(0.024)	(0.005)	(0.046)	(0.029)	(0.029)	(0.028)	(0.029)
Constant	9.494***	2.013***	1.983***	7.955***	7.618***	7.515***	7.509***
	(0.292)	(0.064)	(0.547)	(0.352)	(0.358)	(0.342)	(0.352)

Table C.5—continued

	Dependent Variable						
Item	Overall Satisfaction	Currently Looking for Job	Likely to Look in Next Year	Info Interest Army Jobs	Info Interest Army Careers	Informed Info Interest Army Jobs	Informed Info Interest Army Careers
R^2	0.140	0.049	0.036	0.025	0.046	0.015	0.030
Adjusted R^2	0.135	0.043	0.029	0.020	0.041	0.010	0.024
Residual Std. Error	1.855	0.406	2.627	2.238	2.278	2.171	2.238
	(df = 1,267)	(df = 1,267)	(df = 985)	(df = 1,267)	(df = 1,267)	(df = 1,267)	(df = 1,267)

NOTE: N = 1,275. SAD is the sum of the absolute values of the differences in perceptions of one's actual job characteristics minus one's ratings of the corresponding preferred job characteristics across the 16 job characteristics. $*p < 0.10$; $**p < 0.05$; $***p < 0.01$.

TABLE C.6

Interest in Army Civilian Jobs and Willingness to Recommend One by Gap in Perceived Characteristics and Job Type for Students

	Dependent Variable				
Item	Info Interest Jobs	Info Interest Careers	Informed Info Interest Jobs	Informed Info Interest Careers	Recommend Army to Friend
SAD_ArmyMinusPref	-0.138***	-0.147***	-0.109***	-0.118***	-0.119***
	(0.017)	(0.018)	(0.018)	(0.018)	(0.016)
Civil Engineer	-0.570	-0.476	-0.635	-0.301	-0.291
	(0.472)	(0.474)	(0.478)	(0.479)	(0.430)
Electronics Engineer	0.308	0.427	0.527	0.854*	0.469
	(0.457)	(0.459)	(0.463)	(0.463)	(0.416)
Information Technology Manager	0.437	0.221	0.196	0.314	0.298
	(0.448)	(0.450)	(0.454)	(0.454)	(0.408)
SAD_ArmyMinusPref:Civil Engineer	0.030	0.028	0.035	0.016	0.022
	(0.026)	(0.027)	(0.027)	(0.027)	(0.024)
SAD_ArmyMinusPref: Electronics Engineer	-0.020	-0.031	-0.038	-0.050**	-0.029
	(0.025)	(0.025)	(0.025)	(0.025)	(0.023)
SAD_ArmyMinusPref: Information Technology Manager	-0.035	-0.020	-0.022	-0.026	-0.028
	(0.023)	(0.023)	(0.023)	(0.024)	(0.021)
Constant	9.078***	9.406***	8.769***	9.099***	8.941***
	(0.325)	(0.327)	(0.330)	(0.330)	(0.296)

Table C.6—continued

Item	Info Interest Jobs	Info Interest Careers	Informed Info Interest Jobs	Informed Info Interest Careers	Recommend Army to Friend
			Dependent Variable		
R^2	0.165	0.174	0.112	0.138	0.158
Adjusted R^2	0.161	0.171	0.108	0.134	0.155
Residual Std. Error (df = 1,568)	2.346	2.356	2.377	2.378	2.137
F Statistic (df = 7; 1,568)	44.120***	47.342***	28.290***	35.835***	42.120***

NOTE: N = 1,576. SAD is the sum of the absolute values of the differences in perceptions of Army civilian job characteristics minus one's ratings of the corresponding preferred job characteristics across the 16 job characteristics. $^*p < 0.10$; $^{**}p < 0.05$; $^{***}p < 0.01$.

TABLE C.7

Interest in Army Civilian Jobs and Willingness to Recommend One by Gap in Perceived Characteristics and Job Type for Younger Professionals

	Dependent Variable				
Item	Info Interest Jobs	Info Interest Careers	Informed Info Interest Jobs	Informed Info Interest Careers	Recommend Army to Friend
SAD_ArmyMinusPref	-0.171***	-0.172***	-0.154***	-0.159***	-0.132***
	(0.022)	(0.022)	(0.022)	(0.021)	(0.019)
Civil Engineer	-0.889	-1.101**	-1.087*	-0.907*	-0.602
	(0.554)	(0.556)	(0.556)	(0.542)	(0.488)
Electronics Engineer	-1.041*	-0.550	-0.767	-0.348	-0.285
	(0.565)	(0.567)	(0.567)	(0.552)	(0.497)
Information Technology Manager	-0.053	-0.040	0.225	0.206	0.404
	(0.542)	(0.544)	(0.544)	(0.530)	(0.477)
SAD_ArmyMinusPref:Civil Engineer	0.040	0.048	0.056*	0.045	0.020
	(0.030)	(0.030)	(0.030)	(0.029)	(0.026)
SAD_ArmyMinusPref:Electronics Engineer	0.055*	0.028	0.036	0.019	0.012
	(0.029)	(0.030)	(0.030)	(0.029)	(0.026)
SAD_ArmyMinusPref:Information Technology Manager	0.018	0.009	0.010	0.009	-0.011
	(0.027)	(0.027)	(0.027)	(0.026)	(0.024)
Constant	9.800***	10.054***	9.591***	9.845***	9.475***
	(0.431)	(0.433)	(0.433)	(0.422)	(0.380)

Table C.7—continued

	Dependent Variable				
Item	Info Interest Jobs	Info Interest Careers	Informed Info Interest Jobs	Informed Info Interest Careers	Recommend Army to Friend
R^2	0.128	0.140	0.108	0.129	0.131
Adjusted R^2	0.124	0.136	0.104	0.125	0.127
Residual Std. Error (df = 1,618)	2.495	2.504	2.504	2.439	2.196
F Statistic (df = 7; 1,618)	33.832***	37.529***	27.889***	34.164***	34.814***

NOTE: N = 1,626. SAD is the sum of the absolute values of the differences in perceptions of Army Civilian job characteristics minus one's ratings of the corresponding preferred job characteristics across the 16 job characteristics. *$p < 0.10$; **$p < 0.05$; ***$p < 0.01$.

TABLE C.8

Interest in Army Civilian Jobs and Willingness to Recommend One by Gap in Perceived Characteristics and Job Type for Older Professionals

Item	Info Interest Jobs	Info Interest Careers	Informed Info Interest Jobs	Informed Info Interest Careers	Recommend Army to Friend
			Dependent Variable		
SAD_ArmyMinusPref	-0.140***	-0.130***	-0.117***	-0.123***	-0.086***
	(0.021)	(0.022)	(0.021)	(0.022)	(0.019)
Civil Engineer	-1.157**	-0.765	-0.442	-0.105	0.085
	(0.580)	(0.588)	(0.575)	(0.588)	(0.510)
Electronics Engineer	0.082	0.768	0.048	0.565	0.693
	(0.511)	(0.518)	(0.506)	(0.518)	(0.449)
Information Technology Manager	-0.218	0.109	-1.365**	-1.245**	-0.356
	(0.557)	(0.565)	(0.552)	(0.565)	(0.490)
SAD_ArmyMinusPref:Civil Engineer	0.082**	0.073**	0.034	0.023	0.009
	(0.036)	(0.036)	(0.035)	(0.036)	(0.031)
SAD_ArmyMinusPref:Electronics Engineer	-0.005	-0.032	0.001	-0.025	-0.026
	(0.030)	(0.031)	(0.030)	(0.031)	(0.027)
SAD_ArmyMinusPref:Information Technology Manager	0.010	-0.013	0.078***	0.067**	0.026
	(0.029)	(0.030)	(0.029)	(0.030)	(0.026)
Constant	9.542***	9.486***	9.236***	9.474***	8.857***
	(0.381)	(0.386)	(0.378)	(0.386)	(0.335)

Table C.8—continued

Item	Info Interest Jobs	Info Interest Careers	Dependent Variable		
			Informed Info Interest Jobs	Informed Info Interest Careers	Recommend Army to Friend
R^2	0.111	0.135	0.062	0.090	0.073
Adjusted R^2	0.106	0.131	0.057	0.085	0.068
Residual Std. Error (df = 1,267)	2.137	2.168	2.119	2.167	1.879
F Statistic (df = 7; 1,267)	22.556***	28.347***	12.057***	17.805***	14.227***

NOTE: N = 1,275. SAD is the sum of the absolute values of the differences in perceptions of Army Civilian job characteristics minus one's ratings of the corresponding preferred job characteristics across the 16 job characteristics. *p < 0.10; **p < 0.05; ***p < 0.01.

The results of our factor analyses are shown in Tables C.9–C.11. Positive loadings on the factor are highlighted in green, and negative loadings are highlighted red.

TABLE C.9
Four-Factor Loadings for Younger Professionals

Item	Favorability	Colleagues	Concerns	Challenges
favorability to Army	0.62	0.02	−0.01	0.06
DAC job awareness	−0.01	−0.06	−0.06	−0.04
deployment awareness	−0.11	−0.07	−0.17	−0.02
pension	0.03	−0.70	0.04	−0.17
insurance	0.02	−0.74	0.02	−0.14
salary	−0.13	−0.84	−0.12	−0.17
travel	0.08	0.27	0.21	−0.10
security	0.00	−0.67	−0.12	−0.10
advancement	0.04	−0.27	0.03	0.38
challenges	0.09	0.44	0.11	0.65
balance	−0.11	−0.27	−0.18	−0.39
greatthings	0.01	0.30	0.04	0.55
talents	0.02	0.25	−0.04	0.74
people	0.11	0.85	0.09	0.07
vacation	−0.06	0.08	0.05	−0.66
flexibility	−0.11	0.13	−0.08	−0.62
learnandadvance	−0.03	0.07	−0.11	0.65
collaboration	0.08	0.82	0.06	0.01
colleagues	0.01	0.77	−0.01	−0.30
ArmyPension	0.72	−0.06	0.01	−0.01
ArmyInsurance	0.73	−0.04	0.00	−0.01
ArmySalary	0.76	0.04	0.11	0.04

Table C.9—continued

Item	Favorability	Colleagues	Concerns	Challenges
ArmyTravel	0.66	−0.07	0.09	0.04
ArmySecurity	0.72	−0.05	0.00	0.02
ArmyAdvancement	0.78	0.07	0.18	0.05
ArmyChallenges	0.78	0.00	0.09	0.06
ArmyBalance	0.72	0.16	0.14	0.01
ArmyGreatthings	0.78	0.03	0.05	0.06
ArmyTalents	0.80	0.02	0.08	0.07
ArmyPeople	0.79	0.10	0.11	0.07
ArmyVacation	0.71	0.07	0.11	−0.06
ArmyCollaboration	0.76	0.02	0.10	0.04
ArmyFlexibility	0.70	0.19	0.18	0.02
ArmyLearnandadvance	0.81	0.02	0.09	0.07
ArmyColleagues	0.77	0.11	0.14	0.05
PossibleDeath	0.10	−0.01	0.70	0.01
PossibleTransfer	0.05	−0.06	0.65	−0.02
UndesiredLiving	0.04	−0.02	0.71	−0.05
FamilyOpposition	0.16	0.16	0.68	0.08
NoJobSecurity	0.15	0.04	0.70	0.07
MuchTravel	0.07	0.09	0.67	−0.06
LowSalary	0.04	−0.05	0.68	0.01
PoorBenefits	0.12	0.04	0.72	0.04
SupportMilitary	0.05	0.21	0.69	0.00

TABLE C.10

Four-Factor Loadings for Older Professionals

Item	Favorability	Colleagues	Concerns	Challenges
favorability to Army	0.64	0.03	0.09	−0.04
DAC job awareness	−0.02	−0.16	−0.12	−0.03
deployment awareness	−0.14	−0.01	−0.30	−0.10
pension	−0.01	−0.68	−0.10	−0.33
insurance	−0.03	−0.71	−0.11	−0.30
salary	−0.13	−0.85	−0.15	−0.16
travel	0.11	0.26	0.40	0.10
security	−0.03	−0.68	−0.11	−0.12
advancement	0.05	−0.23	0.26	0.56
challenges	0.06	0.39	0.14	0.70
balance	−0.11	−0.25	−0.29	−0.42
greatthings	0.01	0.34	0.00	0.57
talents	0.02	0.26	−0.17	0.64
people	0.13	0.85	0.15	0.05
vacation	−0.03	0.00	0.04	−0.64
flexibility	−0.11	0.17	−0.08	−0.58
learnandadvance	−0.03	0.17	−0.15	0.62
collaboration	0.10	0.82	0.07	−0.06
colleagues	0.06	0.78	−0.07	−0.40
ArmyPension	0.71	−0.05	−0.02	−0.02
ArmyInsurance	0.72	−0.05	0.03	0.03
ArmySalary	0.73	0.08	0.24	0.07
ArmyTravel	0.66	−0.02	0.12	0.02
ArmySecurity	0.70	−0.01	0.03	0.06
ArmyAdvancement	0.78	0.04	0.27	0.07
ArmyChallenges	0.79	0.08	0.11	0.03

Table C.10—continued

Item	Favorability	Colleagues	Concerns	Challenges
ArmyBalance	0.75	0.15	0.18	0.08
ArmyGreatthings	0.78	0.04	0.12	0.03
ArmyTalents	0.81	0.08	0.10	0.03
ArmyPeople	0.77	0.13	0.17	0.03
ArmyVacation	0.74	0.06	0.14	0.03
ArmyCollaboration	0.78	0.05	0.12	0.02
ArmyFlexibility	0.70	0.14	0.26	0.05
ArmyLearnandadvance	0.79	0.06	0.15	0.06
ArmyColleagues	0.79	0.12	0.13	0.01
PossibleDeath	0.18	0.10	0.75	0.03
PossibleTransfer	0.08	0.01	0.67	−0.09
UndesiredLiving	0.12	−0.01	0.73	−0.07
FamilyOpposition	0.23	0.20	0.74	0.09
NoJobSecurity	0.16	0.10	0.76	0.04
MuchTravel	0.15	0.11	0.73	−0.07
LowSalary	0.06	−0.05	0.70	−0.01
PoorBenefits	0.13	0.09	0.77	0.02
SupportMilitary	0.19	0.24	0.72	0.10

TABLE C.11

Five-Factor Loadings for Students

Item	Favorability	Colleagues	Concerns	Use Own Talents/Learn	Challenges/ Advancement
favorability to Army	0.59	0.00	0.04	−0.03	0.08
DAC job awareness	0.05	−0.01	−0.19	0.04	−0.01
deployment awareness	−0.05	−0.10	−0.14	−0.01	−0.22
pension	0.06	−0.49	0.04	−0.61	0.11
insurance	0.04	−0.59	0.02	−0.50	−0.06
salary	−0.03	−0.78	−0.03	−0.13	−0.24
travel	0.00	0.36	−0.01	−0.36	0.48
security	0.07	−0.66	0.05	0.12	−0.09
advancement	0.08	−0.36	0.07	−0.06	0.63
challenges	0.09	0.29	0.02	0.40	0.61
balance	−0.09	−0.29	−0.03	0.16	−0.68
greatthings	−0.05	0.01	−0.04	0.57	0.00
talents	0.04	0.05	−0.03	0.83	0.05
people	0.04	0.83	0.04	−0.05	0.20
vacation	−0.12	0.25	−0.06	−0.63	−0.28
flexibility	−0.12	−0.04	−0.02	−0.22	−0.69
learnandadvance	−0.01	−0.01	−0.05	0.76	−0.07
collaboration	0.03	0.85	0.04	0.06	0.19
colleagues	−0.02	0.84	−0.03	−0.03	−0.26
ArmyPension	0.72	−0.08	0.04	−0.04	−0.07
ArmyInsurance	0.76	−0.08	0.06	0.00	−0.09
ArmySalary	0.76	−0.03	0.12	−0.02	0.03
ArmyTravel	0.65	−0.04	0.07	0.10	−0.05
ArmySecurity	0.76	−0.08	0.02	0.02	−0.06
ArmyAdvancement	0.78	0.04	0.12	0.00	0.17
ArmyChallenges	0.76	−0.08	0.06	0.04	−0.02
ArmyBalance	0.71	0.13	0.13	−0.07	0.20
ArmyGreatthings	0.78	−0.05	0.02	0.08	0.03
ArmyTalents	0.80	−0.02	0.05	0.07	0.01

Table C.11—continued

Item	Favorability	Colleagues	Concerns	Use Own Talents/Learn	Challenges/ Advancement
ArmyPeople	0.77	0.02	0.12	−0.04	0.12
ArmyVacation	0.71	0.07	0.06	−0.12	0.15
ArmyCollaboration	0.78	0.02	0.09	0.05	0.05
ArmyFlexibility	0.67	0.15	0.14	−0.11	0.26
ArmyLearnandadvance	0.80	−0.03	0.06	0.05	0.00
ArmyColleagues	0.78	0.07	0.12	−0.01	0.10
PossibleDeath	0.16	−0.08	0.73	0.11	−0.06
PossibleTransfer	0.14	−0.12	0.68	0.07	−0.19
UndesiredLiving	0.10	−0.08	0.74	0.03	−0.08
FamilyOpposition	0.13	0.16	0.66	−0.02	0.24
NoJobSecurity	0.11	0.03	0.71	−0.03	0.14
MuchTravel	0.12	0.03	0.65	−0.06	0.03
LowSalary	0.12	−0.06	0.69	−0.01	0.01
PoorBenefits	0.15	−0.02	0.71	−0.05	0.11
SupportMilitary	0.03	0.21	0.57	−0.04	0.35

Tables C.12–C.14 show the relationship of the factors and awareness of Army civilian jobs and civilian deployment practices to perceptions of Army civilian job characteristics relative to one's preferences.

TABLE C.12a

Relationship of Factors and Awareness of Army Civilian Jobs to Perceptions of Army Civilian Job Characteristics Relative to Students' Preference

	Dependent Variable				
Item/Factor	Pension_ Army MinusPref	Insurance_ ArmyMinus Pref	Salary_Army Minus Pref	Travel_Army Minus Pref	Security_ Army Minus Pref
DAC Awareness	−0.005 (0.022)	−0.006 (0.023)	−0.007 (0.026)	0.031 (0.030)	−0.056** (0.028)
Deployment Awareness	−0.018 (0.023)	0.013 (0.024)	0.051* (0.028)	−0.121*** (0.032)	0.055* (0.030)
Favorability	0.081*** (0.002)	0.080*** (0.003)	0.081*** (0.003)	0.085*** (0.003)	0.081*** (0.003)
Colleagues	0.066*** (0.005)	0.096*** (0.005)	0.182*** (0.006)	−0.071*** (0.007)	0.147*** (0.006)
Concerns	−0.014*** (0.005)	−0.010** (0.005)	0.000 (0.006)	0.020*** (0.007)	−0.034*** (0.006)
Use Talents	0.108*** (0.006)	0.119*** (0.006)	0.015** (0.007)	0.186*** (0.008)	−0.048*** (0.008)
Be Challenged	−0.102*** (0.008)	−0.074*** (0.008)	0.022** (0.010)	−0.257*** (0.011)	−0.054*** (0.010)
Constant	−0.004 (0.066)	−0.317*** (0.068)	−1.081*** (0.079)	0.918*** (0.089)	−0.400*** (0.085)
R^2	0.533	0.573	0.646	0.565	0.533
Adjusted R^2	0.531	0.571	0.645	0.563	0.531
Residual Std. Error	0.745 (df = 1,568)	0.769 (df = 1,568)	0.886 (df = 1,568)	1.005 (df = 1,568)	0.745 (df = 1,568)
F Statistic	255.959*** (df = 7; 1,568)	300.003*** (df = 7; 1,568)	409.252*** (df = 7; 1,568)	290.718*** (df = 7; 1,568)	187.683*** (df = 7; 1,568)

NOTES: $N = 1,576$; *$p < 0.10$; **$p < 0.05$; ***$p < 0.01$.

TABLE C.12b

Relationship of Factors and Awareness of Army Civilian Jobs to Perceptions of Army Civilian Job Characteristics Relative to Students' Preference

Item/Factor	Dependent Variable					
	Advancement_ Army Minus Pref	Challenge_ Army Minus Pref	Balance_ Army Minus Pref	Great Things _Army Minus Pref	Talents_ Army Minus Pref	People_ Army Minus Pref
DAC Awareness	−0.010 (0.024)	−0.014 (0.023)	−0.015 (0.023)	0.033 (0.025)	−0.003 (0.020)	−0.060*** (0.022)
Deployment Awareness	−0.035 (0.026)	−0.022 (0.024)	0.111*** (0.025)	−0.018 (0.027)	−0.016 (0.021)	−0.034 (0.023)
Favorability	0.095*** (0.003)	0.089*** (0.003)	0.068*** (0.003)	0.088*** (0.003)	0.081*** (0.002)	0.080*** (0.002)
Colleagues	0.124*** (0.005)	−0.020*** (0.005)	0.045*** (0.005)	0.001 (0.006)	0.008* (0.004)	−0.142*** (0.005)
Concerns	0.002 (0.005)	0.001 (0.005)	−0.024*** (0.005)	−0.024*** (0.006)	−0.016*** (0.004)	−0.013*** (0.005)
Use Talents	0.005 (0.007)	−0.085*** (0.006)	−0.083*** (0.007)	−0.128*** (0.007)	−0.165*** (0.005)	0.016*** (0.006)
Be Challenged	−0.216*** (0.009)	−0.214*** (0.008)	0.260*** (0.009)	−0.012 (0.009)	−0.031*** (0.007)	0.006 (0.008)
Constant	0.091 (0.072)	0.526*** (0.069)	−0.984*** (0.070)	−0.177** (0.076)	−0.194*** (0.059)	0.760*** (0.066)
R^2	0.456	0.537	0.591	0.717	0.506	0.631
Adjusted R^2	0.453	0.534	0.589	0.715	0.504	0.629
Residual Std. Error	0.957 (df = 1,568)	0.813 (df = 1,568)	0.774 (df = 1,568)	0.793 (df = 1,568)	0.860 (df = 1,568)	0.665 (df = 1,568)
F Statistic	259.341*** (df = 7; 1,568)	323.441*** (df = 7; 1,568)	566.823*** (df = 7; 1,568)	229.671*** (df = 7; 1,568)	382.745*** (df = 7; 1,568)	394.843*** (df = 7; 1,568)

NOTES: N = 1,576; *$p < 0.10$; **$p < 0.05$; ***$p < 0.01$.

TABLE C.12c

Relationship of Factors and Awareness of Army Civilian Jobs to Perceptions of Army Civilian Job Characteristics Relative to Students' Preference

Item/Factor	Dependent Variable				
	Vacation_ Army Minus Pref	Collaboration _Army Minus Pref	Flexibility_ Army Minus Pref	Learn and Advance_ Army Minus Pref	Colleagues_ Army Minus Pref
DAC Awareness	−0.012 (0.027)	0.036* (0.021)	0.005 (0.027)	−0.019 (0.022)	−0.034* (0.020)
Deployment Awareness	0.059** (0.028)	−0.034 (0.023)	0.071** (0.028)	0.001 (0.023)	−0.011 (0.021)
Favorability	0.079*** (0.003)	0.079*** (0.002)	0.065*** (0.003)	0.083*** (0.002)	0.071*** (0.002)
Colleagues	−0.070*** (0.006)	−0.153*** (0.005)	−0.015*** (0.006)	0.013*** (0.005)	−0.146*** (0.004)
Concerns	−0.022*** (0.006)	−0.015*** (0.005)	−0.025*** (0.006)	−0.016*** (0.005)	−0.013*** (0.004)
Use Talents	0.130*** (0.007)	0.016*** (0.006)	0.009 (0.007)	−0.170*** (0.006)	0.013** (0.006)
Be Challenged	0.143*** (0.010)	−0.016** (0.008)	0.317*** (0.010)	−0.005 (0.008)	0.127*** (0.007)
Constant	0.051 (0.080)	0.793*** (0.064)	−0.311*** (0.080)	0.036 (0.065)	0.480*** (0.060)
R^2	0.638	0.583	0.664	0.679	0.606
Adjusted R^2	0.636	0.581	0.663	0.677	0.604
Residual Std. Error	0.741 (df = 1,568)	0.903 (df = 1,568)	0.722 (df = 1,568)	0.901 (df = 1,568)	0.731 (df = 1,568)
F Statistic	313.123*** (df = 7; 1,568)	443.293*** (df = 7; 1,568)	472.808** (df = 7; 1,568)	344.511*** (df = 7; 1,568)	504.791*** (df = 7; 1,568)

NOTES: N = 1,576; *p < 0.10; **p < 0.05; ***p < 0.01.

TABLE C.13a

Relationship of Factors and Awareness of Army Civilian Jobs to Perceptions of Army Civilian Job Characteristics Relative to Younger Professionals' Preferences

Item/Factor	Dependent Variable				
	Pension_ Army MinusPref	Insurance_ ArmyMinus Pref	Salary_Army Minus Pref	Travel_Army Minus Pref	Security_ Army Minus Pref
DAC Awareness	0.045* (0.024)	0.040* (0.023)	−0.032 (0.026)	0.008 (0.040)	0.011 (0.029)
Deployment Awareness	0.050** (0.025)	0.042* (0.025)	−0.015 (0.028)	0.046 (0.042)	0.081*** (0.030)
Favorability	0.073*** (0.003)	0.074*** (0.002)	0.085*** (0.003)	0.075*** (0.004)	0.069*** (0.003)
Colleagues	0.071*** (0.005)	0.092*** (0.005)	0.205*** (0.005)	−0.097*** (0.008)	0.113*** (0.006)
Concerns	−0.041*** (0.005)	−0.044*** (0.005)	−0.010* (0.005)	−0.047*** (0.008)	−0.017*** (0.006)
Use Talents	−0.001 (0.007)	−0.011 (0.007)	0.011 (0.008)	0.069*** (0.012)	−0.005 (0.009)
Constant	−0.466*** (0.071)	−0.618*** (0.069)	−1.144*** (0.077)	0.816*** (0.118)	−0.586*** (0.084)
R^2	0.470	0.523	0.735	0.229	0.476
Adjusted R^2	0.468	0.521	0.734	0.227	0.474
Residual Std. Error	0.838 (df = 1,619)	0.812 (df = 1,619)	0.909 (df = 1,619)	1.386 (df = 1,619)	0.995 (df = 1,619)
F Statistic	239.168*** (df = 6; 1,619)	295.765*** (df = 6; 1,619)	748.714*** (df = 6; 1,619)	80.310*** (df = 6; 1,619)	244.663*** (df = 6; 1,619)

NOTES: N = 1,576; *$p < 0.10$; **$p < 0.05$; ***$p < 0.01$.

TABLE C.13b

Relationship of Factors and Awareness of Army Civilian Jobs to Perceptions of Army Civilian Job Characteristics Relative to Younger Professionals' Preferences

Item/Factor	Dependent Variable					
	Advancement_ Army Minus Pref	Challenge_ Army Minus Pref	Balance_ Army Minus Pref	Great Things _Army Minus Pref	Talents_ Army Minus Pref	People_ Army Minus Pref
DAC Awareness	0.023 (0.027)	−0.016 (0.022)	0.019 (0.031)	−0.033 (0.025)	−0.057*** (0.020)	−0.036* (0.021)
Deployment Awareness	0.029 (0.028)	0.024 (0.023)	−0.040 (0.033)	0.051** (0.026)	0.005 (0.021)	−0.032 (0.022)
Favorability	0.086*** (0.003)	0.094*** (0.002)	0.085*** (0.003)	0.101*** (0.003)	0.095*** (0.002)	0.090*** (0.002)
Colleagues	0.070*** (0.005)	−0.053*** (0.004)	0.052*** (0.006)	−0.031*** (0.005)	−0.019*** (0.004)	−0.135*** (0.004)
Concerns	−0.002 (0.006)	−0.019*** (0.005)	0.020*** (0.006)	−0.021*** (0.005)	−0.004 (0.004)	−0.003 (0.004)
Use Talents	−0.127*** (0.008)	−0.147*** (0.007)	0.074*** (0.009)	−0.123*** (0.007)	−0.148*** (0.006)	0.020*** (0.006)
Constant	−0.222*** (0.078)	0.244*** (0.065)	0.919*** (0.091)	−0.148** (0.072)	−0.192*** (0.060)	0.642*** (0.063)
R^2	0.491	0.578	0.525	0.530	0.623	0.625
Adjusted R^2	0.489	0.576	0.524	0.528	0.622	0.624
Residual Std. Error	0.922 (df = 1,619)	0.769 (df = 1,619)	1.074 (df = 1,619)	0.853 (df = 1,619)	0.701 (df = 1,619)	0.742 (df = 1,619)
F Statistic	260.565*** (df = 6; 1,619)	368.995*** (df = 6; 1,619)	298.582*** (df = 6; 1,619)	304.172*** (df = 6; 1,619)	446.067*** (df = 6; 1,619)	449.533*** (df = 6; 1,619)

NOTES: N = 1,576; $*p < 0.10$; $**p < 0.05$; $***p < 0.01$.

TABLE C.13c

Relationship of Factors and Awareness of Army Civilian Jobs to Perceptions of Army Civilian Job Characteristics Relative to Younger Professionals' Preferences

	Dependent Variable				
Item/Factor	Vacation_ Army Minus Pref	Collaboration _Army Minus Pref	Flexibility_ Army Minus Pref	Learn and Advance_ Army Minus Pref	Colleagues_ Army Minus Pref
DAC Awareness	0.083*** (0.027)	−0.019 (0.022)	−0.003 (0.031)	−0.008 (0.022)	−0.010 (0.022)
Deployment Awareness	0.002 (0.029)	−0.005 (0.023)	−0.022 (0.033)	−0.013 (0.023)	−0.028 (0.024)
Favorability	0.084*** (0.003)	0.082*** (0.002)	0.087*** (0.003)	0.094*** (0.002)	0.084*** (0.002)
Colleagues	−0.027*** (0.005)	−0.135*** (0.004)	−0.022*** (0.006)	0.002 (0.004)	−0.125*** (0.004)
Concerns	−0.014** (0.006)	0.003 (0.005)	0.027*** (0.007)	0.006 (0.005)	0.017*** (0.005)
Use Talents	0.125*** (0.008)	0.027*** (0.007)	0.165*** (0.009)	−0.147*** (0.007)	0.102*** (0.007)
Constant	−0.041 (0.081)	0.870*** (0.065)	−0.137 (0.092)	−0.005 (0.064)	0.462*** (0.066)
R^2	0.499	0.585	0.541	0.593	0.609
Adjusted R^2	0.497	0.584	0.539	0.592	0.607
Residual Std. Error	0.950 (df = 1,619)	0.761 (df = 1,619)	1.082 (df = 1,619)	0.753 (df = 1,619)	0.781 (df = 1,619)
F Statistic	269.023*** (df = 6; 1,619)	380.707*** (df = 6; 1,619)	317.955*** (df = 6; 1,619)	393.732*** (df = 6; 1,619)	419.879*** (df = 6; 1,619)

NOTES: N = 1,626; *$p < 0.10$; **$p < 0.05$; ***$p < 0.01$.

TABLE C.14a

Relationship of Factors and Awareness of Army Civilian Jobs to Perceptions of Army Civilian Job Characteristics Relative to Older Professionals' Preferences

Item/Factor	Dependent Variable				
	Pension_ Army MinusPref	Insurance_ ArmyMinus Pref	Salary_Army Minus Pref	Travel_Army Minus Pref	Security_ Army Minus Pref
DAC Awareness	−0.029 (0.025)	0.021 (0.025)	−0.028 (0.029)	−0.033 (0.044)	0.097*** (0.030)
Deployment Awareness	−0.030 (0.024)	0.010 (0.025)	−0.012 (0.029)	−0.002 (0.043)	0.046 (0.030)
Favorability	0.060*** (0.003)	0.058*** (0.003)	0.062*** (0.003)	0.081*** (0.005)	0.051*** (0.003)
Colleagues	−0.042*** (0.005)	−0.032*** (0.005)	−0.010* (0.005)	−0.093*** (0.008)	−0.029*** (0.006)
Concerns	0.070*** (0.005)	0.080*** (0.005)	0.216*** (0.006)	−0.063*** (0.009)	0.127*** (0.006)
Use Talents	0.029*** (0.007)	0.041*** (0.007)	−0.001 (0.008)	−0.015 (0.012)	0.003 (0.008)
Constant	−0.067 (0.077)	−0.421*** (0.079)	−0.897*** (0.090)	1.108*** (0.138)	−0.659*** (0.095)
R^2	0.519	0.557	0.771	0.232	0.516
Adjusted R^2	0.516	0.555	0.770	0.228	0.514
Residual Std. Error	0.709 (df = 1,268)	0.727 (df = 1,268)	0.829 (df = 1,268)	1.262 (df = 1,268)	0.875 (df = 1,268)
F Statistic	227.591*** (df = 6; 1,268)	266.015*** (df = 6; 1,268)	712.519*** (df = 6; 1,268)	63.812*** (df = 6; 1,268)	225.556*** (df = 6; 1,268)

NOTES: N = 1,275 *p < 0.10; **p < 0.05; ***p < 0.01.

TABLE C.14b

Relationship of Factors and Awareness of Army Civilian Jobs to Perceptions of Army Civilian Job Characteristics Relative to Older Professionals' Preferences

	Dependent Variable					
Item/Factor	Advancement_ Army Minus Pref	Challenge_ Army Minus Pref	Balance_ Army Minus Pref	Great Things _Army Minus Pref	Talents_ Army Minus Pref	People_ Army Minus Pref
DAC Awareness	0.003 (0.029)	−0.018 (0.023)	0.014 (0.032)	−0.006 (0.026)	−0.004 (0.023)	−0.036 (0.024)
Deployment Awareness	−0.050* (0.028)	0.041* (0.023)	0.073** (0.031)	0.017 (0.026)	−0.007 (0.023)	0.036 (0.023)
Favorability	0.083*** (0.003)	0.084*** (0.002)	0.066*** (0.003)	0.085*** (0.003)	0.079*** (0.003)	0.082*** (0.003)
Colleagues	−0.040*** (0.005)	−0.021*** (0.004)	0.030*** (0.006)	−0.004 (0.005)	0.010** (0.004)	−0.002 (0.004)
Concerns	0.071*** (0.006)	−0.031*** (0.004)	0.024*** (0.006)	−0.037*** (0.005)	−0.017*** (0.005)	−0.139*** (0.005)
Use Talents	−0.163*** (0.008)	−0.152*** (0.006)	0.106*** (0.008)	−0.120*** (0.007)	−0.128*** (0.006)	0.026*** (0.006)
Constant	0.177* (0.090)	0.288*** (0.072)	−0.730*** (0.099)	0.050 (0.082)	−0.158** (0.073)	0.611*** (0.074)
R^2	0.509	0.610	0.591	0.541	0.599	0.604
Adjusted R^2	0.507	0.609	0.589	0.539	0.597	0.602
Residual Std. Error	0.828 (df = 1,268)	0.656 (df = 1,268)	0.911 (df = 1,268)	0.752 (df = 1,268)	0.671 (df = 1,268)	0.681 (df = 1,268)
F Statistic	219.508*** (df = 6; 1,268)	331.137*** (df = 6; 1,268)	305.102*** (df = 6; 1,268)	248.996*** (df = 6; 1,268)	315.690*** (df = 6; 1,268)	322.750*** (df = 6; 1,268)

NOTES: N = 1,275; *$p < 0.10$; **$p < 0.05$; ***$p < 0.01$.

TABLE C.14c

Relationship of Factors and Awareness of Army Civilian Jobs to Perceptions of Army Civilian Job Characteristics Relative to Older Professionals' Preferences

Item/Factor	Dependent Variable				
	Vacation_ Army Minus Pref	Collaboration _Army Minus Pref	Flexibility_ Army Minus Pref	Learn and Advance_ Army Minus Pref	Colleagues_ Army Minus Pref
DAC Awareness	0.045 (0.028)	−0.068*** (0.022)	0.047 (0.034)	−0.037 (0.024)	−0.019 (0.022)
Deployment Awareness	0.019 (0.027)	0.026 (0.022)	0.003 (0.034)	−0.047** (0.023)	0.009 (0.022)
Favorability	0.072*** (0.003)	0.075*** (0.002)	0.077*** (0.004)	0.078*** (0.003)	0.073*** (0.002)
Colleagues	−0.022*** (0.005)	0.0004 (0.004)	0.023*** (0.006)	0.012*** (0.004)	0.016*** (0.004)
Concerns	−0.031*** (0.005)	−0.135*** (0.004)	−0.062*** (0.007)	−0.012*** (0.005)	−0.140*** (0.004)
Use Talents	0.143*** (0.007)	0.046*** (0.006)	0.171*** (0.009)	−0.119*** (0.006)	0.115*** (0.006)
Constant	0.231*** (0.086)	0.948*** (0.070)	−0.023 (0.106)	0.299*** (0.074)	0.526*** (0.069)
R^2	0.540	0.606	0.557	0.589	0.655
Adjusted R^2	0.538	0.605	0.555	0.587	0.654
Residual Std. Error	0.793 (df = 1,268)	0.639 (df = 1,268)	0.976 (df = 1,268)	0.684 (df = 1,268)	0.633 (df = 1,268)
F Statistic	248.030*** (df = 6; 1,268)	325.591*** (df = 6; 1,268)	265.662*** (df = 6; 1,268)	302.833*** (df = 6; 1,268)	401.738*** (df = 6; 1,268)

NOTES: N = 1,275; *p < 0.10; **p < 0.05; ***p < 0.01.

Tables C.15–C.17 show the relationship of the factors and awareness of Army civilian jobs to the gap between perceptions of Army civilian job characteristics and respondents' preferences.

TABLE C.15

Relationship of Factors and Awareness of Army Civilian Jobs to Gap Between Perceptions of Army Civilian Job Characteristics and Students' Preferences

Item/Factor	Dependent Variable SAD_Army Minus Pref
DAC Awareness	−0.077 (0.148)
Deployment Awareness	0.041 (0.159)
Favorability	−0.321*** (0.016)
Colleagues	−0.582*** (0.033)
Concerns	0.170*** (0.033)
Use Talents	0.420*** (0.042)
Be Challenged	−0.408*** (0.054)
Constant	17.302*** (0.446)
Observations	1,576
R^2	0.464
Adjusted R^2	0.461
Residual Std. Error	5.036 (df = 1,568)
F Statistic	193.596*** (df = 7; 1,568)

NOTES: SAD is the sum of the absolute values of the differences in perceptions of Army civilian job characteristics minus one's ratings of the corresponding preferred job characteristics across the 16 job characteristics.
$^*p < 0.10$; $^{**}p < 0.05$; $^{***}p < 0.01$.

TABLE C.16

Relationship of Factors and Awareness of Army Civilian Jobs to Gap Between Perceptions of Army Civilian Job Characteristics and Younger Professionals' Preferences

Item/Factor	Dependent Variable SAD_Army Minus Pref
DAC Awareness	−0.211
	(0.148)
Deployment Awareness	0.043
	(0.156)
Favorability	−0.381***
	(0.016)
Colleagues	−0.390***
	(0.029)
Concerns	0.084***
	(0.031)
Use talents	0.145***
	(0.045)
Constant	18.381***
Observations	1,626
R^2	0.413
Adjusted R^2	0.410
Residual Std. Error	5.141 (df = 1,619)
F Statistic	189.478*** (df = 6; 1,619)

NOTES: SAD is the sum of the absolute values of the differences in perceptions of Army civilian job characteristics minus one's ratings of the corresponding preferred job characteristics across the 16 job characteristics.
$^*p < 0.10$; $^{**}p < 0.05$; $^{***}p < 0.01$.

TABLE C.17

Relationship of Factors and Awareness of Army Civilian Jobs to Gap Between Perceptions of Army Civilian Job Characteristics and Older Professionals' Preferences

Item/Factor	Dependent Variable SAD_Army Minus Pref
DAC Awareness	−0.109
	(0.151)
Deployment Awareness	0.240
	(0.150)
Favorability	−0.200***
	(0.016)
Concerns	−0.016
	(0.028)
Colleagues	−0.427***
	(0.030)
Use talents	0.049
	(0.040)
Constant	16.254***
	(0.475)
Observations	1,275
R^2	0.424
Adjusted R^2	0.421
Residual Std. Error	4.358 (df = 1,268)
F Statistic	155.472*** (df = 6; 1,268)

NOTES: SAD is the sum of the absolute values of the differences in perceptions of Army civilian job characteristics minus one's ratings of the corresponding preferred job characteristics across the 16 job characteristics.
$^*p < 0.10$; $^{**}p < 0.05$; $^{***}p < 0.01$.

Tables C.18–C.20 show the relationship of the factors and awareness of Army civilian jobs and civilian deployment practices to respondents' concerns about Army civilian jobs.

TABLE C.18a

Relationship of Factors and Awareness of Army Civilian Jobs to Students' Concerns About Army Jobs

	Dependent Variable				
Item/Factor	Possible Death	Possible Transfer	Undesired Living Location	Family Opposition	No Job Security
DAC Awareness	−0.092* (0.048)	0.073 (0.045)	0.123*** (0.044)	0.085 (0.060)	0.201*** (0.054)
Deployment Awareness	−0.013 (0.051)	−0.033 (0.048)	−0.059 (0.047)	0.152** (0.064)	0.232*** (0.057)
Favorability	−0.024*** (0.005)	−0.015*** (0.005)	−0.040*** (0.005)	−0.058*** (0.007)	−0.060*** (0.006)
Colleagues	−0.026** (0.011)	−0.021** (0.010)	−0.021** (0.010)	0.077*** (0.013)	0.006 (0.012)
Concerns	0.438*** (0.011)	0.388*** (0.010)	0.424*** (0.010)	0.457*** (0.013)	0.456*** (0.012)
Use Talents	0.110*** (0.013)	0.073*** (0.012)	0.039*** (0.012)	−0.019 (0.017)	−0.018 (0.015)
Be Challenged	−0.140*** (0.018)	−0.231*** (0.016)	−0.142*** (0.016)	0.161*** (0.022)	0.068*** (0.020)
Constant	7.634*** (0.144)	7.357*** (0.134)	7.122*** (0.133)	5.751*** (0.179)	5.792*** (0.162)
R^2	0.578	0.545	0.575	0.543	0.538
Adjusted R^2	0.576	0.543	0.573	0.541	0.536
Residual Std. Error	1.624 (df = 1,568)	1.513 (df = 1,568)	1.496 (df = 1,568)	2.023 (df = 1,568)	1.825 (df = 1,568)
F Statistic	306.494*** (df = 7; 1,568)	267.898*** (df = 7; 1,568)	302.830*** (df = 7; 1,568)	265.794*** (df = 7; 1,568)	261.110*** (df = 7; 1,568)

NOTES: N = 1,576; *p < 0.10; **p < 0.05; ***p < 0.01.

TABLE C.18b

Relationship of Factors and Awareness of Army Civilian Jobs to Students' Concerns About Army Jobs

Item/Factor	Dependent Variable			
	Much Travel	Low Salary	Poor Benefits	Don't Want Support Military
DAC Awareness	0.128** (0.061)	0.076 (0.052)	0.120** (0.053)	0.175*** (0.067)
Deployment Awareness	−0.054 (0.065)	0.200*** (0.055)	0.084 (0.056)	0.148** (0.072)
Favorability	−0.037*** (0.007)	−0.040*** (0.006)	−0.043*** (0.006)	−0.100*** (0.007)
Colleagues	0.032** (0.013)	−0.024** (0.011)	−0.016 (0.012)	0.088*** (0.015)
Concerns	0.433*** (0.014)	0.413*** (0.012)	0.439*** (0.012)	0.416*** (0.015)
Use Talents	−0.048*** (0.017)	0.006 (0.014)	−0.028* (0.015)	−0.054*** (0.019)
Be Challenged	−0.062*** (0.022)	−0.050*** (0.019)	0.035* (0.019)	0.334*** (0.025)
Constant	6.332*** (0.183)	6.640*** (0.155)	6.419*** (0.158)	5.187*** (0.202)
R^2	0.445	0.494	0.540	0.496
Adjusted R^2	0.442	0.492	0.538	0.493
Residual Std. Error	2.063 (df = 1,568)	1.751 (df = 1,568)	1.782 (df = 1,568)	2.285 (df = 1,568)
F Statistic	179.528*** (df = 7; 1,568)	218.496*** (df = 7; 1,568)	262.904*** (df = 7; 1,568)	220.206*** (df = 7; 1,568)

NOTES: N = 1,576; *$p < 0.10$; **$p < 0.05$; ***$p < 0.01$.

TABLE C.19a

Relationship of Factors and Awareness of Army Civilian Jobs to Younger Professionals' Concerns About Army Jobs

	Dependent Variable				
Item/Factor	Possible Death	Possible Transfer	Undesired Living Location	Family Opposition	No Job Security
DAC Awareness	−0.118** (0.059)	0.060 (0.056)	0.126** (0.051)	−0.137** (0.064)	0.012 (0.060)
Deployment Awareness	−0.008 (0.062)	0.145** (0.058)	0.212*** (0.054)	−0.034 (0.067)	0.036 (0.063)
Favorability	−0.050*** (0.006)	−0.051*** (0.006)	−0.056*** (0.005)	−0.038*** (0.007)	−0.038*** (0.006)
Colleagues	−0.076*** (0.011)	−0.080*** (0.011)	−0.058*** (0.010)	0.026** (0.012)	−0.052*** (0.012)
Concerns	0.468*** (0.012)	0.392*** (0.012)	0.423*** (0.011)	0.469*** (0.013)	0.480*** (0.013)
Use Talents	0.006 (0.018)	−0.006 (0.017)	−0.037** (0.015)	0.045** (0.019)	0.057*** (0.018)
Constant	7.213*** (0.173)	6.769*** (0.164)	6.316*** (0.150)	6.117*** (0.188)	5.922*** (0.178)
R^2	0.508	0.427	0.510	0.519	0.525
Adjusted R^2	0.506	0.425	0.508	0.517	0.523
Residual Std. Error	2.037 (df = 1,619)	1.931 (df = 1,619)	1.768 (df = 1,619)	2.211 (df = 1,619)	2.096 (df = 1,619)
F Statistic	278.093*** (df = 6; 1,619)	201.367*** (df = 6; 1,619)	280.589*** (df = 6; 1,619)	291.103*** (df = 6; 1,619)	298.236*** (df = 6; 1,619)

NOTES: N = 1,626; *p < 0.10; **p < 0.05; ***p < 0.01.

TABLE C.19b

Relationship of Factors and Awareness of Army Civilian Jobs to Younger Professionals' Concerns About Army Jobs

Item/Factor	Dependent Variable			
	Much Travel	Low Salary	Poor Benefits	Don't Want Support Military
DAC Awareness	0.162** (0.064)	0.121** (0.056)	0.013 (0.058)	0.086 (0.068)
Deployment Awareness	0.135** (0.067)	0.249*** (0.059)	0.120** (0.061)	−0.062 (0.072)
Favorability	−0.058*** (0.007)	−0.060*** (0.006)	−0.050*** (0.006)	−0.083*** (0.007)
Colleagues	0.004 (0.012)	−0.089*** (0.011)	−0.047*** (0.011)	0.084*** (0.013)
Concerns	0.470*** (0.013)	0.441*** (0.012)	0.487*** (0.012)	0.527*** (0.014)
Use Talents	−0.076*** (0.019)	0.020 (0.017)	0.029 (0.017)	−0.041** (0.021)
Constant	5.512*** (0.188)	6.163*** (0.166)	6.002*** (0.170)	5.158*** (0.202)
R^2	0.471	0.479	0.540	0.524
Adjusted R^2	0.470	0.477	0.538	0.523
Residual Std. Error	2.218 (df = 1,619)	1.951 (df = 1,619)	2.006 (df = 1,619)	2.373 (df = 1,619)
F Statistic	240.696*** (df = 6; 1,619)	247.721*** (df = 6; 1,619)	316.258*** (df = 6; 1,619)	297.496*** (df = 6; 1,619)

NOTES: N = 1,626; *$p < 0.10$; **$p < 0.05$; ***$p < 0.01$.

TABLE C.20a

Relationship of Factors and Awareness of Army Civilian Jobs to Older Professionals' Concerns About Army Jobs

Item/Factor	Dependent Variable				
	Possible Death	Possible Transfer	Undesired Living Location	Family Opposition	No Job Security
DAC Awareness	−0.138** (0.063)	0.053 (0.063)	−0.007 (0.058)	0.078 (0.066)	0.104* (0.063)
Deployment Awareness	−0.012 (0.062)	0.159** (0.062)	0.116** (0.057)	0.045 (0.066)	0.145** (0.062)
Favorability	−0.060*** (0.007)	−0.064*** (0.007)	−0.060*** (0.006)	−0.055*** (0.007)	−0.071*** (0.007)
Concerns	0.406*** (0.012)	0.344*** (0.012)	0.371*** (0.011)	0.443*** (0.012)	0.433*** (0.012)
Colleagues	−0.040*** (0.012)	−0.051*** (0.012)	−0.076*** (0.011)	0.023* (0.013)	−0.038*** (0.012)
Use Talents	−0.018 (0.017)	−0.083*** (0.017)	−0.073*** (0.015)	0.023 (0.018)	−0.005 (0.017)
Constant	7.252*** (0.196)	6.840*** (0.198)	6.943*** (0.182)	5.574*** (0.208)	5.764*** (0.196)
R^2	0.601	0.461	0.550	0.658	0.613
Adjusted R^2	0.599	0.458	0.547	0.656	0.611
Residual Std. Error	1.803 (df = 1,268)	1.816 (df = 1,268)	1.669 (df = 1,268)	1.910 (df = 1,268)	1.803 (df = 1,268)
F Statistic	318.034*** (df = 6; 1,268)	180.490*** (df = 6; 1,268)	257.883*** (df = 6; 1,268)	406.173*** (df = 6; 1,268)	335.174*** (df = 6; 1,268)

NOTE: $N = 1,275$. *$p < 0.10$; **$p < 0.05$; ***$p < 0.01$.

TABLE C.20b

Relationship of Factors and Awareness of Army Civilian Jobs to Older Professionals' Concerns About Army Jobs

Item/Factor	Dependent Variable			
	Much Travel	Low Salary	Poor Benefits	Don't Want Support Military
DAC Awareness	−0.013 (0.064)	0.239*** (0.061)	0.065 (0.061)	0.107 (0.072)
Deployment Awareness	0.106* (0.063)	0.331*** (0.061)	0.176*** (0.060)	0.100 (0.071)
Favorability	−0.065*** (0.007)	−0.078*** (0.007)	−0.079*** (0.007)	−0.074*** (0.008)
Concerns	0.402*** (0.012)	0.385*** (0.011)	0.436*** (0.011)	0.450*** (0.013)
Colleagues	−0.011 (0.013)	−0.098*** (0.012)	−0.041*** (0.012)	0.057*** (0.014)
Use Talents	−0.104*** (0.017)	−0.012 (0.016)	−0.016 (0.016)	0.028 (0.019)
Constant	6.490*** (0.201)	5.884*** (0.192)	6.054*** (0.192)	5.174*** (0.226)
R^2	0.570	0.509	0.617	0.626
Adjusted R^2	0.568	0.507	0.615	0.624
Residual Std. Error	1.841 (df = 1,268)	1.760 (df = 1,268)	1.760 (df = 1,268)	2.075 (df = 1,268)
F Statistic	279.614*** (df = 6; 1,268)	219.510*** (df = 6; 1,268)	340.083*** (df = 6; 1,268)	353.101*** (df = 6; 1,268)

NOTE: N = 1,275. *p < 0.10; **p < 0.05; ***p < 0.01.

Tables C.21–C.23 provide fit information for the student, younger professional, and older professional factors, respectively.

TABLE C.21
Fit Information for Student Factors

	RC1	RC2	RC3	RC4	RC5
SS Loadings	9.58	4.45	4.41	3.10	2.78
Proportion Var	0.22	0.10	0.10	0.07	0.06
Cumulative Var	0.22	0.42	0.42	0.49	0.55
Proportion Explained	0.39	0.18	0.18	0.13	0.11
Cumulative Proportion	0.39	0.58	0.76	0.89	1.00

NOTES: Mean item complexity = 1.3. Test of the hypothesis that 5 components are sufficient. The root mean square of the residuals (RMSR) is 0.05 with the empirical chi square 6,740.38 with prob < 0. Fit based upon off diagonal values = 0.97.

TABLE C.22
Fit Information for Younger Professional Factors

	RC1	RC2	RC3	RC4
SS Loadings	9.57	4.95	4.66	3.06
Proportion Var	0.22	0.11	0.11	0.07
Cumulative Var	0.22	0.33	0.44	0.51
Proportion Explained	0.43	0.22	0.21	0.14
Cumulative Proportion	0.43	0.65	0.86	1.00

NOTES: Mean item complexity = 1.3. Test of the hypothesis that 5 components are sufficient. The root mean square of the residuals (RMSR) is 0.06 with the empirical chi square 10,687.54 with prob < 0. Fit based upon off diagonal values = 0.95.

TABLE C.23
Fit Information for Older Professional Factors

	RC1	RC3	RC2	RC4
SS Loadings	9.76	5.77	4.99	3.35
Proportion Var	0.22	0.13	0.11	0.08
Cumulative Var	0.22	0.35	0.47	0.54
Proportion Explained	0.41	0.24	0.21	0.14
Cumulative Proportion	0.41	0.65	0.86	1.00

NOTES: Mean item complexity = 1.3. Test of the hypothesis that 4 components are sufficient. The root mean square of the residuals (RMSR) is 0.06 with the empirical chi square 7,436.1 with prob < 0. Fit based upon off diagonal values = 0.96.

Addressing Potential Applicants' Concerns About Army Civilian Employment

In our survey, respondents rated their level of the following concerns about Army civilian employment:

- possibility of involuntary deployment
- possibility of being transferred involuntarily
- required to live in undesirable places
- possibility of injury/death
- low salary
- poor benefits packages
- too much travel
- not enough job security
- opposition by family/friends
- do not want to support the military.

Of these ten concerns, we address four directly and two indirectly in this appendix: the possibility of involuntary deployment (which is related to too much travel, though not equivalent), the possibility of involuntary transfer (related to concerns about a requirement to live in undesirable places), the possibility of injury or death, and inadequate job security. Salary and benefits are covered in Chapter Five. The two remaining concerns, rated at the bottom of respondents' concerns, involve opposition to the military and therefore lie outside of the Army's immediate control, although they potentially can be reduced through branding.

Likelihood of Injury, Death, or Deployment

For the most part, potential applicants' concerns are intuitive but ill-founded. For example, given the Army's mission, it makes sense to be concerned that Army civilians might be injured or killed in the course of combat operations. But the reality is that only 21 civilians—from all of DoD—have died in overseas contingency operations since 2001. Of those 21, only 13 died from hostile action (DoD, 2022).

Some of the concerns are possible in theory but not operative in practice. There is no avoiding the reality that DoD policy theoretically allows the involuntary deployment of DoD civilians. DoD Directive 1400.31 (2003) permits "management . . . to direct and assign civilian employees, either voluntarily, involuntarily or on an unexpected basis to accomplish the DoD mission." At the same time, DoD policy also stresses reliance on volunteers. Directive Type Memorandum 17-004 (2021) notes that "While management has the authority to direct and assign any DoD civilian . . . every effort will be made to make such assignments on a voluntary basis." Department of the Army policy currently in effect requires reliance on volunteers. Not only must individuals volunteer for overseas assignments in support of contingency operations, but their supervisors must also release them—accepting the consequent degradation of the parent organization's ability to execute its assigned mission—and the gaining combatant command accept them (DoD, Defense Civilian Personnel Advisory Service, undated). In short, Army civilians cannot be assured that they would be able to deploy even if they want to go. They are highly unlikely to be involuntarily deployed. In practice, deployment is less a risk to be avoided than an opportunity afforded to only a few. It might not be particularly helpful for Army marketing to highlight unpleasant things that are not going to happen. Still, these were significant concerns among potential applicants and should be addressed in order to increase the likelihood of inquiries about and applications for Army civilian employment. Army officials charged with recruiting civilians might also find it helpful to have information that allays such concerns available to them.

We analyzed two additional potential sources of injury or death: We compared Army rates of lost time due to injury with those of service-providing industries in the private sector using data from the Occupational

Safety and Health Administration (OSHA). We also used OSHA statistics on workplace facilities to estimate the percentage of those killed on the job for reasons unrelated to combat operations.

Because Army civilians—like employees in many other enterprises—do dangerous things even when not deployed, we compared Army rates of time lost due to injury to those of service-providing industries in the private sector. Even though the Army as a whole undertakes a whole range of industrial activities, including manufacturing, transportation, and distribution, we felt that this would be the most stringent comparison.

Army rates of job-related fatalities are generally lower than in the private sector, with both rates being extremely low. Figure D.1 compares the rates per 100,000 employees of fatal injuries for the Army and with service-providing

FIGURE D.1

Comparison of Army and Private-Sector Service-Providing Industries Fatality Rates

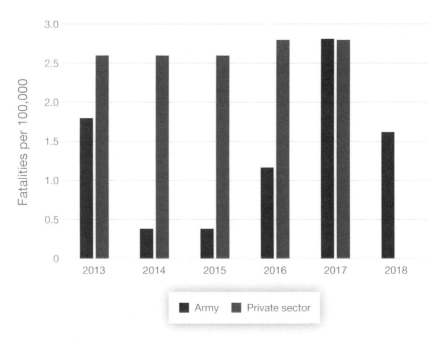

SOURCES: U.S. Department of Labor, Bureau of Labor Statistics, undated; U.S. Department of Labor, Occupational Safety and Health Administration, undated.
NOTE: Private-sector data for 2018 were not available.

industries. In the private sector, the rates tend to hover between 2.6 fatalities per 100,000 employees and 2.8. As the figure indicates, Army rates seldom approach that level.

Similarly, Army rates of job-related injuries that cause lost time tend to be lower than those of private-sector service-providing industries. Figure D.2 compares the private-sector rates of "Cases with days away from work, job transfer, or restriction" with the rates of cases in which the Army lost time due to injury for the period from 2013–2018. The major takeaway from this comparison is that the rates are reasonably similar (with the Army's somewhat lower), indicating that potential Army employees do not incur significantly higher risks of serious injury on the job.

FIGURE D.2

Comparison of Army Rates of Injuries Causing Lost Time with Those of Private-Sector Service-Providing Industries

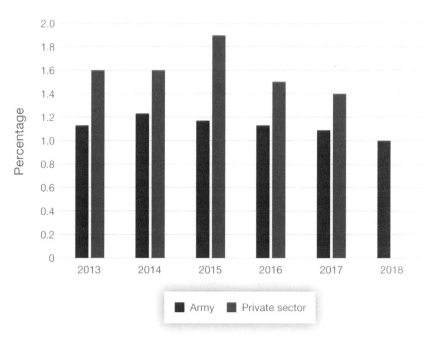

SOURCES: U.S. Department of Labor, Bureau of Labor Statistics, undated; U.S. Department of Labor, Occupational Safety and Health Administration, undated.
NOTE: Private-sector data for 2018 were not available.

Army Civilians Are Unlikely to Be Involuntarily Transferred, Especially to Undesirable Locations

Potential applicants have expressed concerns with involuntary relocation. Such involuntary relocation is possible, but unlikely. To be sure, federal agencies—including the Army—have substantial authority to involuntarily reassign and also relocate employees (5 CFR 335.102).

According to the Office of Personnel Management, federal agencies may reassign employees if there is a legitimate organizational reason for the reassignment and the position to which the employee is being reassigned is at the same grade or rate of pay. Agencies may terminate employees who decline relocation (OPM, undated-d). It is important to note, however, that neither the Army nor any other federal agency can impose criminal sanctions for declining relocation. It is equally important to note that the Army almost never makes use of this authority. An analysis of DCPDS data for the four occupations considered indicates that fewer than 0.89 percent of incumbents had been reassigned to another organization and relocated to another area, the combination of action codes we interpreted as indicating a potential involuntary relocation.[1] This estimate is almost certainly an upper bound, since reassignment can be either voluntary or involuntary.

Army Civilians Are Extremely Unlikely to Be Involuntarily Terminated

Respondents expressed concern about job insecurity. In reality, federal workers are generally assumed to have very high levels of job security. We verified that assumption with respect to Army workers. Table D.1 depicts the percentage of involuntary termination of Army civilians for FYs 2013–2018 in percentage terms. Involuntary terminations hovered at little more than 1 percent of total civilian strength on a year-to-year basis.

---

[1] We analyzed DCPDS transaction records to identify occasions on which employees were reassigned—nature of action code (NAC) 0721—and to a new duty zip code, the first two digits of which differed from the former zip code. A change in the first two digits would indicate a different state, a different region, or potentially both.

TABLE D.1

Involuntary Separations of Army Civilian Employees as a Percentage of Total Army Civilian Employment, Fiscal Years 2013–2018

Reason for Involuntary Termination	FY					
	2013	2014	2015	2016	2017	2018
Retirement—in lieu of involuntary action	0.06	0.06	0.06	0.05	0.07	0.04
Resignation—in lieu of involuntary action	0.01	0.01	0.01	0.01	0.01	0.02
Removal	0.20	0.23	0.20	0.19	0.21	0.20
Separation—reduction in force	0.08	0.03	0.04	0.00	0.01	0.01
Termination	0.86	0.72	0.76	0.57	0.55	0.53
Termination during probation/trial period	0.10	0.09	0.15	0.13	0.15	0.18
Suspension—indefinite	0.01	0.01	0.01	0.01	0.01	0.01
Total involuntary departures	1.33	1.15	1.23	0.98	1.01	0.99
Army civilian strength	289,742	287,551	283,588	282,697	286,893	287,961

Conclusion

Beginning an appeal by asserting that an applicant almost certainly will not be killed in the line of duty would probably do little to increase the allure of an Army civilian career. In fact, it might raise a concern where none had existed before. The same applies to counters to some of the other concerns expressed by potential applicants. Nonetheless, potential applicants have these concerns, and Army officials must be prepared to address them, both proactively to increase interest in Army civilian jobs and to encourage those requesting information and with interest in applying and possibly choosing to work for the Army. Fortunately, the external markets' concerns identified in our analysis appear to be largely groundless. The chances of being killed as an Army civilian for any reason are lower than in the private sector, as is the chance of being injured. For the foreseeable future, Army civilians face little likelihood of involuntary deployment. And, while the possibility of involuntary transfer does exist, it occurs at an extremely low rate. None of these are positive reasons to consider an Army civilian career, but they should not serve as deterrents, either.

Estimating Salary and Compensation Profiles

To examine the relative economic attractiveness of Army civilian jobs in our study occupations, we estimated the salary and compensation profiles with respect to workforce experience for civilian employees in the Army and private sector. This appendix describes the sample that was used and the estimation method.

Sample

Our sample for estimating salary profiles for Army civilian employees came from the Defense Civilian Personnel Data System (DCPDS). We used all employees who worked in the Army from 2016 to 2018 for more than 35 hours per week in one of the four study occupations. For these individuals, in addition to information about hours worked and the occupation in which they were employed, we used information about their education level, salary (including locality adjustment rate), gender, veteran status, and veteran era. Salary information was adjusted for inflation to 2019 dollars. All workers from occupations 1101 and 2210, regardless of educational attainment, were used. Only workers with at least a bachelor's degree were used from the other occupations, in order to focus on the labor market of this more highly skilled portion of employees.

Our sample for estimating salary profiles for private-sector employees came from the Public Use Micro Sample (PUMS) of the American Community Survey (ACS), which was conducted by the U.S. Census Bureau. This survey is an ongoing representative sample of the U.S. population used for estimating detailed demographic and economic information about U.S. residents. We used all waves of the survey from 2015 through 2017, in order to have a sufficiently large sample of private-sector workers.

The ACS, like all Census Bureau products, uses a different occupational coding system than the OPM occupation codes that are used by DCPDS. We used an occupational code crosswalk provided by the Census Bureau to select occupations from the ACS that are most like the occupations analyzed in this study. As with the DCPDS sample, we obtained information for the ACS sample on the demographic characteristics, educational attainment and veteran status, imposed the same restrictions regarding educational attainment and adjusted for inflation.

The sample sizes are listed in Table E.1.

TABLE E.1
Sample Size for Regressions

Occupation	Army	Private Sector
810	6,641	5,862
855	2,687	4,146
1102	7,204	5,001
2210	13,860	12,265

Estimation Method

We used ordinary least squares multiple regression to estimate the relationship between salary and experience for each occupation and each type of employer. Our specification follows Mincer (1974): Years of experience are calculated as age minus years of education minus six, based on the assumption common in labor market analysis that all adult years of life that are not spent in school are available for work experience. Experience is entered as a quadratic in the regression equation. The multiple regression also includes controls for years of education, gender, and veteran status separately by pre-Vietnam, Vietnam, and post-Vietnam eras. The dependent variable is natural logarithm of annual salary. These regressions explain from 14.8 to 60.2 percent of the variation in log salary.

We calculated the expected salary for workers with 1 through 40 years of experience, using the most common case for the control variables: male, bachelor's degree (i.e., years of education equal to sixteen), nonveteran. Expected salary was calculated by exponentiating the predicted value from the regression and adding the expected value of the exponentiated error term (Duan, 1983).

We calculated expected compensation by adding an amount to each expected salary that is equivalent to the average percentage of salary paid as benefits by federal and private-sector employers. To obtain expected compensation for Army employees, we added 61.6 percent to expected salary as suggested by Falk (2012) for federal employees. For private-sector workers, we added 42.8 percent (Falk, 2012).

The expected salaries and compensation are presented in Figures 5.1–5.12 in the main body of the report.

Abbreviations

AcqDemo	Acquisition Demonstration Project
ACS	American Community Survey
AMRG	Army Marketing and Research Group
CP	career program
DA	Department of the Army
DAWIA	Defense Acquisition Workforce Improvement Act
DHA	direct hiring authority
DoD	U.S. Department of Defense
EHA	expedited hiring authority
FAR	Federal Acquisition Regulation
FEVS	Federal Employee Viewpoint Survey
FY	fiscal year
GS	General Schedule
OPM	U.S. Office of Personnel Management
RIM	RAND Inventory Model
SAD	sum of the absolute values of the differences
SME	subject-matter expert
USACE	U.S. Army Corps of Engineers
YORE	years relative to retirement eligibility

References

Allen, David G., James R. van Scotter, and Robert F. Otondo, "Recruitment Communications Media: Impact on Prehire Outcomes," *Personnel Psychology*, Vol. 57, No. 1, 2004, pp. 143–171.

Allen, David G., Raj V. Mahto, and Robert F. Otondo, "Web-Based Recruitment: Effects of Information, Organizational Brand, and Attitudes Toward a Web Site on Applicant Attraction," *Journal of Applied Psychology*, Vol. 92, No. 6, 2007, pp. 1696–1708.

Alonso, Pablo , and Gregory B. Lewis, "Public Service Motivation and Job Performance: Evidence From the Federal Sector," *American Review of Public Administration*, Vol. 31, No. 4, December 2001, pp. 363–380.

Ambler, Tim, and Simon Barrow, "The Employer Brand," *Journal of Brand Management*, Vol. 4, No. 3, 1996, pp. 185–206.

Anastasoff, Jennifer, and Jennifer Smith, *Mobilizing Tech Talent: Hiring Technologists to Power Better Government*, Washington, D.C.: Partnership for Public Service, September 2018.

Backhaus, Kristin, "Employer Branding Revisited," *Organization Management Journal*, Vol. 13, No. 4, 2016, pp. 193–201.

Braddy, Phillip W., Adam W. Meade and Christina M. Kroustalis, "The Effects of Organizational Familiarity, Website Usability, and Website Attractiveness on Viewers' Impressions of Organizations," *Computers in Human Behavior*, Vol. 24, September 2008, pp. 2992–3001.

Bright, Leonard, "Public Employees with High Levels of Public Service Motivation: Who Are They, Where Are They, and What Do They Want?" *Review of Public Personnel Administration*, Vol. 25, June 1, 2005, pp. 138–154.

Bright, Leonard, "Does Public Service Motivation Really Make a Difference on the Job Satisfaction and Turnover Intentions of Public Employees?" *American Review of Public Administration*, Vol. 38, No. 2, 2008, pp. 149–166.

Bright, Leonard, "Why Do Public Employees Desire Intrinsic Nonmonetary Opportunities?" *Public Personnel Management*, Vol. 38, No. 3, Fall 2009.

Brinkerhoff, John R., *The Institutional Army, FY 1975–FY 2002*, Alexandria, Va.: Institute for Defense Analyses, IDA Document D-2695, 2002.

CBO—*See* Congressional Budget Office.

Cober, Richard T., Douglas J. Brown, Lisa M. Keeping, and Paul E. Levy, "Recruitment on the Net: How Do Organizational Web Site Characteristics Influence Applicant Attraction?" *Journal of Management*, Vol. 30, No. 5, October 2004, pp. 623–646.

Code of Federal Regulations, Title 5, Administrative Personnel; Chapter 1, Office of Personnel Management; Subchapter Bm Civil Service Regulations; Part 332, Recruitment and Selection Through Competitive Examination. As of January 20, 2022:
https://www.ecfr.gov/current/title-5/part-332

Congressional Budget Office, *Comparing the Compensation of Federal and Private-Sector Employees, 2011 to 2015*, Washington, D.C., April 2017. As of August 15, 2019:
https://www.cbo.gov/system/files/115th-congress-2017-2018/reports/52637-federalprivatepay.pdf

DCPDS—*See* Defense Civilian Personnel Advisory Service.

Defense Civilian Personnel Advisory Service, homepage, undated. As of January 22, 2022:
https://www.dcpas.osd.mil/

Department of Defense Directive 1400.31, *DoD Civilian Work Force Contingency and Emergency Planning and Execution*, Washington, D.C.: U.S. Department of Defense, April 28, 1995, current as of December 1, 2003.

Directive Type Memorandum 17-004, *Department of Defense Expeditionary Civilian Workforce*, Washington, D.C.: U.S. Department of Defense, January 25, 2017, incorporating Change 4, effective April 19, 2021.

Duan, Naihua, "Smearing Estimate: A Nonparametric Retransformation Method," *Journal of the American Statistical Association*, Vol. 78, No. 383, 1983, pp. 605–610.

Emmerichs, Robert M., Cheryl Y. Marcum, and Albert A. Robbert, *An Operational Process for Workforce Planning*, Santa Monica, Calif: RAND Corporation, MR-1684/1-OSD, 2004. As of January 26, 2022:
https://www.rand.org/pubs/monograph_reports/MR1684z1.html

Equal Employment Opportunity Commission, "Federal Sector Occupation Cross-Classification Table," January 2013. Accessed January 13, 2015:
http://www.eeoc.gov/federal/directives/00-09opmcode.cfm

Facebook, website, undated. As of January 27, 2022:
https://www.facebook.com/

Falk, Justin, *Comparing Benefits and Total Compensation in the Federal Government and the Private Sector*, Washington, D.C.: Congressional Budget Office, Working Paper Number 2012-4, 2012.

Fort Belvoir, Facebook page, undated. Accessed September 30, 2019:
https://www.facebook.com/fortbelvoir/

Gansler, Jacques S., David J. Berteau, David M. Maddox, David R. Oliver, Jr., Leon M. Salomon, and George T. Singley III, *Urgent Reform Required: Army Expeditionary Contracting—Report of the "Commission on Army Acquisition and Program Management in Expeditionary Operations"*, Washington, D.C.: Department of the Army, Office of the Assistant Secretary of the Army for Acquisition, Logistics, and Technology, October 1, 2007.

Geren, Pete, *U.S. Army Smart Contracting: Report to Congress*, Washington, D.C.: Headquarters, Department of the Army, 2008.

GoArmy.com, website, undated. As of September 22, 2022:
https://www.goarmy.com/

Guest, David E., "Perspectives on the Study of Work-Life Balance," *Social Science Information*, Vol. 42, No. 2, June 2002, pp. 255–279.

Houston, David J., "Public Service Motivation: A Multivariate Test," *Journey of Public Administration Research and Theory*, Vol. 10, No. 4, October 2000, pp. 713–727.

Kalliath, Thomas, and Paula Brough, "Work-Life Balance: A Review of the Meaning of the Balance Construct," *Journal of Management and Organization*, Vol. 14, July 2008, pp. 323– 327.

Keller, Kevin Lane, and Donald R. Lehmann, "Brands and Branding: Research Findings and Future Priorities," *Marketing Science*, Vol. 25, No. 6, November– December 2006, pp. 740–759.

Kjeldsen, Anne Mette, and Christian Bøtcher Jacobsen, "Public Service Motivation and Employment Sector: Attraction or Socialization?" *Journal of Public Administration Research and Theory*, Vol. 23, No. 4, 2012, pp. 899–926.

Lamont, Thomas R., Assistant Secretary of the Army for Manpower and Reserve Affairs, "Department of the Army Hiring Freeze and Release of Terms and Temporary Civilian Personnel," memorandum to principal officials, Headquarters, Department of the Army and commanders of Army commands, direct reporting units, and Army service component commands, January 22, 2013.

Law, Jonathan, ed., *A Dictionary of Business and Management*, 5th edition, Oxford: Oxford University Press, 2009.

Lewis, Jennifer Lamping, Laura Werber, Cameron Wright, Irina Elena Danescu, Jessica Hwang, and Lindsay Daugherty, *2016 Assessment of the Civilian Acquisition Workforce Personnel Demonstration Project*, Santa Monica, Calif.: RAND Corporation, RR-1783-OSD, 2017. As of January 26, 2022:
https://www.rand.org/pubs/research_reports/RR1783.html

LinkedIn, website, undated-a. As of January 26, 2022:
https://www.linkedin.com/

LinkedIn, search results for "Civil Engineer Army" in United States, undated-b. Accessed September 27, 2019: https://www.linkedin.com/jobs/search/?currentJobId=972377938&f_C=1224&geoId=103644278&keywords=civil%20engineer%20army

Lyons, Sean T., Linda E. Duxboury, and Christopher A. Higgins, "A Comparison of the Values and Commitment of Private Sector, Public Sector, and Parapublic Sector Employees," *Public Administration Review*, Vol. 6, No. 4, July–August 2006, pp. 605–618.

McHugh, John M., Secretary of the Army, "Delegation of Authority–Expedited Hiring Authority for Acquisition Positions," memorandum for the Assistant Secretary of the Army for Manpower and Reserve Affairs, May 30, 2012.

McHugh, John M., Secretary of the Army, "Army Directive 2014-01 (Army Conference Policy)," memorandum to principal officials, Headquarters, Department of the Army and commanders of Army commands, direct reporting units and Army service component commands, December 18, 2013.

McHugh, John M., Secretary of the Army, "Delegation of Authority–Direct Hire Authority for Scientific and Engineering Positions Within Designated Personnel Demonstration Laboratories," memorandum to the Assistant Secretary of the Army for Manpower and Reserve Affairs, June 18, 2014. Accessed January 2, 2015: http://cpol.army.mil/library/general/DelegationMatrix/memos/20140618-SA-Del-DHA-for-SE-Positions-Demo-Labs.pdf

McHugh, John M., and Raymond T. Odierno, *2014 Army Posture Statement*, Washington, D.C.: Headquarters, Department of the Army, 2014.

McPhie, Neil A.G., *Federal Appointment Authorities: Cutting Through the Confusion*, Washington, D.C.: U.S. Merit System Protections Board, 2008.

Mincer, Jacob, *Schooling, Experience, and Earnings*, New York: National Bureau of Economic Research, 1974.

Monster, website, undated. As of January 26, 2022: https://www.monster.com/

Moore, Jack, "OPM's Focus in Hiring Reform Shifting from Speed to Quality," Federal News Network, March 26, 2014. Accessed January 7, 2015: http://www.federalnewsradio.com/520/3590759/OPMs-focus-in-hiring-reform-shifting-from- speed-to-quality

Mosely, Richard W., "Customer Experience, Organisational Culture and the Employer Brand," Journal of Brand Management, Vol. 15, No. 2, November 2007, pp. 123–134.

Muzellec, Laurent, and Mary C. Lambkin, "Corporate Branding and Brand Architecture: A Conceptual Framework," *Marketing Theory*, Vol. 9, No. 1, March 2009, pp. 39–54.

Naff, Katherine C., and John Crum, "Working for America: Does Public Motivation Make a Difference?" *Review of Public Personnel Administration*, Fall 1999.

National Science Foundation, Committee on Science, Technology, Engineering, and Mathematics Workforce Needs for the U.S. Department of Defense and the U.S. Defense Industrial Base, *Assuring the US Department of Defense a Strong Science, Engineering, and Mathematics (STEM) Workforce*, Washington, D.C., 2012.

Niskanen, William A., *Bureaucracy and Representative Government*, Livingston, N.J.: Transaction Publishers, 1971.

OPM—*See* U.S. Office of Personnel Management.

Organization for Economic Cooperation and Development, "Work-Life Balance," webpage, undated. As of August 15, 2019:
http://www.oecdbetterlifeindex.org/topics/work-life-balance/

Partnership for Public Service, "Best Places to Work in the Federal Government: Government-Wide Analysis, Overall Findings and Private Sector Comparison," webpage, undated. As of August 15, 2019:
https://bestplacestowork.org/analysis/

Partnership for Public Service, "The Hiring Process," July 19, 2005.

Partnership for Public Service, *California's Talent Gap: Recruiting and Hiring a New Generation of Federal Employees*, Washington, D.C., September 2019.

Partnership for Public Service and Booz Allen Hamilton, *The Biggest Bang Theory: How to Get the Most Out of the Competitive Search for STEMM Employees*, McLean, Va., May 2013.

Partnership for Public Service and LinkedIn, *Post and Pursue: Improving Federal Hiring Using Data and Targeted Recruitment*, April 2017.

Perry, James L., and Lois Recascino Wise, "The Motivational Bases of Public Service," *Public Administration Review*, Vol. 50, No. 3, 1990, pp. 367–373.

Perry, James L., Annie Hondeghem, and Lois Recascino Wise, "Revisiting the Motivational Bases of Public Service: Twenty Years of Research and an Agenda for the Future," *Public Administration Review*, Vol. 70, No. 5, 2010, pp. 681–690.

Phillips, William N., Secretary of the Army, "Director, Army Acquisition Corps Guidance Memorandum #6," memorandum to principal officials, Headquarters, Department of the Army and commanders of Army commands, direct reporting units, and Army service component commands, July 8, 2010. Accessed December 1, 2014:
http://asc.army.mil/docs/programs/852/Memo_DACM_6.pdf

Pichler, Florian, "Determinants of Work-Life Balance: Shortcomings in the Contemporary Measurement of WLB in Large-Scale Surveys," *Social Indicators Research*, Vol. 92, No. 3, July 2009, pp. 449–469.

Pursley, Martin , James Cadwell, Eileen Chaisson, Michelle Earley, Kenneth Pickler, and Michael F. Brosnan, *Post and Posture: Improving Federal Hiring Using Data and Targeted Recruitment*, Washington, D.C.: Partnership for Public Service, Linked, April 2015.

Reiter, Natalie, "Work Life Balance: What DO You Mean? The Ethical Ideology Underpinning Appropriate Application," *Journal of Applied Behavioral Science*, Vol. 43, No. 2, June 2007, pp. 273–294.

Ritz, Adrian, Gene A. Brewer, and Oliver Neumann, "Public Service Motivation: A Systematic Literature Review and Outlook," *Public Administration Review*, Vol. 76, No. 3, 2016, pp. 414–426.

Schneider, Karl, Acting Assistant Secretary of the Army for Manpower and Reserve Affairs, "Delegation of Civilian Human Resources Authorities, Version 05-2014, effective June 16, 2014: Revision to Delegation of Civilian Human Resources Authorities Matrix and Execution, Publication and Transmission of Delegations #26 through #36," memorandum to principal officials, Headquarters, Department of the Army and commanders of Army commands, direct reporting units, and Army service component commands, June 13, 2014.

Smith, Aaron, and Monica Andersen, "Social Media Use in 2018," Pew Research Center, March 1, 2018.

Tausig, Mark, and Rudy Fenwick, "Unbinding Time: Alternate Work Schedules and Work-Life Balance," *Journal of Family and Economic Issues*, Vol. 22, No. 2, Summer 2001, pp. 101–119.

USACE—*See* U.S. Army Corps of Engineers.

USAJOBS, website, undated-a. As of January 26, 2022:
https://www.usajobs.gov/

USAJOBS, "Civil Engineer, Department of the Army, US Army Corps of Engineers," webpage, undated-b. Accessed September 27, 2019:
https://www.usajobs.gov/job/512494600

USAJOBS, "Contract Specialist (ACWA), Department of the Army, US Army Contracting Command," webpage, undated-c. Accessed September 27, 2019:
https://www.usajobs.gov/job/545389000

USAJOBS, "Federal Occupations by College Major," undated-d. Accessed September 27, 2019:
https://www.usajobs.gov/Help/working-in-government/unique-hiring-paths/students/federal-occupations-by-college-major

U.S. Army, "Careers & Jobs," webpage, undated. Accessed September 27, 2019: https://www.goarmy.com/careers-and-jobs/army-civilian-careers.html

U.S. Army Acquisition Support Center, website, undated-a. As of January 26, 2022: https://asc.army.mil

U.S. Army Acquisition Support Center, "Civilian Contracting Career Model," undated-b. As of September 27, 2019: https://asc.army.mil/web/wp-content/uploads/2018/08/Career-Model-Contracting-Rev-8-18.pdf

U.S. Army Civilian Human Resources Agency, *Civilian Hiring Reform Process Guide*, January 2013.

U.S. Army Contracting Command, "Home," LinkedIn page, undated-a. Accessed September 27, 2019: https://www.linkedin.com/company/u-s-army-contracting-command/

U.S. Army Contracting Command, "About," LinkedIn page, undated-b. Accessed September 27, 2019: https://www.linkedin.com/company/u-s-army-contracting-command/about/

U.S. Army Corps of Engineers, website, undated-a. As of January 26, 2022: https://www.usace.army.mil

U.S. Army Corps of Engineers, "Careers," webpage, undated-b. Accessed September 27, 2019: https://www.usace.army.mil/Careers

U.S. Army Corps of Engineers, LinkedIn page, undated-c. Accessed September 27, 2019: https://www.linkedin.com/company/us-army-corps-of-engineers/

U.S. Army Engineer Research and Development Center, Facebook page, undated. Accessed September 30, 2019: https://www.facebook.com/ArmyERDC/

U.S. Army Fort Bragg, "For Civilians," webpage, undated. As of September 27, 2019: https://home.army.mil/bragg/index.php/my-fort-bragg/civilians

U.S. Army, Office of the Assistant Deputy Chief of Staff, G-1 (Civilian Personnel), "Army Personnel Demonstration Projects," updated April 2012.

U.S. Army, Office of the Assistant Deputy Chief of Staff, G-1 (Civilian Personnel), *Army Green Ceiling: Perceptions and Trends*, October 2013.

U.S. Army Research Laboratory, "Career Opportunities," webpage, undated. Accessed September 27, 2019: https://www.arl.army.mil/careers/career-opportunities/

U.S. Bureau of the Labor Statistics, "American Time Use Survey (ATUS)," data files, 2013– 2017. As of August 15, 2019:
https://www.bls.gov/tus/#data

U.S. Census Bureau, "American Community Survey," webpage, undated. As of January 22, 2022:
https://www.census.gov/programs-surveys/acs

U.S. Census Bureau, "EEO Tabulation 2006–2010 (5-Year ACS) and 2008–2010 (3-Year ACS) Occupation Code Crosswalk to Aggregated Occupations," April 26, 2013.

U.S. Code, Title 5, Government Organization and Employees, Part III, Employees.

U.S. Code, Title 5, Government Organization and Employees, Part III, Employees; Subpart A, General Provisions; Section 2301, Merit System Principles.

U.S. Department of Defense, Office of the Under Secretary of Defense for Acquisition and Sustainment, *DOD Civilian Acquisition Workforce Personnel Demonstration Project Operating Guide*, Washington, D.C., June 7, 2018.

U.S. Department of Defense, Office of the Under Secretary of Defense for Acquisition and Sustainment, "Casualty Status," accessed April 25, 2022. As of May 1, 2022:
https://www.defense.gov/casualty.pdf

U.S. Department of Defense, Defense Civilian Personnel Advisory Service, "Become an Expeditionary Civilian," webpage, undated. As of May 1, 2022:
https://www.dcpas.osd.mil/policy/expeditionarycivilians/
becomeexpeditionary

U.S. Department of Labor, Bureau of Labor Statistics, "Injuries, Illnesses and Fatalities," webpage, undated. As of May 1, 2022:
https://www.bls.gov/iif/oshcfoi1.htm#other

U.S. Department of Labor, Occupational Safety and Health Administration, "Federal Employee Programs," webpage, undated. As of May 1, 2022:
https://www.osha.gov/enforcement/fap/statistics

U.S. Government Accountability Office, *Federal Hiring: OPM Needs to Improve Management and Oversight of Hiring Authorities*, Washington, D.C., GAO-16-521, 2016.

U.S. Government Accountability Office, *Human Capital: Improving Federal Recruiting and Hiring Processes*, Washington, D.C., GAO-19-696T, 2019a.

U.S. Government Accountability Office, *Federal Workforce: Key Talent Management Strategies for Agencies to Better Meet Their Missions*, Washington, D.C., GAO-19-181, 2019b.

U.S. Government Accountability Office, *Defense Acquisition Workforce: DOD Increased Use of Human Capital Flexibilities but Could Improve Monitoring*, GAO-19-509, 2019c. As of August 20, 2019:
https://www.gao.gov/assets/710/700927.pdf

U.S. Merit Systems Protection Board, Office of Policy and Evaluation, *Attracting the Next Generation: A Look at Federal Entry-Level New Hires*, Washington, D.C., 2008a.

U.S. Merit Systems Protection Board, Office of Policy and Evaluation, *In Search of Highly Skilled Workers: A Study on the Hiring of Upper Level Employees from Outside the Federal Government*, Washington, D.C.: 2008b.

U.S. Merit Systems Protection Board, Office of Policy and Evaluation, *Reforming Federal Hiring: Beyond Faster and Cheaper*, Washington, D.C., 2010.

U.S. Office of Personnel Management, "Hiring Information: Direct Hire Authority," webpage, undated-a. As of January 26, 2022:
http://www.opm.gov/policy-data-oversight/hiring-information/direct-hire-authority/

U.S. Office of Personnel Management, "Hiring Information: Students and Recent Graduates," webpage, undated-b. Accessed November 10, 2014:
http://www.opm.gov/policy-data-oversight/hiring-information/students-recent-graduates/

U.S. Office of Personnel Management, "Hiring Reform: Recruitment Elements," undated-c. Accessed November 10, 2014:
http://www.opm.gov/policy-data-oversight/human-capital-management/hiring-reform/recruitmentelements.pdf

U.S. Office of Personnel Management, "Workforce Restructuring: Summary of Reassignment," webpage, undated-d. As of August 15, 2019:
https://www.opm.gov/policy-data-oversight/workforce-restructuring/Summary-of-Reassignment/

U.S. Office of Personnel Management, 2010 Federal Employee Viewpoint Survey: Report by Agency, 2010.

U.S. Office of Personnel Management, 2011 Federal Employee Viewpoint Survey: Report by Agency, 2011.

U.S. Office of Personnel Management, 2012 Federal Employee Viewpoint Survey: Report by Agency, 2012.

U.S. Office of Personnel Management, 2013 Federal Employee Viewpoint Survey: Report by Agency, 2013.

U.S. Office of Personnel Management, 2014 Federal Employee Viewpoint Survey: Report by Agency, 2014.

U.S. Office of Personnel Management, 2015 Federal Employee Viewpoint Survey: Report by Agency, 2015.

U.S. Office of Personnel Management, 2016 Federal Employee Viewpoint Survey: Report by Agency, 2016.

U.S. Office of Personnel Management, 2017 Federal Employee Viewpoint Survey: Report by Agency, 2017.

U.S. Office of Personnel Management, 2018 Federal Employee Viewpoint Survey: Report by Agency, 2018.

U.S. Office of Personnel Management, 5 CFR Parts 213, 302, 315, 330, 334, 362, 531, 536, 537, 550, 575, and 890, Excepted Service, Career and Career-Conditional Employment; and Pathways Programs, Section 362.204, Applicability, May 11, 2012.

U.S. Office of Personnel Management, *The 2015 Guide to Federal Benefits for Federal Civilian Employees*, revised November 2014. Accessed January 20, 2015:
http://www.opm.gov/healthcare-insurance/healthcare/plan-information/guide/2015-guides/70-1.pdf

Wilson, Elaine, "Obama Calls for Federal Government Hiring Reform," American Forces Press Service, May 11, 2010. Accessed November 21, 2014:
http://www.defense.gov/news/newsarticle.aspx?id=59113

Wright, Bradley E., and Robert K. Christensen, "Public Service Motivation: A Test of the Job Attraction–Selection–Attrition Model," *International Public Management Journal*, Vol. 13, No. 2, 2010, pp. 155–176.

Wright, Bradley E., Shahidul Hassan, and Robert K. Christensen, "Job Choice and Performance: Revisiting Core Assumptions about Public Service Motivation," *International Public Management Journal*, Vol. 20, No. 1, 2017, pp. 108–131.